HOW SHOULD A GOVERNMENT BE?

Also by Jaideep Prabhu

Do Better with Less: Frugal Innovation for Sustainable Growth
(with Navi Radjou), 2019.

Frugal Innovation: How to Do More with Less
(with Navi Radjou), 2015.

Jugaad Innovation: Think Frugal, Be Flexible,
Generate Breakthrough Growth
(with Navi Radjou and Simone Ahuja), 2012.

HOW SHOULD A GOVERNMENT BE?

The new levers of state power

JAIDEEP PRABHU

P

PROFILE BOOKS

First published in Great Britain in 2021 by
Profile Books Ltd
29 Cloth Fair
London
ECIA 7JQ

www.profilebooks.com

A CIP catalogue record for this book is available from the British Library.

ISBN 978 1 78816 137 4
eISBN 978 1 78283 485 4

Typeset in Sabon by MacGuru Ltd
Printed and bound in Britain by Clays Ltd, Elcograf S.p.A.

FSC
www.fsc.org
MIX
Paper from
responsible sources
FSC® C018072

For my parents and grandparents, and for civil service families like theirs around the world that are striving to make their governments work better.

Contents

Introduction

'So, what does all this mean for governments?'

It was December 2012, and I was in New Delhi, delivering a talk at the Ministry of Finance's Annual Economics Conference. I had just finished speaking about how technology was turning the world of business upside down when this question came at me from the depths of the audience. In my talk, I had spoken about how start-ups were using new technologies and new forms of organising to build digital empires that were 'disrupting' incumbent firms across sectors worldwide. I had spoken about how these upstarts had pioneered a new way of doing business: working backwards from what customers wanted and then building organisations that used data from users to relentlessly improve their offerings. I had described how this revolutionary approach had upended the twentieth-century model that favoured large corporations with big budgets who had dominated their sectors by developing technology (sometimes for its own sake) and then pushing it onto mostly passive consumers. The world of business, I argued, now belonged to frugal, nimble, customer-centric firms; the top-down, 'bigger is better' behemoths were a relic of the past.

I had spoken entirely about the private sector, but the voice in the audience wanted to know: 'What does all this mean for governments?'

At first, I was taken aback by the question. It was clearly important and relevant. What's more: the person asking it was a senior member of the Indian government. As a business school academic, I hadn't until then given the implications of technology for government much thought. Somehow, that day, I managed a response that I knew barely scratched the surface of a profound and deep issue. But the question would come back to me in various guises in the years to come.

What does all this mean for governments?

When I was first asked that question in December 2012, I had spent nearly two decades researching and writing about innovation – how firms use technology to develop new and better products for consumers and how they organise for it. In roughly the first half of my career I had studied how such innovation was done in the affluent West by large corporations. Through my research, I became familiar with the classic twentieth-century model of innovation in which bigger was believed to be better: innovation was about large projects – big teams with massive budgets – great secrecy and structured processes that took time to unfold.

Then, in the new millennium, I began to study innovation in emerging economies like India, where I had grown up. What I found there surprised me. In contrast to the Western 'bigger is better', highly structured model, firms in emerging markets were frugal and agile in how they went about innovation. They were good at doing more with less and at improvising and moving quickly with the market.

Inspired by this difference and vitality, I wrote a book about innovation in emerging markets and what Western organisations could learn from them. My co-authors and I called the book *Jugaad Innovation*, after the Hindi word *jugaad*, which is often used in India to describe such frugal and agile innovation. The book struck a chord with readers around the world. Translated into Portuguese, Dutch, French, Italian, Japanese and Mandarin, an early indication of its popularity came when pirated copies showed up on the sidewalks of Mumbai.

Soon after *Jugaad Innovation* came out, I began to notice a great deal of interest in frugal innovation in the West *for* the West. This was partly driven by the increasing numbers of Western consumers, already feeling the effects of decades of stagnant incomes, who were now reeling from the aftermath of the financial crisis and government austerity.

But there were positive drivers too. More and more 'ordinary' people were increasingly empowered by a raft of new tools and resources to develop solutions to problems which only large corporations or governments could have taken on a decade or so before. This democratisation of innovation was giving rise to a frugal economy, underpinned by trends such as the sharing economy and the maker movement. What was exciting to see was how the internet – along with social media, smartphones, cheap computers and software, 3D printers, maker spaces and Fab Labs, accelerators and crowdfunding – was making it possible for small teams to engage in the entire innovation process from originating and developing solutions to manufacturing, promoting and distributing them to a global market. From this revolution came 'frugal' services such as Airbnb and WhatsApp as well as products such as the Square Reader, an internet-of-things device that can accept credit card payments through a smartphone's audio jack. (WhatsApp, for instance, was developed by four people in about nine months and with about $250,000 in seed funds.)

Inspired by this revolution sweeping across Western cities and campus towns, I wrote a second book, *Frugal Innovation*, in which my co-author and I described what large and small organisations were doing in this space and the principles that underpinned their efforts. That book, too, was translated into various languages, including French, Mandarin, Turkish, Ukrainian, Italian and Russian.

Once again, however, as in December 2012 in New Delhi, wherever I went, in talks I gave about these books, there was the inevitable question from someone in the audience: So, what does all this mean for governments? More often than not, someone in the audience would also furnish me with answers by speaking about what *was* happening in governments around the world. And so, though my books and career had until then focused on the private sector, I became increasingly aware of a parallel revolution taking place in the state.

I argue that it's not the companies/state changing, but the people; they can now access the necessary info to design + demand change.

Looking back, it's now clear to me that the seeds of my interest in government had been sown at an earlier point in my career. In 2008 I had been elected to a chair in business at the University of Cambridge. The chair had been endowed by the Indian government in honour of India's first prime minister, Jawaharlal Nehru, who had studied natural sciences at Cambridge one hundred years before. While the focus of the chair was business, I knew that it would also be necessary to look at how governments worked and examine the links between the public and the private sectors. Growing up in India in the 1970s and 1980s, I had been acutely aware of the importance of the state in driving business and growth. On a more personal level, my father had been a civil servant and from a young age I had observed the bureaucracy's crucial role at close quarters.

But from 2012 onwards I started to look for and find opportunities to study government more systematically. I began to teach a master's course on government and technology at Cambridge. Shortly afterwards, I became the academic director of a leadership programme for senior Indian civil servants and taught on similar programmes for bureaucrats and political leaders from the UAE, Nigeria, Malaysia and Kazakhstan. I also became an associate fellow of the Centre for Science and Policy, which had been set up to bring academics and policymakers from Europe together to address issues of mutual interest. From that time on, I would meet and speak at length to several hundred civil servants from various parts of the world, including the UK, North America, the European Union and the Commonwealth.

Introduction

The more I thought about the question of technology and government, the more I realised that it had at least three facets to it. First, there were the positive implications for how government itself functioned. How could the state use new technology and ways of organising to deliver services to its citizens better, and do this faster and cheaper? If Amazon, Google and Facebook could make the customer experience so seamless, could harness big data and analytics to do this quickly and cheaply, could coordinate huge numbers of actors on both the demand and supply side of the economy, bringing efficiency and prosperity in their wake, and keep on relentlessly doing all this better, then surely governments could do the same? But I also realised there was a second, darker side to the issue. Perhaps governments could also then use these very tools to gain greater control over their citizens, to monitor and surveil them, and accrue even more power. If Amazon, Google and Facebook had been able to gain so much influence over the lives of people, then how much more dangerous could those same tools be in the hands of governments? And third, of course, there was the question of how governments should view and manage the use of such tools by the private sector. What should governments do about the digital giants and their immense power? And how should states engage with start-ups and social entrepreneurs to stimulate innovation and drive inclusive growth? How, in brief, should a government be in the twenty-first century?

*

'The nine most terrifying words in the English language,' Ronald Reagan once said, 'are: "I'm from the government and I'm here to help."' Are governments really so bad at getting things done? And if they are, what should their scale and scope be? That question is the most bitterly contested in contemporary politics.

On one side of the argument are the libertarians, for whom

governments are incompetent and inefficient at best, and dangerous at worst. For them, the only good state is a small one that leaves much of the work of running an economy to the market and civil society. This is the intellectual tradition of Friedrich von Hayek and Milton Friedman, and of politicians from Ronald Reagan and Margaret Thatcher to the Tea Party Republicans.

Ranged against them are the statists: those who believe in the inherent benevolence of the government and wish to grow its powers and use them to influence society and the economy. This is the tradition of the Fabian socialists and central planners as well as contemporary politicians like Bernie Sanders and Elizabeth Warren and movements such as Syriza, Five Star and Podemos. For them, governments are the only force that can redress the vagaries and injustices of the market and ensure that all lives are valued properly.

It is no surprise that these factions should disagree, and it is no surprise that they might both be wrong. But what this book sets out to argue is that they are also both, in a sense, right. There is, in fact, a way in which governments can be both big and small, generous and frugal, deeply involved in the lives of their citizens while stopping short of meddlesome intrusion. This is true in times of stability when the economy and society are ticking along nicely. But it is even more true in times of crisis, during financial downturns or pandemics, when the state has a crucial role to play but must do so efficiently and effectively. During the financial crisis of 2007–08, for instance, some governments did better than others at responding to the problems at hand in how they introduced and managed rescue packages and bailouts. The consequences of this response lived well beyond the immediate aftermath of the downturn. So, too, with the Covid-19 pandemic of 2020. Some governments were noticeably better than others at harnessing their resources to respond quickly, humanely and effectively to the health and economic consequences of the crisis. The best governments were able to balance the imperatives of securing public

6

health with ensuring their economies did not grind to a halt. How did they do so?

In good times and in bad, there are many ways a government can achieve *more* for their citizens with *less*. Some of these are obvious, but many, I argue, are new and depend on new technologies or developments in the theory of organisations. If we put them all together, we have a recipe that just might change the world for the better.

Whether we like it or not, there really are transformational technologies that are altering the potential scale and scope of both government and private enterprise. Moreover, there are new forms of organising that go hand in hand with these technological changes. All this has consequences for old arguments about the scale and scope of the state. For example, for good or ill, we can now have a vastly intrusive state apparatus at low cost. And so this book sets out to help the reader discover the real landscape of alternatives that we face today: a world in which vast, unaccountable bureaucracies can be assembled in a bedroom; the machinery of surveillance is privatised, globalised and unaccountable; and there are both worrying potential downsides as well as upsides to the new means available to governments. And, of course, if our governments don't use these means, others will. The question of how a government should be has changed, and this book sets out to show how.

In doing so, it aims to be largely apolitical. Of course, there will always be political arguments about what kinds of issues a government ought to involve itself in. My subject, however, is the relatively apolitical question of how it should set about accomplishing its goals once these issues have been decided upon. I realise that this question is not wholly apolitical, of course. The desire for effectiveness breaks down at the extremes of left and right. For example, those who are fiercely opposed to government at any scale may see little point in helping it do its work better; they might even cherish its specific inefficiencies and failures as proof of its intrinsically flawed nature, or actively attempt to sabotage it. On the other hand, those who support an extreme form of statism may be comfortable with government inefficiency; they may even believe that the only way to address social inequities is by throwing ever more (of someone else's) money at the many problems that societies today face.

This book isn't meant for either of these factions. If, however, you do think there are legitimate things for governments to do, and you want them done safely, efficiently and in a way that is responsive to democratic correction, then this book is for you. It will contain models for how governments can do things, which you can use as examples if you happen to work in government, or as standards to hold your representatives to if you care about how well a government does its job. The book will also show – in a cautious way, consistent with the desire not to express substantive opinions about political questions – where the dangers may lie. Indeed, more often than not, the success of government programmes depends not on the ideology that underpins them but on the competence with which these programmes are implemented. The best plans can be sunk by poor implementation, while even mediocre ideas can be made to work if they are implemented well. How to make governments better at implementation is, I believe, an eminently practical question, of which both libertarians and statists can appreciate the value.

The book's structure reflects these aims. Chapter 1 describes India's Unique ID project and illustrates what governments can do today in terms of creating digital infrastructure and programmes on a huge scale with limited budgets and with effectiveness and efficiency. Chapter 2 steps back to survey the field of twentieth-century political thought: the battlefield of ideas between the libertarians who have argued for small states and the statists who have argued for big ones. It makes the case that this binary argument no longer holds and that, as Aneesh Chopra, the first chief technology officer of the US government and author of

Introduction

Innovative State, puts it, states 'must leave behind the tired arguments between those who enthusiastically espouse bigger and those who staunchly support smaller government, arguments that create adversaries and animosity but little advancement'.[1] Arguing with Chopra, Chapter 2 asserts that: 'This isn't about bigger. This isn't about smaller. This is about smarter.'

Chapter 3 returns to India's Unique ID project and surveys similar developments in other countries around the world, particularly China. It looks at positive examples of governments doing more and better with less but also examines the dark side of what the ability to do so implies. If governments can do more to serve their citizens, surely they can also misuse this powerful apparatus to conduct surveillance, monitor and police, and eventually oppress their people. What are the implications of this power for governments and societies?

Chapters 4 to 8 look in greater detail at how governments should be in the twenty-first century. They explore four key principles of how governments can be more responsive to citizens; more inclusive; more experimental; and learn to steer and not row, both in how they regulate and cultivate private enterprise.

More specifically, Chapter 4 explores how states can put citizens first – both by using new technology and by making government hierarchies flatter – and deliver public services faster, better and cheaper.

In many parts of the world, people feel abandoned by the state. Equally, where markets rule, people have felt the power of these markets to alienate. Chapter 5 explores 'social security' and how governments at different levels can be more inclusive in their approach to diverse groups in society.

Chapter 6 looks at how states today can use their privileged access to the public to conduct experiments and learn from the results. How can governments – as the digital giants do with their customers – use new technology, data and behavioural science to nurture their relationship with citizens in smart and nimble ways?

How can they quickly scale up solutions that have been proven to work at the experimental stage, and look across domains to share best practices across different levels of the state?

Chapter 7 explores how states can steer their economies by *regulating* industry and new technologies in a better way. In the next few decades, the world will see the advent of radical new technologies in many areas: artificial intelligence, robotics, driverless cars, quantum computing, genetic engineering, and so on. These technologies could transform our lives for the better. They could also cause untold disruption and suffering. It will be up to governments to manage and regulate them in clever ways that realise their potential without endangering society and citizens. For economies to be innovative and flourish, Chapter 7 argues that it is necessary for governments to strike a balance between the extremes of a laissez-faire approach to new technologies and heavy-handed regulation that might kill them even before we can assess their potential for positive change.

Chapter 8 looks at how governments can steer and not row in how they *cultivate* industry and enterprise. It shows how governments can tap into the creative potential of their companies and citizens so as to stimulate and not stifle innovation.

To survive and prosper, governments must be able to adapt and change. But government bureaucracies are often resistant to change: they are hierarchical, follow structured processes, suffer from siloed thinking and punish failure, thus discouraging innovation. Chapter 9 looks at how states can change all this by creating structures, attitudes and practices that encourage those within governments to prepare for the future.

Eventually, however, the ultimate driver of change in how states function comes from citizens and how they interact with their governments. What must citizens do to get the government they want? How can they make elected officials sweat, not only during elections but at other times too? Chapter 10 looks at how citizens should choose their leaders, and what counts as useful experience to run a government in the new millennium. The chapter also examines the role of the engaged citizen and citizens' movements in holding governments to account.

Throughout the book, I consider stories and cases from both developed countries (such as the US, the UK, Denmark and Canada) and developing nations (such as India, China, Kenya and Bangladesh). This choice is fuelled by a conviction that cross-country comparisons matter. In important respects, governments are similar wherever they are: they have similar objectives, resources and constraints, and comparable ways of working and processes. But even where they differ, comparisons can be revealing. After all, something that one country does differently and well can inspire people from another to change.

Moreover, I build the book on stories and cases rather than on argumentation alone. This stems from my conviction that things often work differently in practice from what ideology might lead us to expect. Paying close attention to what actually happens when we try to do something in real life can be illuminating and instructive. Most of the stories I've chosen are from the last ten years and therefore relatively recent. Some, however, date from before the financial crisis of 2008. Those older stories, I believe, remain relevant. The basic techniques and possibilities of government don't change that fast. Indeed, in some cases their effects remain for a long time. In still other cases, a certain amount of time must elapse before we can see what the true effects of a change might be.

*

This book is about how to make governments work faster, better and <u>cheaper</u>. As such it has immediate relevance for those who work for or with governments. But it is also written with the general reader in mind. In an age when governments have never been more important, and when public impatience and dissatisfaction with public institutions are growing, this book hopes to inform and inspire people about the transformative potential of the state working in tandem with its citizens.

Teaching, writing and thinking about the question 'What does this mean for governments?' has convinced me that we are on the cusp of a revolution in how states function. We are rapidly moving from an old model of government – top-down, inside-out, expensive and slow – to one that is bottom-up, outside-in, frugal and quick.

For over a century, the most explosive question in political thought has been about the size of the state. Should it expand and take an active role in all sorts of areas of life? Or is that just meddlesome and wasteful? These questions might have made sense in the previous century. Now, with revolutions in technology and organisational structure, a revolution is also coming in the essential business of government. It is of great importance, therefore, that we again ask the question of how a government should be. If we don't, we risk ending up with one we would not wish to be governed by.

1

Foundations

India in the early 1980s was not a great place to start a business. For one thing, money was almost non-existent. To get going, Nandan Nilekani was forced to borrow $250 in starting capital from the wife of one of his co-founders. Then there was the bureaucracy that made it hard to acquire even the most basic technology. A joke at that time was that half the country was waiting for a phone while the other half was waiting for a dial tone. Nilekani was trying to set up a software company, but Infosys, his fledgling firm, had to wait three years to get a licence to import a computer. At every turn, the new business had to grapple with antediluvian government processes, byzantine bureaucracy and petty officials who only worked if their palms had been properly greased. Although Nilekani's father had been a manager at the Minerva Mills, he had subscribed to the Fabian socialist ideals that had driven the newly independent India. And so, growing up in Bangalore, Nilekani had been raised on fine socialist principles. His first encounters with government as a businessman would put them to the test.

It took a decade of hard slog before things began to look up. In the early 1990s, India's economy opened to the world. It became easier to travel abroad, to import machinery and invite consultants from overseas. Gradually, Infosys became a major player in the global software business. The company pioneered a new way of distributing office work around the globe, locating different elements of projects in the cheapest locations before seamlessly delivering the solutions to clients wherever they were. If you worked for a software company anywhere in the world, or scratched under the surface of the software you were using as a consumer, you would have been immediately aware of this revolution. By the end of the decade, Infosys had made a name for itself as the company that had invented the global outsourcing model.

Outgoing, genial and articulate, Nilekani was the international face of the company. In 2002, just over twenty years after he had co-founded it, he became CEO of Infosys. When he took over, the company was worth $500 million. When he stepped down to become co-chairman in 2007, it was worth $3 billion.[1] Such success attracted attention in India. Most people still struggled with the grind of getting ahead; despite reforms, the state still smothered many aspects of life and work, and the country remained poor.

And yet, even as Nilekani's wealth and success put him beyond the reach of bureaucratic hassle, Leviathan tried to lure him back in. In 1999, the chief minister of Karnataka state came to see him. Would he lead a task force to improve the capital city's infrastructure and governance challenges? A few years later the Indian prime minister asked Nilekani to serve on a new National Knowledge Commission, set up to improve India's competitiveness in the global knowledge economy. Around that time, Nilekani also became part of the National Advisory Group on e-Governance and helped co-found the National Association of Software and Service Companies (NASSCOM), India's trade body for the software industry. In 2006, in recognition of these contributions, he was awarded one of India's highest civilian honours, the Padma Bhushan. Writing in *Time* magazine, the journalist Thomas Friedman asked: 'What makes Nilekani unique? For me it comes down to one phrase: great explainer ... [I]f you sit outside his office for a day, you notice that half the people going in are employees looking for instructions or customers looking for deals; the other half are politicians, journalists and ministers from around the world looking for an explanation of what it all means.'[2] It was Nilekani, explaining how Infosys had used technology to go global, who gave Friedman the phrase 'the world is flat', and inspired the New Yorker's paean to globalisation of the same name.

Nilekani's ideas about the power of technology, alongside his experience of government at various levels, kept gnawing away at him. His work for various civic bodies kept his interest in public service alive. His natural curiosity about why things were the way they were and his instincts as a problem-solver kept coming back to him even as Infosys went from strength to strength and his own business reputation grew.

In 2009, he set out his thinking in a book, *Imagining India: The Idea of a Renewed Nation*. In it, Nilekani took on some of the big problems that vexed him and his country alike. One of the most knotty was citizen identification. The problem, Nilekani explained, was that over 500 million Indians, a majority of the population, had no means of proving who they were to anyone who might ask. And many did ask: bank officials, shopkeepers handing out food rations, clerks in government departments providing citizen services. As a result, many Indians could not open bank accounts, take out driving licences, or get access to the land records or the food rations that were their due.] issue

Meanwhile, those who did have access to identification suffered from a surfeit of such schemes, depending on which part of the state they engaged with. There were passports, ration card numbers, a permanent account number for paying taxes, voter ID cards, and so on. All these databases existed in disconnected silos, which made zeroing in on a single, definite identity for every citizen almost impossible. And so the system was full of phantoms. In India, while the intended beneficiaries of government schemes went without, untold numbers of fake identities voted and pulled down government subsidies, defrauding the state of millions. An academic once told Nilekani that there were more below-the-poverty-line ration cards in Karnataka state than its entire population put together. This bureaucratic sprawl and waste reminded Nilekani of Infosys's own struggles in the early 1980s: to gain permits to do business, import computers, borrow foreign currency, and so on.

So, what could be done?

Nilekani had a radical idea. The country needed a unique and universal ID for every Indian. This would not only ensure that the citizens for whom government benefits were intended would actually receive them, in a fair and efficient way, but it would also eliminate fraud in the system and save the state huge sums.

Imagining India became a *New York Times* bestseller. It was clear that Nilekani had ambitions beyond the realms of private enterprise. Barely six months after his book was published, the world would find out just how serious these ambitions were. On 26 June 2009, the newly re-elected prime minister of India, Manmohan Singh, announced that Nilekani would head the newly created Unique Identity Authority of India (UIDAI). Nilekani was venturing into the belly of the biggest beast the world had known.

Getting started on the Unique ID

Speaking to me in March 2017, Nilekani recalled his first heady days in government. In May 2009, there had been a national election. The incumbent Indian National Congress (or Congress party) was re-elected and full of renewed enthusiasm for doing things. The prime minister approached Nilekani about working with his team.

'After a couple of conversations, I realised that working on a unique ID was the right thing for me to do. I could see its value. It was technology intensive, which played to my strengths, and it was measurable in its success. I could say my team had enrolled so many people in so much time, and so on.'[3]

Nilekani met Prime Minister Singh and laid down a few

conditions. He wanted the ID project to be run as a separate entity, an autonomous body created by the law. He also wanted to report to the PM himself, with a post of cabinet rank.

Nilekani had worked on the fringes of government for some time by that point. He knew how city, state and central governments worked. He had seen bureaucrats function and how conscious of hierarchy they could be. If he was going to navigate the system, he would need to have the necessary stature. He also knew that power is an ephemeral thing in public life. 'It is often about who you know and who is supporting you. When I worked on the Bangalore Agenda Task Force, to improve infrastructure in the city, I had the support of the chief minister of the state. But as soon as he lost the elections, no one returned my calls.' Nilekani knew he could only negotiate these things before he joined. Once in government, he would quickly become part of the furniture.

The prime minister accepted all his conditions. On 26 June 2009, Nilekani's appointment was announced to the cabinet. On 9 July, he quit Infosys. On 26 July, he joined the government as chairman of the Unique Identification Authority of India (UIDAI). The inventor of global outsourcing had made the leap from the private to the public sector.

Nilekani arrived with a basic plan of attack. To give every Indian a unique identity he would need something like a unique number linked to biometric data – a photograph, ten fingerprints, iris scans of both eyes – and demographic data such as that person's name, address, gender and date of birth. 'I wanted to keep the solution simple,' he says.

He needed a team. First of all, bureaucrats based in Delhi who knew the system and could oversee the administration of the project, and second, technical people who knew hardware, software and the ins and outs of biometric measurement. Again, speed was of the essence. His past work in government meant that he had friends in the bureaucracy who could help him identify good people. He handpicked ten.

To make sure the technology would meet the challenge, Nilekani did two things. He went to the private sector to build the team, and he based it in Bangalore, the centre of India's computer industry. He looked for people who understood technology, marketing and branding. Sanjay Jain, the chief product manager, came from Google. Pramod Varma, the chief architect, had been at Infosys, Nilekani's old firm. Srikanth Nadhamuni, the head of technology, had worked at Sun and Intel. Vivek Raghavan, the biometric architect, had been a technology entrepreneur in Silicon Valley. They all came to the project attracted by the excitement of doing something different. They had no intention of becoming lifelong government employees. As they all lived and worked in Bangalore, that was where the technical team was based. 'This was my way of letting the technical guys do their job in peace,' says Nilekani. 'In Bangalore it was possible to create an informal culture, away from the rigid formalism of Delhi bureaucracy.'

It was time to make an ambitious statement of intent. In August 2009 Nilekani went public saying that he would enrol 600 million Indians (roughly half the population) in five years. He felt that a commitment like that was important. It would sharpen minds.

Technology matters

Right at the outset, in the very first months of the project, Nilekani had put together a strategy document that set out the UID's goals and guiding principles. His focus was speed and scale. To achieve this, it was important to build simplicity and minimalism into the design.

The UID would represent the largest exercise of its kind in India, and possibly the world. It would be the very manifestation of a vision of government as innovator. A vision of the state – not as a passive follower of technologies pioneered in the private sector – but as a trailblazer, the first not only in the developing world but anywhere on the planet. Information technology would be the driver. It would underpin the three key processes of enrolling people, ensuring there was no duplication of identities on the system, and then being able to authenticate people online in real time. Ensuring security throughout was paramount.

Vivek Raghavan, the biometric architect, describes the approach as follows: 'We knew we couldn't do many of these things on our own, and nor was this desirable. Our team would build the core software system but for everything else we would work in partnership with others. And so we created an entire eco-system to work with us.'[4]

Sanjay Jain, the chief product manager, adds: 'There were three components of this ecosystem.' First there were 'registrars' whose role was to collect the biometric data and enrol citizens in the field: these could be state governments, the postal service, banks, insurance and telecommunications companies, and agencies involved with right-to-work schemes or the public distribution system. Then there were software companies developing the apps that would use the UID for banking, health, the public distribution service, and so on. Finally there were companies developing devices and the hardware needed to do the enrolment and run the applications.[5]

The UIDAI wouldn't itself get into procurement; the enrolling agencies would do that – they would buy from the hardware companies. The role of the UID team was to ensure that the enrolling agencies bought hardware that was compatible with the standards that the UID team had laid down.

As a result, even at its height, the team had less than 100 people in it. This was remarkable by government standards anywhere, where new projects are often bogged down by massive teams and bloated budgets. However, in the larger ecosystem around the UID, there were thousands of people involved. 'It was these other people who did the bulk of the work and helped us achieve so much in so little time,' says Jain.

How did they get all this support? And how did they know they were on the right track?

The first year was spent creating the technical, administrative and legal framework for the project. While Ram Sewak Sharma, a civil servant from the elite Indian Administrative Service, ran the team in Delhi, and the engineers in Bangalore built the technology platform, Nilekani launched a one-man campaign to win over key players throughout the country. He travelled to every state and met with all the chief ministers and chief secretaries. He spoke to bank officials, members of chambers of commerce, and even the heads of fertiliser associations (agriculture being a big part of the Indian economy).

'Nandan's role', says Jain, 'was to talk about the project, get support, find applications for the UID and confirm that the principles behind our design were sound. He was all the while testing our principles and refining them. But very soon, wherever he went, there were no new questions being posed, so we knew the design was solid. That was our feedback loop.'

By August 2010, the team was ready to get going. The first enrolments began in September 2010. 'By then,' says Jain, 'we had decided to call the UID Aadhaar, meaning 'foundation', a word that resonated with Indians across the country from various language groups.'

The UID had cleared the first hurdle. But many more obstacles lay ahead.

Bureaucratic and political challenges

The pilot phase of the UID began in September 2010 and came to a close in December 2011. Despite the size of the challenge, it went well. Ram Sewak Sharma, the civil servant who headed the authority in Delhi, describes how Aadhaar began to gain real momentum. 'In little over a year, by December 2011, we had enrolled the first

100 million citizens and had posted each of them a letter with their unique 12-digit number. We then asked the government for permission to do a further 100 million enrolments. At the peak, we were enrolling something like 25 million people a month.'[6]

Enrolment centres were popping up all over the country. [Several states, regardless of their political affiliation, came on board and supported the project. They could see the benefits of Aadhaar: it offered a practical solution to the huge leakages in their benefits programmes and the vast amounts they lost as a result.]

The UIDAI began by paying registrars Rs. 50 (about $1) for every citizen enrolled. Later this was brought down to Rs. 40. The total cost of everything else – software development, the data centres, the biometric de-duplication process, the posting of Aadhaar letters – came to another Rs. 50 or so per ID. In total, each Aadhaar would cost the government about Rs. 100 per citizen: a one-time cost of Rs. 120 billion to enrol all Indians. In contrast, the government spent Rs. 3 trillion a year on subsidies and benefits of various sorts, with something like Rs. 30 billion a year lost to leakages, fakes, duplicates and ghosts. 'The states could see the return on investment and came on board,' says Sharma. 'By August 2012 we had achieved our target of enrolling 200 million people in all. Then the government gave us permission to enrol 400 million more.'

But even as they made progress with enrolment, they began to face a number of existential threats. The biggest of these came from within the government itself.

The Indian Home Ministry had its own scheme to collect biometrics and issue a smart card to every Indian. Linked to the National Population Register (NPR) – a database of the identities of all Indian residents – the focus of the Home Ministry scheme was to establish citizenship and deal with internal security. The NPR project set off a turf war between the UIDAI and the Home Ministry. The latter had the backing of the minister, a powerful politician with prime ministerial ambitions. Meanwhile, the Ministry of

Finance didn't like the idea of two different agencies collecting biometrics for two different purposes: they rightly saw this as a waste of government money. At various times during those months, the [Home Ministry made moves to either shut down the UID project or take it over.] There were many times when they nearly won.

'Then we came under attack from the left wing within the government itself,' says Sharma. Members of the influential National Advisory Council, a think tank that advised the Congress party leader Sonia Gandhi, argued that the UID's biometric data would compromise citizens' privacy and security. The economist Jean Drèze and the social activist Aruna Roy, both members of the council, claimed that by introducing Aadhaar the state was abdicating its responsibility towards social welfare programmes. This was particularly ironic as the UID was designed to *help* the very disenfranchised communities that Roy and Drèze had spent their careers championing. Even so, they took their case to Sonia Gandhi and asked her to stop the project until it had been properly studied by social scientists. These criticisms later provided fodder for activists who took their concerns about privacy and security to the Supreme Court.

The third challenge came from the Bharatiya Janata Party (BJP), the ruling Congress party's main opposition in government.

In 2011, a Standing Committee on Finance was formed to study Aadhaar, headed by a senior member of parliament of the BJP. In late 2011, the committee came out with a scathing report which challenged the UIDAI on legal grounds. 'The report implied, often inaccurately,' says Sharma, 'that Aadhaar used untested technology, that it suffered from various operational problems, that it did not employ robust verification of people's identities, and that it granted foreign nationals, such as Bangladeshi immigrants, legal status. That report was very damaging for us. That was another moment when we thought the UIDAI would die.'

But by far the most critical threat came in late 2013 and early 2014 as national elections loomed.

In early 2014, the BJP, which had been in opposition for ten years, was in the ascendancy. Led by Narendra Modi, the chief minister of Gujarat state, it looked likely that the party would come to power again. Indian voters had grown disenchanted with the Congress and its coalition of rambunctious and disruptive partners. The tireless Modi traversed the length and breadth of the country holding huge rallies where he excoriated the Congress and its allies for being corrupt and inept, and for failing to deliver development and jobs.

In campaign mode, Modi was in imperious form. A formidable orator, he used a full range of taunts and jibes to ridicule the Congress party and its leaders: Rahul Gandhi, the inexperienced inheritor of the Nehru-Gandhi legacy, and Manmohan Singh, the ageing prime minister. Threatening and vigorous, Modi included Aadhaar in his litany of failed Congress projects. His party, he said, had already opposed the project on the grounds that it enabled non-Indians, including illegal immigrants, to benefit from government programmes. In September 2013, at a youth rally in Tiruchirappalli in South India, Modi mocked Aadhaar, calling it a *jadi buti* – a quack's cure – for all of India's problems. He raised the issue of the billions of rupees that had been spent on the project and asked who had really benefited from the scheme. He told the gathered crowds that as chief minister of Gujarat he had written to the prime minister several times over the previous three years raising concerns about Aadhaar and its threats to national security. At a National Security Council meeting, he had asked the prime minister to study questions he had raised about the project. He had warned that the scheme would not work if these questions were not properly addressed.[7]

Long before Donald Trump turned social media into a political weapon, Narendra Modi was already proving a master of the medium, circumventing established newspapers, radio and TV channels, and going direct with his views to the growing millions who followed him on Twitter. On 8 April 2014, Modi tweeted:

'On Aadhaar, neither the team that I met nor PM could answer my Qs on security threat it can pose. There is no vision, only political gimmick.'

Warming to his theme, on 9 April 2014, while campaigning in Bangalore – Nilekani's home-town – Modi again questioned the wisdom of spending money on Aadhaar without addressing the issue of national and border security. The government, he said, must answer for what had been done with the hundreds of millions of rupees meant for the programme. In the end, he warned, the Supreme Court would have to intervene.

Days later, on 16 May 2014, the country voted Modi and the BJP into power. It was the party's biggest victory ever. With over 300 seats, it had won an outright majority in the lower house. This meant it would not have to enter into messy alliances with smaller parties that would weaken its authority. The BJP could do as it pleased. If Prime Minister Modi kept to his campaign story, the Aadhaar project was dead.

The vultures were circling. After four years and billions of rupees spent, after nearly 600 million Indians had been enrolled across the length and breadth of the country, after thousands of enrolment booths had done their work and bureaucrats and technical people had slaved for months: after all this, it now looked as if the project would come to nothing. Nilekani explained:

> At bottom, we had designed Aadhaar as a way to bring the government closer to the people. It was meant to put power in the hands of citizens and make the state more responsive and accountable to them. What better way was there to embed democratic principles – government of, for and by the people – than this? And yet, ironically, the democratic process itself would now put paid to this reinvention of the government's relationship with its people. The foundation had been laid but no one would be able to build on it. It seemed a sad way to end.

Then, when all seemed lost, someone from the new government appeared. He was there to help.

UID: from underdog to top dog

On 16 May 2014, Narendra Modi became the 14th prime minister of India. Throughout the campaign that had led up to his victory, Modi had been critical of Aadhaar. There were indications that, now he was in power, he would dismantle it completely. Indeed, shortly after the BJP's victory, its spokesperson, Prakash Javadekar, had told the press: 'Our concerns with Aadhaar are two-fold: the lack of a legal backing and the security implications.'[8]

A few weeks later, however, in a significant volte-face, Modi made a public declaration, stating that he would seek to enrol one billion Indians under Aadhaar 'at the earliest'.

What had changed his mind?

In the weeks after winning the election, Modi had met with both Nilekani and Ram Sewak Sharma, the senior civil servant who had been Nilekani's right-hand man in the UIDAI's early years. Sharma, now in charge of the Department of Information Technology, had convinced him that the UID project could save huge amounts of money. At a meeting with Modi he did a back-of-the-envelope calculation. The government of India, he pointed out, spent about $60 billion on individual subsidies. At a minimum, some 10 per cent of these individuals were 'ghosts'. If they were removed, this would result in an annual saving of $6 billion.

What's more, and unknown to either Nilekani or Sharma, Modi had in fact tried out a programme similar to Aadhaar at a regional level when he was chief minister of Gujarat, with positive results. As it turned out, Modi was not as opposed as they had feared. The UID project lived to fight another day.

This was just the beginning. In the months to follow, the BJP government, despite having been previously critical of the project, would go about embedding Aadhaar in several of its programmes. It would make the programme the centrepiece of reforms to the public distribution system for food and subsidies for the poor and link it to financial inclusion programmes and even the tax system.

Arun Jaitley, the finance minister, kicked things off by allotting $280 million to the project for the fiscal year 2014–15, up from the previous year's budget of $220 million. Then, on 10 September 2014, the Cabinet Committee on Economic Affairs approved the enrolment process in the states of Bihar, Uttar Pradesh, Uttarakhand and Chhattisgarh. The aim was to sign up one billion people across India by the end of 2015.

Another committee was assigned to review the Direct Benefits Transfer Scheme for government subsidies for cooking gas. This scheme was redubbed PAHAL in November 2014, and it was decided that the Aadhaar number could be used to credit subsidies directly to purchasers' bank accounts. By March 2015, the PAHAL scheme would grow to cover over 100 million of the 145 million active users of cooking gas in the country. Arvind Subramanian, the chief economic adviser to the Ministry of Finance, would hail the scheme a 'game changer' for India. He claimed that it had resulted in a 24 per cent reduction in the sale of subsidised gas, as it ensured that 'ghost beneficiaries' were excluded from the system.[9] The savings to the government in 2014–15 alone were calculated to be nearly $2 billion, more than the Aadhaar project had cost until then. In September 2015, the government extended the use of direct cash transfers to food subsidies in three territories: Puducherry, Chandigarh, and Dadra and Nagar Haveli. Now, instead of providing subsidised food to the poor through intermediary 'ration shops', cash transfers were made directly to Aadhaar-linked bank accounts of beneficiaries. Speaking about these reforms, Peeyush Kumar, the civil servant in charge, announced that: 'While initially, Rs. 500–700 per household will be transferred to the bank accounts of beneficiaries as food subsidy, at a later stage, kerosene will also be brought under direct benefit transfer.'[10] By 2016, direct bank transfers in food subsidies were estimated by another high-level committee to have saved the exchequer $4.8 billion annually, out of a central food subsidy bill of about $19 billion.

Another major initiative was the government's financial inclusion drive. When the BJP came to power, more than 40 per cent of Indians, many of them poor farmers or landless labour, had little or no access to the banking system. In an attempt to remedy this, on 15 August 2014 Modi launched the *Pradhan Mantri Jan Dhan Yojana* (the Prime Minister's People's Wealth Plan), a financial inclusion programme aimed at expanding citizens' access to bank accounts, remittances, credit, insurance and pensions.[11] Run by the Department of Financial Services, over 15 million bank accounts were opened on inauguration day, an achievement that made it to *Guinness World Records 2015*.

Forcing banks to open accounts was one thing. Getting citizens to use them was another. Bank accounts with no useful purpose were destined to remain dormant. One way to make them useful was to use direct bank transfers for benefits. But there was a further impediment: how to ensure that beneficiaries would be able to access the money from these accounts? For most rural Indians, the nearest bank branch was still too far away to reach in person. This was where mobile banking came in. As the finance minister, Arun Jaitley, put it:

> If we can realize the government's JAM – Jan Dhan, Aadhaar, Mobile – vision we can ensure that money goes directly and more quickly into the pockets of the poor and from the savings we achieve, we can put even more money for the poor. If we can be careful in our design and implementation, we can extend Direct Bank Transfer to other commodities, so that the poor get more money to spend for their upliftment.[12]

arguing gov could provide more benefits due to less financial waste

The floodgates had been opened. [As more and more Indians enrolled, and the central government pushed ahead with direct bank transfers for food and gas subsidies, different parts of the government began to find other uses for Aadhaar.]

In July 2014, government offices introduced Aadhaar-enabled biometric attendance to control absenteeism, and published the data online on attendance.gov.in. That month, the Employees' Provident Fund Organisation of India began linking pension accounts with Aadhaar numbers. In August, the prime minister directed the Planning Commission of India to enrol all prisoners in India under the UIDAI. In November, the Department of Tele-communications asked all telecom operators to collect Aadhaar numbers from new purchasers of SIM cards. In December, the Minister for Women and Child Development, Maneka Gandhi, proposed that Aadhaar be made mandatory for men creating pro-files on marriage and dating websites.

In 2015, various arms of the state found further uses for Aadhaar. In February, the Ministry for External Affairs announced that those with an Aadhaar number would get their passports issued within ten days, as this sped up verification and made it easier to check the National Crime Records Bureau data-base if applicants had criminal records. In March, the Election Commission began its National Electoral Roll Purification and Authentication Programme that linked the photo IDs of regis-tered voters to their Aadhaar number, thus removing duplicates and creating an error-free voter identification system. The same month, an Aadhaar-linked DigiLocker service was launched, allowing citizens to scan and save their documents in the cloud, and share them with government officials electronically.

And so it went.

So much so that, by early 2016, Aadhaar had expanded well beyond its original goals. Intended as a voluntary scheme, it had now become practically mandatory, not only for a number of government services but also for certain private services such as mobile phone connections and bank accounts. Critics began to worry that the project was on its way to becoming a Frankenstein's monster. Because its uses had leaped ahead of any laws passed to make it compatible with constitutional freedoms and rights, it potentially threatened the foundations of India's liberal democracy and even possibly violated elements of the constitution.

Moreover, was this to be the fate of other countries too? As in India, governments around the world had woken up to the immense possibilities of biometrics and related digital technologies – such as closed-circuit television and GPS tracking linked to apps – not only to deliver government services but also potentially to monitor and control their populations. Were we now in a "brave" new world of unlimited government ability and power? And what would happen in countries that didn't have the protections of democracy? → democracy is a lie...

Important as these questions are, they raise more basic ones about what a government is for and how it should be. What does political thought tell us about how governments should organise and use technology to achieve their aims and those of society? We now turn to that subject in Chapter 2.

2

How should a government be?

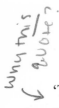

Why this/quote?

'The problem with socialism is that you eventually run out of other people's money.'

Margaret Thatcher

'I react pragmatically. Where the market works, I'm for that. Where the government is necessary, I'm for that. I'm deeply suspicious of somebody who says, "I'm in favor of privatization," or, "I'm deeply in favor of public ownership." I'm in favor of whatever works in the particular case.'

John Kenneth Galbraith

Why can't they be separate?

What historically motivates this?

In the 1930s, as Europe and the world hurtled towards the nightmare of the Second World War, a prelude to those real conflicts was taking place on the battlefield of ideas: ideas about how a government should be. Ranged against each other from left to right, east to west, were the communism of the Soviets, the fascism of Germany and Italy, and the liberal democracy of the West.

Even though there were many differences in these visions of the state, they all more or less agreed on one thing: the crucial importance of the government in directing the economy. Soviet Russia had central planning and state ownership of the means of production. Nazi Germany had a dominant role for the state at the helm of a war economy, including a four-year plan led by Hermann Göring. And the United States, reeling from the Great

Depression and the excesses of market capitalism, had launched the New Deal with huge state spending on ambitious public works programmes. All three movements – fascism, communism and the New Deal – were, in one way or another, responses to a fundamental problem at the heart of capitalism: the problem of business cycles in which bust follows boom as supply and demand fall out of sync with each other.

As its main rivals took up state intervention with gusto, Britain too began to edge in the same direction. The question of whether industry should be nationalised had been reopened. At the centre of the debate was one of the world's leading academic institutions: the London School of Economics. And at the heart of the battle, arguing the case against nationalisation and state planning, was an Austrian émigré by the name of Friedrich Hayek.

Vienna and London

Born in 1899, Hayek had grown up in a Vienna that was a global centre of ideas and culture. As a boy he had shown an academic bent and had enjoyed links with the intelligentsia – his cousin was the philosopher Wittgenstein. In 1917, while still a teenager, Hayek fought in the First World War, on the Italian front. When the war ended, he returned to Vienna, determined to pursue an academic career. Later he would reflect on how the war had been a decisive influence on his life and had drawn his attention to the importance of political organisation.

At the University of Vienna, under the influence of the economist Friedrich von Wieser, Hayek first developed broadly socialist leanings. But then he read Carl Menger's *Principles of Economics* and began drifting towards classical liberalism. Menger had taught political economy at the University of Vienna from 1873 to 1903. One of the most influential economists of his time, he had trained a generation of economists, including Ludwig von Mises, who would become a major influence on Hayek.

Hayek read Mises's *Socialism* and began attending his seminars. Mises then hired Hayek to work for the Austrian government on the legal and economic aspects of the Treaty of Saint-Germain, which dissolved the Austro-Hungarian Empire and created the new Republic of Austria. In 1923–24, Hayek travelled to the US to work on a project compiling macroeconomic data on the American economy and the operations of the Federal Reserve. On returning to Vienna, with the help of Mises, Hayek founded and served as director of the Austrian Institute for Business Cycle Research, before moving to the London School of Economics (LSE). In London, he would soon be recognised as one of the leading economists of his generation, in particular for his work on the coordination function of prices.

Battles with Keynes

The LSE in the 1930s was in fierce rivalry with Cambridge and its reigning monarch, John Maynard Keynes. Lionel Robbins, the director of the LSE, set up Hayek to be a foil to Cambridge and Keynes. In 1930, Keynes published his two-volume *A Treatise on Money* which examined the relationship between unemployment, money and prices. Its central idea was that high interest rates would cause unemployment to rise, partly because consumers would want to save rather than spend, making it difficult for producers to make a profit and thus hire workers.

Robbins, the editor of *Economica*, the premier journal of its time, invited Hayek to review *A Treatise on Money*. Hayek's review was harsh. He criticised both the analysis and the style. 'The *Treatise*', he wrote, 'proves to be so obviously the expression of a transitory phase in a process of rapid intellectual development that it would be decidedly unfair to regard it as anything but experimental.'[1] In a further twist of the knife, Hayek added: 'The exposition is ... difficult, unsystematic and obscure ...'[2]

Keynes responded in the very next issue, first attacking Hayek's piece before launching into his own review of Hayek's *Prices and Production,* which had just been published. In this book, Hayek had argued that business cycles resulted because central banks pumped more money into the economy than was needed, leading to lower interest rates and poor allocation of capital. He claimed that 'the past instability of the market economy is the consequence of the exclusion of the most important regulator of the market mechanism, money, from itself being regulated by the market process.'[3] Keynes called *Prices and Production* 'one of the most frightful muddles I have ever read'.[4] He added that the book was 'an extraordinary example of how, starting with a mistake, a remorseless logician can end in Bedlam'.[5]

The battle would soon spill over into the public domain, beyond the pages of *Economica.*

Keynes had been critical of the British government's austerity measures during the Great Depression. He believed that governments should spend more than they earned and run deficits during downturns. In October 1932, Keynes and several Cambridge economists wrote a letter to *The Times* in favour of public investment to fight the depression. Hayek and some of his LSE colleagues promptly wrote a rejoinder in favour of the government's balanced budget policy. They argued that private investment in public markets was a better road to wealth and economic coordination than government spending programmes could ever be.

As the 1930s drew on, Hayek got caught up in a debate with others over the 'economic calculation problem'. Ludwig von Mises had written in his *Economic Calculation in the Socialist Commonwealth* that: 'Every step that takes us away from private ownership of the means of production and from the use of money also takes us away from rational economics.'[6] Building on Mises, Hayek argued that planners in a centrally directed economy could never have the information they needed to carry out their duties reliably. An efficient allocation of resources could only occur through the price mechanism in free markets. In 1935, Hayek published *Collectivist Economic Planning*, a collection of essays from an earlier debate that Mises had initiated. In this book, Hayek included an essay in which Mises argued that rational planning was impossible under socialism. On the book's publication, socialists like Oskar Lange and H. D. Dickinson attempted to disprove Mises's thesis. They noted that the difference between a planned and a free-market system lay in who was responsible for solving the demand and supply equations. If some prices chosen by socialist managers were wrong, gluts or shortages would result, acting as signals to adjust prices up or down, just as would happen in a free-market economy. Through trial and error, a socialist economy could therefore be made to mimic the efficiency of a free market while avoiding its problems.

Hayek challenged these arguments. In a 1937 essay 'Economics and knowledge', he pointed out that economic theory assumed that all agents had full and correct information. In the real world, however, different people had different bits of knowledge, and some of what they believed could be wrong. Human knowledge, for Hayek, was contingent and dispersed. The complexity of the industrial economy meant that it was 'impossible for any man to survey more than a limited field'.[7] Building on Mises's work on the price mechanism, Hayek argued that, without it, socialism would have no way to allocate resources so as to reconcile the preferences of millions of people. Further, because it was unable to satisfy the huge variety of people's wants, a centrally planned economy would end up being innately coercive. By concentrating economic power, it would also concentrate political power. A *competitive* economy and polity, in contrast, was 'the only system designed to minimise by decentralisation the power exercised by man over man'. Democracy was a 'device for safeguarding freedom'.

In 1936, Keynes published his magnum opus: *The General*

Theory of Employment, Interest and Money. In it he argued that slowdowns like the Great Depression were caused by depressed consumption and excessive saving. Depressed demand decreased the incentive for businesses to invest, causing unemployment to rise. To stimulate the economy, it was necessary for the state to intervene by stimulating demand through spending. Such expansionary strategies would reignite industry, returning the economy to health. The implications of Keynes's analysis were clear. The best way to respond to the Great Depression was for the state to intervene and to spend. With the publication of his book, Keynes's academic reputation rose and rose, while Hayek's began to fade. Perhaps in reaction, Hayek now turned his attention to other themes.

The Road to Serfdom

In 1940, as the Battle of Britain raged, the London School of Economics moved to Cambridge, to premises at the university's oldest college, Peterhouse. Hayek too moved, first into rooms that Keynes secured for him in King's College, and then to a converted barn where he would live with his family until the end of the war. The lighter teaching load at Cambridge and the shorter distances to work gave Hayek time to write and think. He grew closer to Keynes on a personal level; they discussed books at weekends and took turns on certain nights to watch for fires from the roof of King's College.

Between 1940 and 1943, Hayek worked on the book that would become *The Road to Serfdom*. Inspired by the French liberal philosopher Alexis de Tocqueville's writings on the 'road to servitude', Hayek was concerned that the problems of capitalism were driving Britain and the West too far in the other direction. Convinced from his own experience that this would be a mistake, Hayek wrote in his introduction that the book was a 'product of an experience as near as possible to twice living through the same period – or at least twice watching the same evolution of ideas'.[8] Right after the First World War, both Austria and Germany had passed nationalisation acts. Now again, during the Second World War, Hayek feared the same would happen in Britain. As he well knew, the Great Depression had shaken the faith of citizens and intellectuals alike in the ability of the market system to provide. The mass unemployment and destitution it had brought had increased popular support for socialism in Europe and the US. Capitalism's failings had led to the failure to preserve democratic government in Germany and, before that, Russia. For Hayek, however, only capitalism made democracy possible. 'We have progressively abandoned that freedom in economic affairs,' he wrote, 'without which personal and political freedom have never existed in the past.'

Against the tide of socialist opinion, Hayek sounded a battle cry. But he didn't simply make the economic argument that central planning was inefficient. He extended his critique to the political sphere: economic planning and state direction of the economy would lead to totalitarianism. To properly plan and run an economy, the state would need to assume dictatorial powers. Further, there was no such thing as allowing the state to manage economic activity *only*. If planning really did free citizens from less important cares and enabled plain living and high thinking, who would wish to belittle such an ideal? But, Hayek warned, 'the ultimate ends of the activities of reasonable beings are never economic'.

The nationalisation of industry would lead to the nationalisation of thought. The planning of wartime would extend into peacetime. And there was no point in hoping that the best would run the government. Rather, in a totalitarian system, only the worst would have the ruthlessness and drive to make it to the top. Even if these leaders started out with good intentions, absolute power would corrupt them absolutely. The practice of private

36

Nate prop → tools of production (land. factory. intell prop
social prop → personal belongings

ownership was essential, not only for prosperity, but also for freedom and democracy.

As Alan Ebenstein notes in his biography of Hayek, the argument wasn't merely 'that capitalism is justified because it is more economically productive than classical socialism, but that capitalism is justified because classical socialism is inimical to liberty'.[9] In *The Road to Serfdom*, Hayek drove home a specific point relentlessly: that collectivism and the longing for a society with a grand common purpose was both misguided and dangerous to freedom.

It's dangerous to want collectivism?

Fame

The Road to Serfdom was published in Britain in March 1944. It was widely reviewed and sold well. Ironically, given its argument, the wartime rationing of paper meant the publishers struggled to keep up with demand, leading Hayek to dub it 'that unobtainable book'.

On 28 June 1944, Keynes wrote to congratulate Hayek on his 'grand' achievement. 'You will not expect me to accept quite all the economic dicta in it. But morally and philosophically, I find myself in agreement with virtually the whole of it; and not only in agreement with it, but in a deeply moved agreement.'[10] Keynes's only criticism was that 'there is a question of knowing where to draw the line', because Hayek's argument meant that 'so soon as one moves an inch in the planned direction you are necessarily launched on the slippery path which will lead you in due course over the precipice', a conclusion with which Keynes clearly disagreed. George Orwell, not a likely supporter, wrote that in the 'negative part of Professor's Hayek's thesis there is a great deal of truth'.[11] *→ not an argument... Orwell is a socialist*

In the US, the book achieved greater popularity than in Britain. In April 1945, the *Reader's Digest* put out an abridged version, which brought it to a wide audience. A planned academic tour in

why does / have that choice?

exactly... • why does / have that choice?

the spring of 1945 turned into a huge success. Wherever Hayek went, he was interviewed by the press and on the radio. His ideas seem to have uncovered a deep well of unmet demand.

In 1950, Hayek left Britain to take up a position at the University of Chicago. At Chicago, Hayek would conduct a series of influential seminars, inspiring several academics to work on projects sympathetic to his own. Along with three leading stalwarts of the economics department – Frank Knight, Milton Friedman and George Stigler – Hayek would go on to form the Mont Pelerin Society, an international forum for libertarian economics. Hayek and Friedman would also support the Intercollegiate Society of Individualists, an American student organisation devoted to the spread of libertarian ideas.

Friedman and the Chicago men

Ever since its eighteenth-century origins, the US has had a strong strand of libertarianism running through its veins. In the 1940s, home-grown journalists and writers like Isabel Paterson, Rose Wilder Lane, and Ayn Rand helped spread the libertarian ideas to which Hayek and Friedman later gave academic respectability. Wilder Lane, who had travelled through the Soviet Union with the Red Cross, became a committed opponent of communism. Her initial writings on individualism and the libertarian state led to the publication of *The Discovery of Freedom* in 1943. Lane opposed the New Deal, and worried about 'creeping socialism' through social security and all forms of taxation. That year also saw the publication of *The Fountainhead* by Ayn Rand and *The God of the Machine* by the literary critic Isabel Paterson. Together, these three women built the foundations of the modern libertarian movement in America.

But despite the popular success of these ideas, the world of academia and policy remained dazzled by Keynesianism. Long after his death in 1946, most economists would accept Keynes's argument in favour of state intervention in the economy, especially during downturns. Meanwhile, the federal government in the US would kick into tax and spend overdrive. From 1950 onwards, as the economy grew, so too did the state's spending: on defence, and the wars in Korea and Vietnam, as well as on health, education and social security. For decades to come, the US would grow accustomed to running budget deficits on a grand scale, backed by the academic beliefs of the time.

A notable exception to Keynesian dominance was the economics department of the University of Chicago. Led by Milton Friedman, Chicago launched a libertarian counter-attack against the Keynesian mainstream. A small man with a giant reputation, Friedman was not only a good technical economist who made fundamental contributions to economic science but also a pugnacious debater unafraid to speak in public and write in the popular press.

As Micklethwait and Wooldridge put it in *The Fourth Revolution*: 'Friedman loathed the liberal conceit that government was the embodiment of reason and benevolence; he only saw muddle and selfishness. He believed there was a direct correlation between government intervention and national decline.'[12] Friedman also took on the idea that politicians and bureaucrats were more noble in their intentions than their counterparts in business. In many ways, Friedman was more combative than Hayek. Where Hayek had been at pains to produce a sober critique of his socialist contemporaries and his friends like Keynes, Friedman was not averse to more startling arguments. In 1962, he wrote *Capitalism and Freedom*, in which he proposed slashing big government programmes when they were at their very height. (Kennedy, who had inherited a $289 billion federal government debt from Eisenhower, had just added a further $23 billion by spending on farm subsidies and employment offices.) Friedman argued for the abolition of the minimum wage and farm subsidies and even the elimination of border controls.

Friedman also hobnobbed with politicians to further his cause. In 1964, he advised Barry Goldwater, and subsequently became an ally of Ronald Reagan. Nevertheless, in the 1960s and the first half of the 1970s, Friedman, Hayek and the Chicago school were still mostly wading against the dominant stream of opinion and practice.

But all that would soon change.

Thatcher and Reagan

The first signs that the tide against big government was turning came in February 1975 when Margaret Thatcher was elected leader of the UK Conservative Party. Shortly after she became leader, Thatcher met Hayek in London. In the summer of 1975, when a speaker at the Conservative Research Department argued that she should choose a pragmatic 'middle way' between the extremes of left and right, Thatcher reached into her bag and held a book aloft. It was Hayek's *The Constitution of Liberty*, published in 1960, in which he argued that liberty was the pre-condition for wealth and growth, and not the other way around. 'This is what we believe,' Thatcher said, banging the book down on the table for emphasis.[13]

When Thatcher came to power in 1979, Britain's economy was on its back, wracked by inflation and unemployment. She launched an immediate reversal of the state's control of the economy, privatising whole sectors, reforming industrial relations, and introducing changes to taxation. Competition policy was given more weight than industrial policy. Along with privatisation came financial deregulation. Exchange controls were abolished in 1979, and the Big Bang of 1986 removed many constraints on the London Stock Exchange.

On the macro-economy, Thatcher was influenced by Friedman's monetarist thinking. Direct income taxes were lowered while indirect taxes increased. Interest rates were raised to slow the growth of the money supply and lower inflation; limits on public spending were introduced; and spending on social services such as education and housing was reduced.

In 1982, at the Conservative Party Conference, Thatcher would say that her government had done 'more to roll back the frontiers of socialism than any previous Conservative government'. The following year she claimed that the British people had completely rejected state socialism and understood that 'the state has no source of money other than money which people earn themselves ... There is no such thing as public money; there is only taxpayers' money.' *vuae*

A recession in the early 1980s saw unemployment rise, but the subsequent recovery, when it came, brought annual growth of over 4 per cent in the late 1980s, leading to claims of a British 'economic miracle'. By 1987, unemployment was falling and the economy was stable. Inflation, which had reached a high of 27 per cent in 1975, fell to 2.5 per cent by 1986, and the top rate of tax fell to 40 per cent in 1988 from 98 per cent in 1979. Privatisation improved performance in many cases, through greater labour productivity. In 1987, Thatcher was re-elected for a third successive term. Many of her policies would remain in place for decades. Even the Labour Party, which had once vehemently opposed her policies, dropped its opposition to many of them when it came to power in the late 1990s.

In the US, Ronald Reagan became president in 1980. Like Thatcher, he was sceptical of government, and listed Hayek among the two or three people who had most influenced him. Like Thatcher, Reagan launched a Hayekian programme of deregulation. He advocated free-market fiscal policies, and sought to stimulate the economy with across-the-board tax cuts. Opposed to government intervention, Reagan reduced spending on non-military programmes such as Medicaid, food stamps, federal education and the Environmental Protection Agency. To manage

Cutting all
non-military
programs?
stupid!

41

the central bank, Reagan appointed Alan Greenspan chairman of the Federal Reserve in August 1987. A member of Ayn Rand's inner circle since the 1950s, Greenspan would describe himself as a 'lifelong libertarian Republican'.

As in the UK with Thatcher, after the early 1980s recession, the US economy under Reagan grew quickly, posting an annual rate of 7.9 per cent from 1982 to 1988. Unemployment, which had peaked at 10.8 per cent in December 1982, fell during the rest of Reagan's presidency. Sixteen million new jobs were created, and inflation decreased significantly.

Are we going to talk about the bad?

The rest of the world

But perhaps the greatest successes for Hayek, Friedman and their libertarian ideas would come from behind the Iron Curtain. In the 1970s and 1980s, books like *The Road to Serfdom* would prove a major influence on the future leaders of the 'velvet revolutions' of Central and Eastern Europe. Many of these then dissenters would become classical liberals like Hayek, having learned from him the importance of economic freedom. One of them, Václav Klaus, described how, as a graduate student in Italy, he had read Hayek, and then returned to Czechoslovakia with a deep appreciation for the principles of the market. Klaus would eventually become president of the Czech Republic.

Milton Friedman would claim that no one had had more influence 'on the intellectuals behind the Iron Curtain' than Friedrich Hayek. 'His books', Friedman said, 'were translated and published by the underground and black market editions were read widely, and [undoubtedly influenced the climate of opinion that ultimately brought about the collapse of the Soviet Union.'[14]]

you're delusional??

Indeed, the collapse of the Soviet Union laid bare all the pitfalls of centrally planned economies; and not only their economic

that isn't how the USSR fell...

drawbacks – the waste, stasis and inefficiency – but also their political and moral consequences. Very much as Hayek had warned, the communist bloc had used its hold over the economy to consolidate power in the hands of a monolithic state that then controlled all aspects of life. The road to serfdom had led to a nightmarish reality of gargantuan proportions. The fall of the Iron Curtain, when it came, was a liberating force greeted with almost universal relief. → pretty sure the people in that region not would agree

Close on the heels of the Soviet bloc came many post-colonial countries in Asia, Africa and Latin America. Under the influence of the Soviets, and in reaction to a capitalism which they associated with imperialism, many of these countries had, between the 1950s and 1990s, adopted central planning and state ownership of the economy. Now they saw the damage that central planning had done. Moreover, in East Asia, they saw how market economics had led to spectacular growth in Japan, Taiwan, South Korea, Hong Kong and Singapore. Afraid of turning into the Soviet Union and inspired by these Asian tigers, the developing economies of Asia, Africa and Latin America began in the 1990s to dismantle state ownership and open up to domestic and foreign competition. The sweeping away of controls brought a flourishing unlike the world had ever seen before. From 1990 onwards, some of the new emerging markets – not least China and India – began to see double-digit growth.

By the dawn of the new millennium, there were very few countries in the world where the state still dominated the economy. Globally, a liberal consensus prevailed. Hayek and his acolytes had won. The libertarians, it would seem, had vanquished the state.

Or had they?

The state never went away

In the late twentieth century, despite the victories of Hayek and Friedman, and despite the relentless progress of the market, the state persisted. Indeed, states would only grow in importance alongside markets. After all, governments were needed to guide and manage the economy. If anything, as markets grew in importance, the role of governments became even more crucial.

In the US, from the 1950s onwards, the federal government began running a seemingly permanent budget deficit. Even as the economy grew and prosperity spread, state spending on social programmes and defence increased. John F. Kennedy added $23 billion to the $289 billion debt he inherited from Eisenhower by spending on state highways, farm price supports, tax refunds, a Food Stamp programme and employment offices. Lyndon Johnson added a further $42 billion to the national debt with the founding of Medicare and Medicaid, and urban renewal. This was nearly double what Kennedy had added, but would be less than a third of President Nixon's increase. In fact, with only one exception, every president since Johnson has grown the national debt by 30 per cent or more. Even Ronald Reagan – that famous advocate of limited government – would end up presiding over an expanding state and increased spending. His policy of 'peace through strength' involved a 40 per cent real increase in defence spending between 1981 and 1985, a peacetime record. (The only exception to this trend would be Bill Clinton, who ended his second term with a budget surplus: an achievement that was quickly reversed by George W. Bush's tax cuts.)

In the UK under Thatcher, the privatisation of industry needed state regulation to ensure fairness and competition. Indeed, regulation expanded significantly during the Thatcher years to compensate for the loss of direct government control. Regulatory bodies such as the Office of Telecommunications (Oftel), the Office of Gas and Electricity Markets (Ofgem), and the National Rivers Authority were formed in 1984, 1986 and 1989, respectively.

In the 1990s, the left-of-centre governments of Bill Clinton in the US and Tony Blair in the UK found an accommodation with the market and the libertarian ideas of Reagan and Thatcher. They valued the prosperity that markets brought and they used this to fund the welfare state. Markets for them were not incompatible with social programmes and state funding of health and education. Clinton reformed the social security system, making it more efficient and fair. Blair invested in social infrastructure – in schools and hospitals – and focused on improving the delivery of these services, reducing waiting times in the NHS and improving educational outcomes in schools. There was also a focus on reducing child poverty and growing inequality. This pragmatic consensus between the state and the market would last for at least two decades, until it all came crashing down in 2007–08.

The financial crisis

Perhaps the most spectacular case for the role of the state would come with the financial crisis of 2007–08, the worst global downturn since the Great Depression.

After several years of growth, and ever-increasing deregulation of financial markets, the chickens came home to roost in a big way in 2007, when subprime homeowners in the US began to default on their mortgages. Then, on 15 September 2008, the excessive risks that banks had taken resulted in the collapse of the Lehman Brothers – the fourth-largest US investment bank. The credit freeze that followed threatened a collapse of the global financial system.

There were many, complex reasons for the crash. Nevertheless, the Financial Crisis Inquiry Commission, set up by the US Congress to investigate, concluded that the main reasons were widespread failures in financial regulation and supervision and the market's inability, on its own, to rein in Wall Street. Specific failures of the state included poor 'preparation and inconsistent action' as well as the deregulation of over-the-counter derivatives, especially credit default swaps; the repeal of the Glass–Steagall Act in 1999 which removed the separation between investment and depository banks in the United States; and laws that were poorly enforced in key parts of the financial system.

As early as 1997, Alan Greenspan, the chairman of the Federal Reserve, had fought to keep the derivatives market unregulated. In 2000, President Clinton and Congress had brought in the Commodity Futures Modernization Act which permitted the self-regulation of the over-the-counter derivatives market. Derivatives such as credit default swaps (CDS) could then be used to hedge against credit risks without requiring ownership of the underlying debt instruments. Between 1998 and 2008, the volume of outstanding CDSs would increase a hundred-fold, with estimates of the debt covered by these contracts ranging from $33 to $47 trillion by November 2008. Meanwhile, by June 2008, the total value of over-the-counter derivatives would rise to $683 trillion.

The state, through its negligence, had helped bring on the crisis. Now it had to step in to mitigate the fallout. The Federal Reserve, along with central banks around the world, immediately expanded the money supply. This, it was hoped, would prevent a deflationary spiral in which lower wages and greater unemployment would cause a self-reinforcing drop in global consumption. Central banks in the US, UK and Europe then launched the largest liquidity injection in world history, purchasing $2.5 trillion of government debt and troubled private assets from banks. Governments in the West rushed to guarantee the debt issued by banks, ultimately purchasing $1.5 trillion of newly issued preferred stock in their major banks. States broadened the number of institutions with liquidity and increased the flexibility with which institutions could tap into such liquidity.

Governments also bailed out a variety of firms, incurring huge financial obligations in the process. Together, various US government departments spent trillions on loans, asset purchases, guarantees and direct spending. The US would eventually execute two stimulus packages, totalling nearly $1 trillion during 2008 and 2009. Other countries launched their own stimulus plans in 2008.

In June 2009, President Obama introduced a series of regulatory proposals. These addressed consumer protection, executive pay, bank financial cushions and capital requirements; expanded regulation of the shadow banking system and derivatives; and gave greater powers to the Federal Reserve to wind down systemically important institutions. In January 2010, Obama proposed further regulations limiting the ability of banks to engage in proprietary trading. In Europe, governments introduced the Basel III regulations that increased capital ratios, imposed limits on leverage and counter-party risk, and introduced new liquidity requirements.

During congressional hearings in 2008, Alan Greenspan would testify that he had 'made a mistake in presuming that the self-interest of organizations, specifically banks and others, were [sic] such that they were best capable of protecting their own shareholders and their equity in the firms'.[15] He went on to grudgingly admit that his free-market ideology might have been flawed.

The financial crisis proved how important governments are to the smooth running of their economies. It demonstrated that when states take their eyes off the ball, the busts that follow booms are inevitable and deeply damaging. Then, in the aftermath of these busts, governments have to step in and clean up the mess. Without such interventions, the world would have seen more and greater catastrophes, cataclysms that would make the Great Depression seem tame in comparison.

Libertarians versus statists

In the last quarter of the twentieth century, the mutual dependence between the state and the market became starkly evident in many parts of the world. The rise of the Asian tigers and then China showed precisely what is possible when the market is managed by the state. Without the state's muscular role, there would not have been an East Asian miracle. In Russia, in contrast, the aftermath of the Soviet Union showed what happens when the state is weak. There, shock therapy and an inattentive government brought with them all the horrors of unbridled, laissez-faire capitalism: the rise of oligarchs and inequality on a grand scale.

But equally, as China shows, the market on its own cannot ensure liberty. For freedom to have deep roots, it is necessary to have constitutional checks and balances on central state power, and a wider culture of independent institutions and transparency. An authoritarian state can manage the economy to generate prosperity as a cynical means to ensure its own monopoly on power.

So, as we enter the third decade of the new millennium, after over a hundred years of boom and bust and seismic political and social change, what have we learned about how a government should be?

On the one hand, through Hayek, Friedman and the libertarians, we have learned about the power of the market to deliver economic dynamism and, in some cases, provide other types of freedom too. But on the other hand, through Keynes and the statists, we have learned about the flaws and limits of markets and the need for government management, regulation and intervention.

The libertarians have won many victories, none more significant than the fall of Soviet communism and (partly) the rise of China. The developing nations that adopted state planning as a central tenet have all begun to liberalise. In those countries, the state has stepped back from running and owning the means of production and opened up to domestic and foreign competition. The space for economic liberty has expanded around the world. In some cases, civil and political liberties have also expanded as a result.

The irony, though, is that while all this has happened, the

statists have won victories of their own. Side by side with the expansion of the market, the world has also seen an expansion of the state, of its duties and responsibilities, and its powers, size and budgets. In addition to their nineteenth-century duties of providing security, defence, and law and order, in the twentieth century, governments became responsible for managing the economy and the business cycle, setting fiscal and monetary policy, providing social security and employment guarantees, spending on infrastructure, health and education, and investing in science and technology.

Now, in the twenty-first century, the list of things that governments must do has grown even longer. Many of the greatest challenges of our time – globalisation, migration, inequality, climate change, pandemics and disruptive technology – can only be dealt with by proactive states that take coordinated action in the public interest, while balancing the competing interests of multiple groups. In addition to everything they have done before, governments must now also stimulate innovation, deal with employment and skills, protect the environment and regulate new technological areas. States are the final backstop against all the spill-overs of the private sector, good and bad.

Around the world, impatience at the inability of governments to respond to changing circumstances has resulted in mass dissatisfaction. Disruptions brought by technology have led to disruptions in politics. This has been further exacerbated by crises such as the financial crash of 2007–08 and the Covid-19 pandemic of 2020. Citizens want their governments to be more responsive, competent and transparent. This requires leaders to make all kinds of pragmatic trade-offs between state intervention and liberty. But, as Ricardo Reis, a professor at the London School of Economics, writing on responses of policy makers to the Covid-19 economic crisis, puts it: 'Across all these trade-offs, the urgency of doing something has drawn in the usual ideologues. For them, there are no trade-offs (now or ever). The emergency either requires a huge permanent expansion in the role of the government, or bailouts to failed but politically connected businesses.'[16]

Ultimately, however, states cannot go on endlessly growing and spending to achieve their objectives. Overspending can have disastrous economic consequences. Increasing the size and complexity of government will also make it slow to change and unresponsive to citizens' needs. Even if governments must spend during the crisis itself, eventually, when the crisis passes, someone has to foot the bill. And so governments have to learn how to do more and better with less, and they have to act quickly, without breaking the bank. But to believe that this requires handing them more power is a mistake. Even the best governments can, in time, turn complacent, arrogant and incompetent.

In 1936, Keynes wrote in *The General Theory of Employment, Interest and Money* that: 'The authoritarian state systems of today seem to solve the problem of unemployment at the expense of efficiency and freedom. But it may be possible by a right analysis of the problem, to cure the disease whilst preserving efficiency and freedom.' That balance between effectiveness, efficiency and freedom is precisely the challenge that this book takes up.

Hayek and friends vs. Amazon and co.

For most of the last hundred years, the question of how governments should be has been fought on the battleground of big and small states. But the area of possibility has now changed for reasons that Hayek, Keynes and Friedman could not have anticipated or known.

Whether we like it or not, states are more important now, even as markets have become more powerful. Technology has made it easier for governments to do more with less. This technology has also made market actors, in some cases, more powerful than states, threatening to destabilise states and markets alike.

To ensure that markets work well, governments must now have a better understanding of technology and how to use it better. But there also need to be checks and balances on what state and market actors can achieve with their newfound power.

Hayek died in March 1992, just before the internet went mainstream worldwide. He did not live to see the rise of the digital giants: the immense power that market efficiency could bring, but also the inequality it could create, the distortions it could bring to democracy and freedom, and the threats it could pose to governments and economies alike. He did not live to see how countries like India – whose governments in the twentieth century had hardly been models of efficiency and effectiveness – could use twenty-first-century technologies and forms of organising to create a powerful digital infrastructure at low cost. And though he had lived through a decade of China's rise, Hayek could not have anticipated how the Chinese government would use the power of the market to deepen its own hold on power, and use technology and organisation to develop a state apparatus to monitor and control its people.

In the 1940s Hayek had argued that economic efficiency and individual freedom were closely allied. A free, decentralised society could allocate resources better than a few central planners; the latter could only guess at the knowledge dispersed among millions of individuals. Today, by contrast, an efficient, centralised system may well be possible. Digital technologies and big data allow firms like Google, Amazon and Facebook to 'view' large parts of the economy and coordinate it far more effectively than the Soviet planners ever could.

Hayek had three arguments against states. The first two were their relative inefficiency and incompetence; the third was their potential to misuse excessive power. However valid his first two critiques might once have been, clearly governments now can do a lot *and* do it well. India's Aadhaar is testament to that. States can also use their privileged access to the public to conduct experiments and learn from the results. They can, as the digital giants do with their customers, use new technology, data and behavioural science to nurture their relationship with citizens in smart and nimble ways. Governments can then quickly scale up solutions that have been proved to work at the experimental stage and look across domains to share best practices across different levels of the state.

Put simply, today there are transformational technologies that Hayek did not anticipate and that are altering the scale and scope both of government and private enterprise. This has consequences for old arguments about the size of the state, in that they no longer make sense as a way of choosing between the options. For instance, for good or ill, we can now have a vastly intrusive state apparatus at low cost.

So, what remains is Hayek's third critique of government, namely, its potential to misuse its power. In some ways, this critique is even more relevant in the twenty-first century. Can governments become too efficient and effective for their own good and that of their citizens? We turn to the potential dark side of the state's ability to use new technology and organisation in Chapter 3.

Hayek → planning (anti-socialism) (libertarianism fandus
Keynes → market manipulation
Friedman → no manipulation & no gov involv in economy

3

Lean Leviathan: is an effective, efficient state only more terrifying?

'Even to observe neutrality, you must have a strong government.'

Alexander Hamilton

'A government big enough to give you everything you want is strong enough to take everything you have.'

Thomas Jefferson

Back in New Delhi, Aadhaar had by 2016 expanded well beyond its original aims. Intended as a voluntary scheme, it had now become practically mandatory for not only a number of government services but also certain private services such as mobile phone connections and bank accounts. Critics from various quarters pointed out that it still didn't have a proper legal basis on which to operate. But any new bill the government introduced would need the approval of the upper house where the BJP, the ruling party, didn't have a majority.

To circumvent this, on 3 March 2016, the finance minister, Arun Jaitley, introduced the Aadhaar Act as a 'money' bill. Such 'money' bills, could be passed using a special provision that linked them to mainly financial matters, allowing them to bypass formal approval from the upper house. A clause in the Act retroactively legalised all previous executive actions of the government related to Aadhaar.

The decision to introduce the Act as a money bill was immediately criticised by the opposition. Ghulam Nabi Azad of the Congress party wrote to Jaitley complaining that it was wrong of the ruling party to bypass the upper house because the BJP did not have the majority there. Tathagata Satpathy of the Biju Janata Dal party raised concerns that the project might be used for mass surveillance or even ethnic cleansing in the future.

Despite this opposition, the Act was passed in the lower house on 11 March 2016. In a debate in the upper house on 16 March, Sitaram Yechury of the Communist Party of India (Marxist) argued that the bill should not have been passed when a case concerning the right to privacy was still in the Supreme Court. On 16 March 2016 the upper house returned the bill to the lower house with some suggested amendments, which the lower house promptly rejected.

Critics: efficacy, security and privacy

As the government and its various arms – in New Delhi and in the states – began to find ever more uses for Aadhaar, India's civil society began to find ever more objections to it. These objections did not go away after the passage of the Aadhaar Act. Indeed, they only gathered momentum, and fell under three main banners: efficacy, security and privacy.

Aadhaar had run into a number of practical problems since its first application in the public distribution of food. Reetika Khera, a development economist and critic, has highlighted three of these. First, while most people had an Aadhaar number, a few of the most vulnerable did not. For them, gaining access to food through the public distribution system was threatened. Even for those who had ID numbers, problems arose because of errors in data entry, because the process of 'seeding' or linking to Aadhaar caused problems due to lack of connectivity, or because unscrupulous middlemen extracted a fee to get this linking done. Further, errors in the demographic data such as misspelt names or incorrect dates of birth could cause problems when there was a mismatch between information in a bank account and the Aadhaar card. Such mismatches could then lead to pension payments, for instance, being disrupted or discontinued.

Khera's views have been backed up by a December 2017 report released by the Center for Global Development. Based on research conducted in the state of Rajasthan, the study found problems with authentication and financial access points, and that some respondents had to pay 'fees' to providers. The report concluded that 'even with the Aadhaar system in place and apparent broad preferences for the new delivery systems, the technological infrastructure creates some bottlenecks'.[1] Of those receiving food rations, 71 per cent could generally authenticate themselves in one or two attempts; for 25 per cent it took three to four attempts; and 4 per cent said that they were unable to do so in a timely manner or not at all. The few who found the new system worse for gas subsidies and pensions cited the inconvenience of accessing bank funds as the main reason.

Jean Drèze, a Belgian economist who has lived in India since 1979, has worked extensively on issues concerning poor urban and rural communities. Since Aadhaar's inception, Drèze has been sceptical of its ability to improve the benefits system. In 2017, with Khera and others, Drèze conducted a survey of 900 households in Jharkhand state comparing villages that used the Aadhaar system for buying grain with those that didn't. Drèze and his co-authors found that 20 per cent of households in the villages where Aadhaar authentication was compulsory failed to obtain any grain, compared to 4 per cent in other villages. They also concluded that Aadhaar had not done much to reduce corruption. Among households that succeeded in buying grain, the levels of corruption were the same – about 7 per cent – in villages with or without the system.

[handwritten margin note: is this research/study done, but what will they do with the findings]

Other critics have objected to Aadhaar being made mandatory for welfare and social services schemes. Indeed, Khera, along with her co-authors, estimates that, since 2014, at least twenty-five people may have died because glitches in the system have them cut off from rations, healthcare or pension payments.[2]

A second major issue was the security of the system and related concerns about privacy. In January 2018, the *Tribune*, an English-language daily, revealed that for about $8 a journalist had managed to gain illegal access to the entire Aadhaar database, except for cardholders' fingerprints and iris scans. For $5 more, she was able to print out ID cards linked to any Aadhaar number.[3] The UIDAI's first response to the news was to file a police report against the reporter and her newspaper. When this resulted in more bad press, the UIDAI changed its tune, reiterated its commitment to press freedom and to finding the culprits, and added more layers of security to the system.

It soon emerged that the journalist from the *Tribune* had been able to breach the system's defences through one of the thousands of private registration providers licensed to process ID applications. Ananth Padmanabhan from the Carnegie Endowment for International Peace believes that having so many private agents is a recipe for disaster and can lead to further problems.[4] For instance, Aadhaar is now linked to more than 150 other databases, many of which include more detailed and less secure citizens' data stored by several Indian states. Some of these databases include information on religious affiliation and use mobile phone data to track citizens' movements. Another flaw emerges from how the UIDAI itself is structured. 'It is a very strange beast,' says Mr Padmanabhan. 'They made the custodian of data the regulator. Those duties should be separated.'[5]

[handwritten margin note: difficult to ensure privacy w/ many private contractors]

Critics have raised concerns about breaches in the security of a database that could eventually store a full profile of a person's lifestyle, friends and purchases. Others worry that crooks or the government itself might misuse such data. These concerns have not proven to be unfounded: over 200 government entities have published private Aadhaar data, and a few firms with access to Aadhaar data have been caught using it for purposes other than those permitted.

Mishi Choudhary, a technology lawyer writing for the BBC, argues that it may be hard to prevent the misuse of the database for state surveillance. Anyone committing data to the system, she says, is essentially 'betting for her lifetime that her government will never become totalitarian or even strongly anti-democratic'.[6] Choudhary points to the case of Xinjiang province in China where state surveillance has resulted in the 'vast collection of DNA samples, fingerprints, iris scans and blood types of people aged 12 to 65'.[7] This information is linked to residents' *hukou*, or household registration cards, and has been used to control people's access to educational institutions, and medical and housing benefits.

Choudhary argues that the risks of catastrophic failure are hard to manage in a centralised single-number system. Because no one can change their genetic data or fingerprints in response to a leak, any compromise of such a database is essentially irreversible for a whole lifetime. Further, no government can definitively claim that such a database will never be compromised. 'In more decentralised approaches,' she says, 'multiple data sources and forms of identification are overlapped to get as high a probability of correct identification as necessary. This means not relying on only one form to confirm a person's identity and allowing for different forms to be used to enable diversification of risk.'[8]

The Supreme Court steps in

By 2018, Aadhaar had become a focal point for debates about privacy, data sovereignty and digital governance in India. Writing in April 2018, Shashi Tharoor, a Congress party member of parliament, argued that the government had effectively made Aadhaar mandatory, while assuring the courts that it was not. The government had even allowed private companies in, so much so that the entire scheme was now 'unconstitutional', despite the backing of the Aadhaar Act, 2016. The Act, accordingly to Tharoor, limited the purpose of authentication to establishing the 'identity of an individual in relation to the receipt of a subsidy, benefit, or service incurred from the Consolidated Fund of India'.[9] How did services provided by private banks and telephone operators fall within these categories? And what interest did the state have in knowing whether an individual had travelled by train or plane, opened a bank account or had a mobile connection? Linking biometric and other sensitive data to a central database, without providing adequate security, was in effect a violation of the right to privacy. Its legality was now a matter for the courts, Tharoor concluded.

The Supreme Court of India had, of course, from the very start been involved in cases linked to Aadhaar. India's constitution – whose text is the longest in the world – provides for the separation of powers: an executive that is accountable to the legislature and an independent judiciary, led by the Supreme Court. As early as July 2015, the Court had noted that some states were insisting on Aadhaar to disburse benefits despite an order against this. In August 2015, it directed the government to publicise in print and electronic media that Aadhaar was not mandatory for any welfare scheme. Eventually, in January 2018, a five-member bench began a hearing of twenty-seven cases challenging the constitutional validity of the system. Stretched over thirty-eight days, this would end up becoming the second-longest case ever presented before the Court.

On 26 September 2018, the bench announced its ruling. With a 4–1 majority, it upheld the legality of the system for welfare programmes, stating that the benefits outweighed the risks to privacy. Acknowledging failures in the system, the ruling said that these constituted only about 0.2 per cent of cases, and that there was no need to 'throw the baby out with the bathwater'. The panel permitted the government to demand Aadhaar numbers when citizens registered to pay tax and filed annual returns.

The Court, however, also ruled that Section 57 of the Aadhaar Act was unconstitutional. This meant that private banks and mobile phone operators could no longer require customers to provide their Aadhaar number to verify their identity when signing up for services. The Court also struck down the so-called 'national security exception' that allowed investigative agencies access to anyone's data without a warrant in exceptional circumstances.

The dissenting voice on the bench – that of Justice D. Chandrachud – highlighted the various risks to privacy that the system posed. In his remarks, he noted that 'constitutional guarantees cannot be compromised by the vicissitudes of technology'. He also disagreed with his fellow justices about whether Aadhaar minimised data collection, noting that it had the 'potential for surveillance' and that its architecture 'posed risks on potential violation of leakage of the database'.

Writing for the BBC, Ronald Abraham and Elizabeth Bennett argue that Chandrachud's dissenting opinion should shape the project's 'future course – and do so with transparency'.[10] They recommend that every time there's a data breach, the government should engage with researchers and critics instead of being in denial about it. The government should also be proactive about releasing information on security, and document both the shortcomings and the steps taken to correct for them. And instead of aggressively expanding the scope of the project, the government should focus on its role as an identity platform, and do that securely and well. This should include making it easier for rural residents to get updates and to eliminate exclusions due to Aadhaar.

The pros and cons of fingerprinting

Despite the controversies it has generated, the Aadhaar project remains popular. In June 2018, Amitabh Kant, the bureaucrat in charge of Niti Aayog, India's top planning body, declared that the government of India had saved $18 billion by digitally transferring money to the beneficiaries of over 400 government schemes. He added that '(The) government is ahead of the private sector in financial inclusion. We have digitised our economy. Unlike the USA, in India data is public owned.'[11] Aadhaar, Kant said, had helped India pole-vault into the top five of fintech (financial technology) economies globally. Indeed, by 2020, India was the world's second-largest fintech hub, with over 2,000 start-ups and a transaction value of over $30 billion in 2016 (expected to grow to over $70 billion by 2020).[12, 13]

Nandan Nilekani, Aadhaar's mastermind, argues that it should be seen not as another project or scheme but as fundamental infrastructure for the digital age. India is now the only country in the world, he points out, where a billion people can do completely paperless, cashless transactions on their mobile phones at dramatically reduced costs. 'If you build the right digital infrastructure then you can leapfrog.'[14]

When seen as critical infrastructure, Aadhaar seems less controversial. The government, argues Nilekani, would never refuse to build a highway because smugglers could potentially drive on it. Nor would anyone argue that we should 'destroy the highways we've already built and millions use, because not everyone owns cars' or that 'only state-owned vehicles, not private car and truck owners, should drive on it'.[15] In the case of Aadhaar, he says, 'universal access is for the greater good'.[16]

Nilekani agrees that there is a need for stronger privacy and security controls. But these needs, he feels, should not be an argument against private access. Instead, they are a reason to allow such access to pass through the state, because doing so would bring universal oversight to the system. 'The democratic checks and balances that we build to regulate private access will also regulate government actions. It is far better, in such cases, to trust the state's institutions with their judicial and parliamentary oversight, than the benevolence of data-driven businesses.'[17]

Indeed, if the state does not produce public goods, the private sector will step in to fill the void. In many countries, the global tech giants are the most popular providers of digital identity. 'It is their stated objective', Nilekani reminds us, 'to know you better than you know yourself, so that they can sell ads and products to you.'[18] Increasingly, these businesses are so profitable that they can cross-subsidise other services and offer them free, in order to collect even more of your data. This data, Nilekani argues, 'does not reside on Indian soil and is accessible to foreign governments. We do not have sovereignty over our own data, and cannot decide what happens to it.'[19]

The benefits of Aadhaar are no doubt many, and there is global acknowledgement of what it has achieved. Paul Romer, Nobel Laureate and former World Bank chief economist, believes that it is best to develop one standardised system so people can carry their IDs wherever they go in the world and that the system in India is the most sophisticated he has seen. Romer also believes that it should be part of the policy of the government to give individuals some control over the data that the private firms collect and some control over how that data is used'.[20] In this, he is on the side of a growing number of human rights activists and policy experts, all of whom agree that giving users control over data is a good way to enable fairness and privacy in its capture and use, whether by governments or private firms.

India is hardly an exception

While remarkable in its scale and scope, in global terms the Unique ID project is by no means unique. The Indian attempt to revolutionise government and its relationship with its citizens has in fact happened alongside – and even been preceded by – similar attempts around the globe.

In 2003, for instance, Brazil introduced the Bolsa Familia programme of direct cash transfers to poor families who kept their children in school and attended regular preventive healthcare sessions. Launched by President Lula da Silva, the programme built on earlier efforts to create a single national database of the beneficiaries of government assistance. It reduced the duplication of benefits and administrative costs across programmes and introduced time limits and graduation criteria for beneficiaries. By 2013, the programme was credited with halving extreme poverty from 9.7 per cent to 4.3 per cent and reducing income inequality by 15 per cent.[21] According to Deborah Wetzel, a senior director at the World Bank, with nearly 50 million beneficiaries, 90 per cent of whom were women, the programme is now widely regarded as a 'global success story' and a 'reference point for social policy around the world'.[22] Most impressively, the exercise didn't cost much. For just 0.6 per cent of GDP, the government had brought efficiency to its social sector – Brazil spends over 20 per cent of GDP on education, health, social protection and social security – and built a platform for further programmes such as Brasil sem Miséria (Brazil without Misery) and Busca Ativa (Active Search). A country which had once been derided for being a place where 'throwing money out of a helicopter' would be a more efficient way to reach its poor, had succeeded in creating a system that brought dignity and autonomy to its people in a quick and frugal way.[23]

Elsewhere in the Americas, Mexico, Chile and Uruguay have made rapid progress in simplifying and digitising public services. In Mexico, 74 per cent of government transactions can now be completed online.[24] In Chile, the cross-government Digital Agenda 2020 aims 'to achieve massive use of online services and to guarantee their quality'.[25] Tools that make it easier to share information between departments have been crucial to delivering citizen-focused services. For example, having a unified system to verify people's identity online makes coordinating services easier. Mexico and Uruguay now have such digital identity systems in place, and citizens can access services using interfaces that are simple and similar to one another. Between 2010 and 2014, Chile launched its ChileAtiende programme, which brings together services from twenty different government institutions. Citizens can access 'all these transactions face-to-face in a single office' or through the programme's 'call centre or web platform'.[26]

Meanwhile, in Europe, Estonia has, since the mid-1990s, pursued a systematic programme of developing and embedding e-governance as a cornerstone of how it is run. A world leader in digitisation, Estonia allows its citizens to do a whole host of things online, including voting, filing tax returns, obtaining identities via e-ID, participating in the census, setting up businesses, signing contracts, managing pensions, obtaining and fulfilling prescriptions, and interacting with the education system. All these services are linked to a single unique ID. The Estonian government estimates that its e-systems save about 2 per cent of GDP per year through efficiency while increasing citizen engagement and delivering one of the highest rates of tax payment in the world. Further, e-ID solutions also allow for better internal tracking of expenditure, reducing improper government payments. A similar approach in a country like the US would result in savings of over $300 billion (2 per cent of US GDP in 2017) and over $100 billion a year in improper government payments.[27] Inspired by this example, Israel is in the process of doing something similar.

Despite the ability of the state to use new technology and organisation to do more for its citizens with less, there is nevertheless a dark side to these developments. As the Aadhaar project shows, such programmes raise legitimate concerns about privacy, security and surveillance. India, however, despite its problems, is a democratic country, with constitutional checks and balances,

[handwritten marginalia: examples of digital public services]

[handwritten marginalia: 1) allows access (will only internet (no house) required)]

an independent judiciary and a (mostly) free press. These checks and balances, as Nilekani argues, can act to ensure transparency and protection of citizens against misuse by the state. But not all countries have such protections, and some very authoritarian governments around the world have taken to the new world of technology and organisation with great enthusiasm.

China's 'Social Credit System'

Since 1978, when its ruling Communist Party opened up to the world, China has enjoyed a remarkable renaissance. The country's achievements not only make it globally important, but they also require us to be nuanced about its complexities and contradictions. In the space of four decades, the country has gone from being a backwater to the second largest economy in the world. Much of this growth has been achieved by a novel form of state-controlled capitalism, whereby the government has encouraged foreign and domestic firms (some of which are state owned) to use the market mechanism to deliver innovation.

At the same time as revitalising private enterprise, the Chinese government has also pushed for change in the public sector. As Yijia Jing and Stephen Osborne describe in *Public Service Innovation in China* (2017), starting around 2003, the Chinese government began promoting a 'service-oriented government' that extends and builds on its core mission of law enforcement. At the central and local levels, public sector institutions have become engaged in service delivery – in improving health, education and citizen services – and citizen satisfaction has become an increasingly important indicator of public performance. Modern techniques have been introduced to help with this: surveys to evaluate performance, and microblogs and WeChat, a social media app, to disseminate information.

Most of these innovations, however, pale in comparison with

the Social Credit System, a national programme designed to assess the economic and social reputation of citizens and businesses. Under the system, all Chinese citizens will be given a credit rating based on their economic and social behaviour. The rating will combine Western-style credit scores with more expansive and potentially intrusive measures. These could include data from online payment providers or scores produced by neighbourhoods for good behaviour. The rating will have consequences for citizens. Those with high scores will receive perks such as favourable bank loans and discounts on heating bills, while those with low scores could be barred from buying plane or high-speed-train tickets.

Launched in 2014, the system focuses on 'honesty in government affairs', 'commercial integrity', 'societal integrity' and 'judicial credibility'. The government sees the system as a way to regulate the economy and as a tool of governance to steer the behaviour of citizens. According to the State Council's founding document, the scheme should 'allow the trustworthy to roam everywhere under heaven while making it hard for the discredited to take a single step'.[28] As of 2020, the plan to have an initial phase of the system in place nationwide seems to have largely been successful.

How it plays out can be seen in Rongcheng, one of three dozen cities across China where the system was first introduced. Rongcheng's City Hall, like the city itself, has a futuristic feel: it is a glass and steel concoction that looks like a spaceship. In a bid to ease bureaucracy, the hall serves as a one-stop shop for citizens seeking permits and licences. To save them from driving from one office to another, residents can speak to officials across departments at their desks in gleaming open-plan spaces. At one of these spaces, they can also pick up their social credit score.

Operated by the deputy director of the Rongcheng Social Credit Management Office and seven other employees, the system works as follows: 1,000 points are assigned to each of the city's 740,000 adult residents at the outset. If you get a traffic ticket, you

[handwritten margin notes: "this doesn't sound like communism"; "that's awful... and sounds just as horrible as the U.S. credit location system"; "Point of point system"]

lose 5 points. If, on the other hand, you earn a city-level award for a 'heroic act', run a good business, or help your family in difficult circumstances, you get 30 points. A department-level award gets you 5 points. You can also earn points by volunteering in city programmes or giving to charity. Anything that affects your score must be backed up by official documents.[29]

Depending on your score, you get a rating from A+++ to D. (Some offences can hurt your rating badly. Drunk driving could cause your rating to drop to a C.) An A+++ rating makes you eligible to rent public bikes without a deposit, receive a $50 heating discount in winter, and get bank loans on good terms. Companies, too, are subject to the system. They can gain points for paying taxes on time but lose them for selling substandard or unsanitary products. Businesses with higher scores benefit from more favourable loan conditions and pass through fewer hoops in winning public tenders.

The system has already been embroiled in much controversy. Across the country, Chinese courts had 'banned would-be travellers from buying flights 17.5 million times by the end of 2018' and 'citizens placed on blacklists for social credit offences were prevented from buying train tickets 5.5 million times'.[30] Others have been banned from admitting their children to certain schools, renting hotel rooms, using credit cards and even finding employment. Citizens have also been punished for their online behaviour – for spending too much time playing games or for their shopping habits – and a whole host of personal acts that have no impact on the wider community.[31] Human Rights Watch calls the programme 'chilling' and filled with arbitrary abuses.[32] Others see it as a frightening mass surveillance and disciplinary machine.

Complicating matters, there is no single system. Currently, each local government has its own system with its own variations. There are also private versions such as Sesame Credit, set up by Ant Financial, a payments firm that was spun out of Alibaba, China's Amazon. In some cases, there are agreements

[handwritten margin notes:] Very detailed. "accu" "rac"? Why do they have programs + resources helping people get out of me

between cities and companies such as Alibaba and Tencent that enable data exchanges which go into citizen assessments. Mareike Ohlberg, a research associate at the Mercator Institute for China Studies, finds this linking of data from private systems to government rankings troubling. Currently, she says, there is a great deal of data moving around with no protection, and no transparency about the algorithms used to produce a score or ranking.[33]

That said, the system isn't entirely unique to China; there are parallels in the West. In the UK, for instance, credit rating systems combine data from a citizen's credit score with phone usage and rent payments to filter job applications or determine access to social services. And companies like Experian track and supply data on how timely we are with debt repayments for use by banks and mortgage lenders. In Germany, data from a universal credit rating system, Schufa, is combined with geo-location and health records to determine access to credit and health insurance. Small businesses in the West are not immune either: those who sell on digital platforms like eBay or Amazon are subject to social-style scores based on shipping times, and Uber drivers and Airbnb renters are routinely rated by customers with consequences for their earnings. But what makes the Chinese system unique is that it extends this idea to all aspects of citizens' lives, including civic behaviour such as jaywalking, paying bills, playing music in public spaces, and so on. Ohlberg does not believe that the use, and abuse, of aggregated data for the analysis of behaviour is itself a Chinese phenomenon. But she does think that if the Chinese system comes together as envisioned, it would be 'both unique and part of a global trend'.[34]

According to the Chinese government, the Social Credit System is about building trust. This claim is not implausible. Jing Zeng, a researcher at the University of Zurich, says that the Chinese economy does have issues concerning, for example, food quality, pollution, or companies not treating their employees fairly. Punishing companies for bad behaviour could improve consumer confidence and improve the efficiency of markets. Credit ratings could also help those outside the financial system gain easier access to credit. As Ohlberg points out: 'Some of the earlier pilots of the social credit system that preceded the major policy plan that was published in 2014, were actually building a social credit system for the countryside. The majority of people there wouldn't have financial banking data on them.'[35] Such a system could also be used for micro-enterprises, whose creditworthiness cannot typically be assessed with traditional criteria.

So far, Chinese citizens seem persuaded of the essential benevolence of the system. A 2018 survey of over 2,200 respondents found that 80 per cent had joined a commercial social credit system.[36] The most popular of these was Sesame Credit, which allows users to opt in. However, only 7 per cent of respondents were aware that they were now also part of a government system. Perhaps most surprisingly, 80 per cent somewhat or strongly approved of social credit systems. The strongest support came from those who were older and more affluent, educated and urban: a group that in the West would value privacy above all. (Online, Chinese citizens appear even more enthusiastic about the approach. When, in 2016, the National Tourism Administration published the names of people who had been banned from air travel for 'bad behaviour', thousands of Chinese 'liked' and reposted the news on the Sina Weibo social media site.)

[It is possible, though, that many Chinese citizens have not thought through the implications of the system.] As Ohlberg points out, the system can also be used to 'enforce vague laws like endangering national security or unity'. Samantha Hoffman, a non-resident fellow at the Australian Strategic Policy Institute, agrees. For her, the Social Credit System is all about government power. 'If solving problems was the real goal, the CCP [Chinese Communist Party] would not need social credit to do it.'[37]

According to Hoffman, the Social Credit System is a 'state-driven program designed to do one thing, to uphold and expand the Chinese Communist Party's power'. In some ways, it is a tech-enabled version of Chairman Mao's 'Mass Line': the method that the party has used to shape and manage society since 1948. 'In Mao's China,' Hoffman says, 'the Mass Line relied on ideological mass mobilisation, using Mao Zedong's personal charisma, to force participation. The CCP could no longer, after the Mao era, rely on ideological mobilisation as the primary tool for operationalising social management.'[38]

Ohlberg also believes that misunderstandings about the system do not mean that it isn't dangerous. The truth, according to her, lies 'somewhere between the people who say the media coverage is inaccurate and that means it's not so bad and the people who see this huge dystopia'.[39]

The surveillance state

In some ways, a preview of a dystopian Chinese future is already on display in Xinjiang: the Central Asian province with a Muslim separatist movement.

Under President Xi Jinping, the Chinese government has vastly expanded domestic surveillance, fuelling a new generation of companies that make sophisticated technology at low prices. In 2017, the Chinese government spent over 1.24 trillion yuan on domestic security, amounting to over 6 per cent of total government spending and more than its military budget.[40] Internal security spending has doubled in regions like Xinjiang and Beijing. Indeed, surveillance techniques are first tested in Xinjiang before being rolled out elsewhere. These techniques include the use of video surveillance systems, database software, smartphone forensics hardware, police glasses with built-in facial recognition, cameras that analyse how people walk, drones and 'intelligent' robots. In 2018, China had 170 million security cameras in use for its so-called Skynet surveillance system, with another 400 million estimated to have come on board by 2020.[41] Integrating these cameras with facial recognition software and artificial intelligence has the potential to create a vast surveillance state.

Local variants to this broad approach crop up all the time. For instance, a recent Human Rights Watch report examines a mobile app that is being used by the authorities in Xinjiang to collect personal data on ethnic minorities in the province.[42] The app is linked to the integrated joint operations platform (IJOP), a Xinjiang policing programme that studies the data and flags individuals who are deemed threatening. IJOP is, in turn, part of a vast surveillance network in Xinjiang that includes checkpoints with face scanners, 'convenience' police stations, and even surveillance cameras inside homes. Data collected includes people's blood type, height and religious practices. Individuals flagged as threatening can end up in re-education camps. Human rights groups estimate about one million Uighurs are currently held in such camps; though the government calls them voluntary 'training centres', survivors have reported being brainwashed, abused and tortured.

According to Maya Wang, author of the Human Rights Watch report: 'The Chinese government is monitoring every aspect of people's lives in Xinjiang, picking out those it mistrusts, and subjecting them to extra scrutiny.'[43]

Here, as in other parts of the economy, the government works closely with companies. The IJOP system and app, for instance, were developed by subsidiaries of China Electronics Technology Group Corporation, a major state-owned military contractor. The app targets over 30 'person types' to which officials pay special attention. These types include those who exhibit behaviours such as 'suddenly returned to hometown after being away for a long time'; 'does not socialise with neighbours, seldom uses front door'; 'collected money or materials for mosques with enthusiasm'; and 'household uses an abnormal amount of electricity'.[44] After filing reports on suspicious individuals, the app prompts the authorities to carry out 'investigative missions'. These enable them to collect even more personal data, such as checking a person's phone for any one of over fifty apps including WhatsApp and virtual private networks (VPNs). The IJOP app might also include data on a person's vehicle, its colour, type and licence plate number. The data is then used to enable surveillance cameras equipped with artificial intelligence to track the vehicle as it travels past checkpoints, the Human Rights Watch report claims.

In China, the Communist Party is already a ubiquitous presence in city halls and boardrooms throughout the land. The use of surveillance across the board, with the aid of technology, extends its reach further. And crises, such as the Covid-19 pandemic of 2019–20, provide the perfect excuse to expand this grip wider and deeper. Long after the initial outbreak of the disease had killed thousands in Hubei province and then subsided, the Chinese government continued to police the movement of its citizens across the country through a colour-coded health app. The state also banned people, including those with residency visas, from returning to their homes from abroad.[45]

Moreover, the Chinese justice system has several inadequacies. As Samantha Hoffman points out: 'There are no genuine protections for the people and entities subject to the system … In China there is no such thing as the rule of law. Regulations that can be largely apolitical on the surface can be political when the Communist Party of China (CCP) decides to use them for political purposes.'[46] According to Amnesty International, China 'has the largest number of imprisoned journalists and cyber-dissidents in the world', a fact that is related to it having 'the world's most sophisticated system for controlling and surveilling the web'.[47]

Meanwhile, technology built for China is now being exported to other countries. By 2019, eighteen countries, including Uzbekistan, Pakistan, the United Arab Emirates and Zimbabwe, were using Chinese intelligent monitoring systems, while more than thirty-five countries had received training in topics like 'public opinion guidance', according to a report from Freedom House.[48]

With such surveillance know-how and equipment spreading across the globe, critics warn of a future of tech-driven authoritarianism, and a loss of privacy on an industrial scale. 'They're selling this as the future of governance; the future will be all about controlling the masses through technology,' says Adrian Shahbaz, research director at Freedom House.[49]

Democratic nations like the UK and the US are clearly not immune. The UK has one of the most extensive surveillance policies in the world, combining a vast network of private and public cameras with considerable traffic enforcement and internet powers. In the US, as the whistle-blower Edward Snowden revealed, the government's surveillance services have harvested data on millions of citizens' phone calls and internet usage. But China's growing global dominance has added a new dimension to the phenomenon. Loans from Beijing have made surveillance technology available to governments that could not afford it before, while China's authoritarian system means that there is little accountability and transparency around its use.

'The West should not copy any aspect of social credit,' says Samantha Hoffman of the Australian Strategic Policy Institute. She points to the comparisons with private applications like Uber and its rating system, but believes that, while private apps are problematic, they are very different from state-sponsored systems. 'The People's Republic of China is an authoritarian country,' she says. 'The Chinese Communist Party [has been] responsible for gross human rights violations for decades – just look at the example of Xinjiang now.'[50]

How should governments in the twenty-first century be?

As India's Aadhaar and China's Social Credit System show, governments around the world can now create and launch vast programmes with great speed and efficiency and at low cost.

On the plus side, these programmes show how it is possible to transcend the ideological opposition between the big and the small state. A government doesn't have to be wasteful, slow and corrupt: it can learn to be efficient, transparent and effective. But they also show the importance of civil society and institutional checks and balances in ensuring that states do not misuse the immense power and efficiency they gain from new technologies and new forms of organisation. Government programmes have to be, in a moral sense, run to different standards than private enterprise.

How states use new technologies and forms of organising in the twenty-first century is of great importance, therefore, not only to those who work for governments but to all citizens. How, then, should governments be in this brave new world? How can we ensure that they do good for their citizens in more effective and efficient ways? The next few chapters examine four principles to guide governments in doing better with less in the twenty-first century. Chapter 4 begins with perhaps the most important of these: how to build a government that is responsive to citizens' needs, namely, one that works outside-in from the citizen's perspective, rather than inside-out from the perspective of the bureaucracy.

4

The responsive state: putting citizens first

'A state should be a service, not an idol.'

Alexander Gabuev

'The worth of the state, in the long run, is the worth of the individuals composing it.'

John Stuart Mill

In 1981, at the age of twenty, Jos de Blok became what was then a rare thing: a male nurse. At university he had studied economics and had interned at the chemical giant Dow, but his heart hadn't been in it. 'It was too much about business and money and not enough about people. As a teenager, I had volunteered at a hospital and that experience had stuck with me. So I decided I would go back to that.'[1]

For the first few years, de Blok cared for people with mental health disabilities in the psychiatric wards of large hospitals. Then, in 1987, he went to work as a district nurse. At that time, as had been the case for much of the twentieth century, healthcare in the Netherlands was built around small communities with neighbourhood nurses at their centre. These nurses worked closely with family doctors and the hospital system. All highly educated, they had a great deal of autonomy, their work was varied, and their focus was firmly on their patients.

Even now, some thirty years later, de Blok is wistful about those years. 'That was the most beautiful time of my life. I worked in a village with a few colleagues. We were a team and organised everything ourselves. We learned to deal with all kinds of problems. We took care of the terminally ill, those with dementia, but we also looked after children. It was an inspiring job.'

Then in 1993 everything changed. To deal with rising costs and an ageing population, Dutch politicians across parties decided that community healthcare should be 'professionalised'. Small home-care groups would be merged to form larger organisations run by professionals. This would bring economies of scale. In a larger group, nurses with complementary skills could do more and bring a wider range of capabilities to the table. Competition would drive down costs, while the quality of care would improve.

For the new system to work, a great deal had to change. Care, which had been integrated, was now split into care for the elderly and for children. Then, the very definition of what work would be done by whom also changed. A lot of the jobs that were done by the nurses themselves became centralised and were moved to a back office where a whole new set of jobs was created. New people were recruited to oversee the intake of patients and assign nurses to them. Others were tasked with being planners who gave nurses their daily schedule and optimised their routes. Call centres were set up to field phone calls from patients.

Soon, managers entered the picture in a big way. By 1995, consolidation meant that the number of care organisations had dropped from nearly 300 to about 85. These larger organisations had a whole cadre of bosses – CEOs, directors and regional managers – to manage and monitor nurses in the field.

To increase efficiency, various care activities came to be defined as 'products'. Each product was in turn split into a number of tasks or interventions. To increase efficiency, each of these interventions was given its own set of time norms. Injections were given ten minutes, and bathing fifteen minutes; wound dressing would take ten minutes; changing compression stockings was allowed no more than two and a half minutes. Stickers with barcodes were put on the doors of patients' rooms. After each visit, nurses would scan these barcodes along with the product they had delivered. This data was time-stamped on a central system so everything could be monitored and assessed remotely.

The whole process of care was split into a number of specialised tasks, carried out by different people. Less educated nurses, who would be cheaper to hire, would do simpler things, while only the more highly educated, and hence more expensive, nurses would handle the more complex ones.

'The entire system changed dramatically,' says de Blok. 'In a very short period of time, the focus shifted from taking care of people to delivering products. And these products proliferated like crazy. There was personal care, personal care extra, personal care special. There was nursing care, nursing care extra, nursing care special. There was guidance, guidance extra, and so on.'

The process became industrial. As part of the change, many of the elderly were moved to old people's homes, and the back offices of the care organisations grew to take on more administration. Functional areas like human resources and marketing sprang up. 'All this changed the perception of what is good care,' says de Blok, 'and what are good solutions. Systems replaced relationships. We had quality control systems, human resource systems, administrative systems. Management layers grew. Back offices grew.'

[Instead of being able to think of patients and how to make their lives better, nurses were driven to distraction by the various activities they had to deliver and the codes to give to each of these.] If a nurse took ten minutes longer to travel to a patient, they had to explain why they had done that: they had to account for all their time as that was how they were paid. These changes resulted in an exodus of highly qualified nurses from the profession and a huge drop in education levels in the remaining workforce. Over the next few years, nearly 50 per cent of nurses educated to bachelor's level in the Netherlands left their jobs.

But if things were bad for nurses, they were even worse for patients.

'For the patients,' says de Blok, 'especially the elderly, some of these changes were a disaster. You could have someone with dementia who had to deal with thirty different people coming to their home in the space of a month. With every new person in their home, they would have to explain again their whole situation and the specific help that they needed.' Care organisations became like factories. Managers took over.

The ultimate irony was that politicians had thought that market forces and competition would drive down costs and that quality of care would improve. Instead, the reverse happened. Costs actually went up, while quality declined. The system was meant to be orderly and managed. But turmoil prevailed. As the care organisations merged and grew, they retreated into themselves and grew further and further away from the very people they were set up to serve.

Buurtzorg: placing people above bureaucracy

Jos de Blok could not escape the cataclysm of 1993. The changes meant that he had to step back from being a district nurse and move into administration. Over the course of the next decade he retrained as a manager. He studied for a master's degree in innovation and took on a series of management roles including director of innovation and eventually managing director. But all the while he was plotting to change the system, to return it to its more humane foundations.

'When I quit as a community nurse in 1994, I had a big argument with my director. And I promised my nursing colleagues and friends that I would not rest until our profession was somehow rebuilt. For ten years, I carried that promise around with me, constantly thinking of how I could make it happen.'

Meanwhile, the organisation he worked for almost went bankrupt. Many of the nurses became coordinators or assessors. Several left the field entirely. Using the skills he had picked up from his master's degree, de Blok tried to change the system from within. He made several attempts to close the gap between nurses and management. His role as director of innovation gave him a licence to do this. But he could only achieve so much. Eventually the system proved too powerful for him.

Things came to head in 2003:

> I had sixteen senior colleagues by then, all directors. All with their own empires. And all focused on their positions and their own advancement. The focus of our meetings was only about how we should compete with other home-care organisations and grow our market share. We were no longer thinking about how we could improve life for our patients.

All around him, de Blok saw a lot of dissatisfied patients and nurses. The time had come to make his move. He would have to start his own organisation and he would have to go back to first principles to do so.

He went back to what he knew and loved best: being a nurse.

> I still felt and thought like a nurse. So I did what a nurse would do and put myself in the shoes of my terminally ill patients. I tried to see the world from their perspective. Some of them would have only a few days to live. What could I do to make those last few days as good as possible?

Starting from the patient's perspective, de Blok asked himself a number of questions. How could one organise the best possible support for patients and their families? How could one help with the mourning process, and give families the best memories of the experience? The answers, when they came, were clear. It wouldn't work for patients and families to have to deal with a system that threw several different people at them all the time, each of whom was assigned to perform one of several different tasks. It would be necessary instead to focus above all on the *relationship* between the carer and the patient. You would need to have a few, highly qualified people, with autonomy, taking care of what the patient and the family needed most in those last few, precious days.

Then de Blok thought about the nurses themselves: how could he make *their* jobs better? How could he ensure that they were focused on their relationship with patients instead of the bureaucracy that had come to dominate their lives? What if one could organise all the bureaucracy in a way that would keep the outside world happy without having to bother the nurses with any of it?

> I thought about how great it would be if we could say to nurses: you do what is needed to focus on care. We will connect your time with different products, but you won't need to deal with any of that. We could still tell the health insurers we were doing things in the same way as other care organisations, that average prices would still be the same, and so on. But the reality for the nurses would be different. Their relationship with patients would be sacrosanct.

Then a final piece of the puzzle came into place. Ard Leferink, a former colleague and expert in information systems, told de Blok that he knew of a way to scale up his idea. At that time, the management information systems in use in most care organisations in the Netherlands had been developed in the 1990s, before the era of the internet. They were clunky and siloed and not particularly user-friendly. Leferink could see how a contemporary, internet-based, Facebook-like platform could be built quickly and cheaply to support the nurses in their work while freeing up their time to focus on care.

But this is what happens when we have 'frugal' governments that expect nurses to clear a million nurses because num won't find more nurses.

'With this approach,' de Blok says, 'we could focus on good patient outcomes based on professional ethics and still reduce costs. The nurses and the patients would both be happy. We would be mixing new forms of organisation and technology with the tried and tested principles that had worked in the 1970s and 1980s, and we could still keep the various players in the system, like the insurers and the politicians, happy.'

And so, in 2006, along with Leferink and Gonnie Kronenberg, his wife, de Blok set up a new care organisation: Buurtzorg. Meaning 'neighbourhood care', the organisation's mission would be to make care patient-centric and to empower nurses. Its motto and guiding principle was simple: humanity above bureaucracy.

Self-managed teams with no boss

At the heart of the Buurtzorg model is a small, self-managed team of ten to twelve nurses serving a well-defined community of about 5,000 people. 'If you work in a community of about 5,000,' says de Blok, 'you might have to deal with about forty elderly patients in need of care. If you have ten to twelve nurses in charge of that community, then each nurse has roughly four to five patients to take care of at any time, a good ratio for quality care.'

At such a scale, nurses could focus on forming deep relationships with their patients and on providing holistic, all-round care. The fragmentation that had bedevilled the managed systems of the larger care organisations became a thing of the past. Nurses became personal guides for their patients, with each patient seeing no more than one or two nurses over the course of their care. At this scale, the nurses could also create better links with others in the community and develop the informal networks they needed to do their work better.

The nurses would get referrals from hospitals, doctors or families and then organise everything themselves, including registering patients, making assessments and scheduling appointments. They would decide among themselves which doctors and pharmacies to work with and how to engage with the hospitals in the area. To assist with various administrative functions such as registration and scheduling, they would access web-based tools on a personal iPad: everything was digital.

But their autonomy didn't stop there. The teams were also allowed, for instance, to choose where to locate their offices and how to decorate them. This created ownership and a sense of entrepreneurialism. 'The moment the teams started to work in this way, they started to think differently,' says de Blok. 'In most large organisations, employees do what they are told. But if it's your own company, you ask: what do I need to do to be successful?'

In the Buurtzorg model, nurses perform a number of tasks that in larger organisations are typically done in a highly regulated way by management or the IT department. Buurtzorg teams are given broad guidelines within which to operate – their office rent should not exceed €500, the budget for office furniture is €1,200 – but they nevertheless have a great deal of autonomy. The main thing is to focus on providing the best possible care and ensuring that the teams are financially healthy. This autonomy enables a number of creative practices: nurses have found new ways of sharing information within their teams, and deal with doctors and hospitals in a similarly flexible way.

A key element of the way the teams are organised is that they have no boss: decisions are made collectively. The teams are self-organising and self-governing. In his book *Reinventing Organizations*, Frederic Laloux, an organisation theorist who has written extensively about the Buurtzorg model, says: 'Anybody who has worked on a team with no boss knows that it can easily turn into a nightmare. Yet that only rarely happens at Buurtzorg. How come?'[2]

The reason, according to Laloux, is that Buurtzorg helps the nurses to help themselves. The nursing teams are given constant support through training, coaching and the use of tools that enable such self-management to work in practice. For instance, all new nurses take a course in 'solution-driven interaction'.[3] During the course, they acquire skills and techniques for group decision-making and learn about different ways of listening and communicating. They also learn how to run meetings and how to support each other in difficult times. Once on the job, nurses get regular help from Buurtzorg coaches who are trained in group dynamics. The nurses are also encouraged to help each other out. Here, too, technology comes to their aid: teams support each other with problems and solutions on the Buurtzorg social networking platform.

Laloux emphasises that the lack of a boss does not mean that all nurses in a team are 'equal'. On any given subject, a particular nurse with the necessary expertise might take the lead, while deferring to other nurses on other subjects. For instance, one nurse might be a great coach or a good listener, while another might have an encyclopaedic knowledge of medical conditions.

The ultimate beneficiaries of all this organisational innovation are the patients themselves. With the Buurtzorg model, the patients get to know their nurses well. They build relationships with their main carers and grow to trust them over time. Their care is no longer a blur of unfamiliar faces and impersonal manoeuvres administered *to* them: an injection here, a bandage there. They are no longer simply a barcode or a number. Not only are their physical needs taken care of, but so too are their emotional and social needs, in a holistic manner. The Buurtzorg model also ensures that patients are involved in their own care. Nurses are trained to help patients to help themselves. Rather than become dependent on their nurses, patients are encouraged to tap into their networks of family, friends and neighbours for support.

Buurtzorg started in 2007 in the small Dutch town of Almelo with a single team of ten nurses. But the model soon proved so successful that by 2014 it was a rapidly growing organisation of

82

9,000 nurses serving over 70,000 patients in more than 800 communities across the Netherlands.[4] By 2018, more than half of all district nurses in the country worked for Buurtzorg.

Light back-office and no middle management

Perhaps the most revolutionary feature of Buurtzorg is how it organises its back-office work. Administration is a highly streamlined affair. Activities that can be done on the frontline by the nursing teams in a quick and seamless way are done on the frontline. The rest – core functions like salary and financial administration – are done by a small office team back in Almelo. From the start the plan was to have no middle management: no separate departments for communication, legal services, human resources, estates management, finance, procurement or information technology.

'Our vision', says de Blok, 'was that anything we can integrate into daily practice should not be done in the back office. If you register data on an IT system, then you don't need people elsewhere to control this workflow. As long as someone on a nursing team checks everything is right, you don't need another group of people to check this again.'

The Buurtzorg back office was built on the founding team's experience of what was essential for administration. Billing hours to health insurers. Contracts. Nurses needing support when they had difficult cases. The watchwords in all this were 'simplify' and 'automate'. This dramatically reduced the need for staff in Almelo. 'We said, we won't use anything from the existing world of care organisations,' says de Blok. 'Human resources became simply contracts for workers. We only did what was absolutely needed.'

In its first years, even as the number of nurses joining the organisation soared, Buurtzorg had only five to ten people dealing with administration. These staff were generalists, with flexible skills and mindsets, who understood the links between human resources and finance and who were happy to do whatever was needed of them, whether this involved client administration or working with insurers. It was never a problem for them to shift from one set of tasks to another.

'We created flexibility and ownership in the back office,' says de Blok. 'Even as we began to grow, with hundreds of nurses coming on board from 2008, we did not say: we have another 1,000 nurses, so we need more people in the back office to support them.'

To make this approach work, all the Buurtzorg nursing teams have their own budgets. Every team also has its own online point-of-sale system or PIN to take care of payments in real time. Going digital has reduced the need for paperwork flying back and forth between the frontline and headquarters.

The organisation has been very careful about how it grows its back office. As of 2018, its ratio has remained fixed at about fifty administrators serving 14,000 nurses. 'We always feel we can do with less,' says de Blok. 'If someone leaves we don't hire another person.' When Buurtzorg stepped in to rescue a failing Dutch care organisation in 2016, it ended up adding another 2,500 nurses to its rolls. Through the merger, three people from the new organisation's back office left the combined entity. 'Even though these three people left, the overall administrative process actually improved,' says de Blok. 'Sometimes when you have too many people in administration, it creates problems. And if you have people, even if you don't need them, it can be hard to get rid of them.'

The antibodies in the system fight back

The Buurtzorg journey has been far from smooth sailing, however. There has been much resistance from the existing system and from entrenched interests. In the early days, many thought that de Blok and his friends were plain crazy. How can you work with more expensive nurses, they said, and still be cheaper? The assumption was that expensive people meant expensive care. Based on this logic, a lot of care organisations had got rid of their expensive nurses. When Buurtzorg came along, they thought: they can take the expensive nurses as long as we still have access to the cheaper ones. Plus, back then Buurtzorg – with only eighty to ninety people – was still not making a big impact, and was hardly a threat to anyone.

But when the organisation began to grow, and as hundreds of nurses in the Netherlands began to join it from other care organisations, opposition started to increase. Some care organisations hired lawyers and threatened to sue if their departing nurses took their patients with them. Buurtzorg began receiving these legal letters from late 2009 onwards.

In 2010, things got worse. Some insurance companies, citing technical reasons, threatened to withhold €4 million in payments to Buurtzorg, and a cash crunch loomed. In reality, the health insurers were ambivalent about the new organisation and its breakneck growth. While some felt that the Dutch health system was ready for something new, others saw Buurtzorg as a gimmick. The Buurtzorg response to all this was: we can deal with this scepticism, as long as the insurers pay. In time, the record would speak for itself.

Support, when it arrived, came from an unexpected quarter. In 2008, the Dutch minister of health had been to visit Buurtzorg and was impressed by what the nurses had said to her. Buurtzorg had the same nurses and patients as other healthcare organisations, the minister had noted, but there was none of the disquiet that was apparent elsewhere. 'We can be ourselves in this work,' the nurses had told the minister. This resulted in an invitation to The Hague to explain to the health ministry how the Buurtzorg model worked. From this visit came an initiative to develop a national policy based on the Buurtzorg model. The insurance companies too, for their part, soon came on board, and eventually disbursed the withheld funds.

Proof of the pudding

In 2009, an independent audit by Ernst & Young found that Buurtzorg patients required 40 per cent fewer hours of care.[5] Patients, the report observed, were encouraged to be more autonomous. The nurses, rather than coddling them, helped them to recover the ability to take care of themselves. Nurses also got their patients to use their own support networks in the healing process, involving friends, family members and neighbours to help on a regular basis. As a result, patients healed faster and needed to spend less time in care. The need for hospital admissions also dropped by a third, and when patients were admitted, their stay was typically shorter. The report found other benefits too: nurse absenteeism and turnover were 60 per cent and 33 per cent lower than in other nursing organisations. Plus, overhead costs were lower than those of other home-care providers: 8 per cent of total costs compared with 25 per cent.[6] The report concluded that if the Buurtzorg model were to be scaled to the whole of the Netherlands, the Dutch social security system would realise overall savings of over €2 billion.[7]

In 2015, a new evaluation by the consultancy KPMG found that although Buurtzorg care was costlier per hour than traditional approaches, it was of higher quality and more highly valued by patients.[8] Crucially, as with the Ernst & Young audit, the KPMG study also found that the Buurtzorg model required only half as much care as was typical. As a result, the model was 30–40 per cent cheaper overall, while patient satisfaction was the highest.[9]

Unsurprisingly, Buurtzorg has been the Netherlands' 'employer of the year' for several years running.

Major proof that the model works has come from its spread to other areas of healthcare and social services in the Netherlands and beyond. In preventive health, for instance, two Buurtzorg nurses created Buurtzorg+, a new approach to prevent older people from falling and getting hurt. Realising that many elderly patients suffer from falls, and that the hip replacements they eventually receive reduce their autonomy, the nurses worked with a physiotherapist and an occupational therapist to develop a protocol of changes in home interiors and habits that would minimise the risk of falling in the first place.

Another variant is Buurtdiensten (Neighbourhood Services) designed to help Alzheimer's patients with household chores. Built around the core model of small teams working in communities, the spinoff had, by 2018, grown to over 1,000 employees in a little over three years.

In 2012, Buurtzorg Jong (Buurtzorg Young) was founded to support vulnerable and neglected children. Again, small teams of carers, working with teachers, nurses, doctors, the police and social workers in families, schools and hospitals help overcome the fragmentation and high overheads that bedevil traditional social services in this area.

In mental health, Buurtzorg T brings therapeutic care to people in the early stages of mental illness in their homes. This reduces the need to place patients in psychiatric hospitals, thus relieving pressures on the formal system.

Moves are now afoot to transform living for older people: to move away from massive, bureaucratic retirement homes to smaller-scale, community units. Hospitals everywhere have grown into large, soulless places, notes de Blok. And so Buurtzorg is driving efforts to create a small, networked set of units around city neighbourhoods.

Impressed by what the organisation has achieved in the Netherlands, other countries are developing their own equivalents of the Buurtzorg model. Since 2010, policymakers, doctors and nurses have come calling from Belgium, China, the Czech Republic, France, Japan, South Korea, Sweden, the UK and the US. 'What I see in a lot of countries is that systems are increasingly complicated and frustrations are becoming worse and worse,' says de Blok. 'I want to show that it's easy to change.'

In all, Buurtzorg has received requests from over forty countries and is helping develop the model in twenty-five of these, via licensing agreements. Buurtzorg delivers the content and translates its IT platform into different languages, but local organisations adapt the model to suit their conditions where it matters most.

Indeed, the Buurtzorg model offers important lessons not only for healthcare but for public services more generally around the world. It shows how better organisation, supported by technology, can make governments more responsive to their citizens in an area that most affects their daily lives: public services. Namely, the provision of health and social care, education, emergency services, law enforcement and security, which constitutes a major part of government work anywhere. Can governments rise to the challenge of the growing demand for better public services within increasingly constrained budgets and in a timely manner?

The global crisis in public services

For over twenty-five years, Mark Thompson has studied and practised organisational transformation in the public sector. After working in the government services division of Andersen Consulting, he went on to set up Methods, a consulting company that he still runs with his co-founders. Along the way, Thompson picked up a master's and a PhD, and is now a professor in digital economy at the University of Exeter, UK. While he has written papers and books on various aspects of change in government, his main focus throughout has been on public services.

For Thompson, a government's ability to deliver public services is of crucial importance for a number of reasons:

> Public services are the point where the state touches the vast majority of citizens. As citizens, we aren't particularly interested in the inner workings of large departments like the Treasury or the Department for Work and Pensions. But what we do care about are everyday issues like: is my rubbish collected on time and are the carers looking after my aged parents properly?[10]

Public services are the public face of governments everywhere. And yet, right across the world, they are under severe strain. Even before the financial crisis, a 2007 McKinsey report highlighted how ageing populations were leading to unsustainable increases in healthcare budgets in the developed and developing world. These pressures have only increased in the last few years. As Thompson puts it: 'In the US, the UK, France, Germany and Japan, public services are the visible sign of how governments are failing their citizens on an almost daily basis.'

There are many reasons for this. On the one hand, you have demographics and the sheer pressures of demand. We are all living longer – but not necessarily healthier – lives. There are simply more people to be taken care of. On the other hand, there's the fact that citizens' expectations have grown even as the treatment they receive is subject to rationing. Side by side with this are constraints on what governments can spend. Many countries in the West are facing a declining share of global GDP, poor productivity figures, and large and growing fiscal deficits. These problems are not going away any time soon. 'We cannot afford to cut frontline services any further,' says Thompson. 'But equally, we cannot pay for these services simply through taxation. No amount of squeezing of the top 5 per cent is going to help square the circle: the numbers are too big. Anyone who thinks that simply upping taxes on "the rich" will sort things out is kidding themselves.'

The situation is particularly bad at the local government level where many public services are delivered. Take the UK, for example. For the last few years there has been a daily chorus in the press of what is wrong with local public services. In particular, social care – the provision of protection or care to children or adults with needs due to illness, disability or poverty – is a major time bomb. A 2018 report by the Institute for Fiscal Studies estimates that social care eats up over a third of local government budgets.[11] Further, central funding for councils has dried up. Non-council tax funding has been cut to zero and some councils have had to fund social care via their savings. By 2020, a few county councils, among them Surrey and Northamptonshire, had gone bust. More are expected to follow.

'The old argument of more taxes or more cuts to public services is a false choice,' says Thompson. 'I believe that there is a third option: the wholesale administrative reform of public services. It is going to happen eventually anyway, but, mysteriously, no one is discussing this openly yet.'

To add to the mystery, a way forward may have been staring us in the face all the time.

The seductive world of Amazon, Netflix and Google

Can governments learn from Amazon, Netflix and Google? At first blush, it may seem odd, even shocking, to hold up technology firms as paragons for governments to follow. Aren't these companies, after all, exemplars of all that is wrong with the use of technology in our contemporary world? Shouldn't governments be protecting us from the excesses of the digital giants rather than mimicking them? And yet, as Mark Thompson argues, there is much that governments can learn from these firms – from how they have used technology and new forms of organising to deliver services to large numbers of people in a highly effective and efficient way.

Indeed, the internet has upended business in a whole range of sectors around the world. In little over a decade, a vast number of digital start-ups have sprung up and grown to be behemoths in areas as diverse as transport, retail, music, film, dating, hospitality, housing and travel.

Just think of Uber, Amazon, Spotify, Netflix, Tinder and Airbnb. Each of these firms has succeeded by building itself around users, and by using new organisational forms and technology to serve consumers in direct, flexible and cost-effective ways. Many are able to relentlessly improve the service they provide by collecting and processing data, and ensuring that they are always giving people exactly what they want. And while most use digital technology, doing so is merely a means to an end: to enhance the relationship with customers, rather than replace or reduce it.

Whether we like it or not, the secret to the success of these firms is that they have disrupted the way whole industries are organised. Almost all of them have succeeded partly by removing large swathes of middlemen in sectors where the incumbents spent far too much time duplicating things and too little time creating value for people.

'In industry after industry,' Thompson says, 'digital start-ups have applied these principles and repeated the trick across markets.' He believes that the same ideas can be applied to the public sector with huge dividends for citizens and governments alike. To do that, however, public services will have to focus relentlessly on activities that citizens value, and standardise the rest. Much as Buurtzorg has done, they will have to constantly improve the former while streamlining the latter using the web.

'We need to fundamentally reorganise how public services are delivered and administered,' says Thompson, 'and we need to use digital technology to help us do that. We can learn a lot from firms like Amazon, Netflix and Google.'

Take Amazon, for example. The behemoth creates huge value for its users by designing its services around their needs and their 'consumption journey' – the way they search for, evaluate, pay for and receive services – and by delivering all this in an integrated, simple, easy-to-use way. It then uses the shared plumbing of the internet to realise vast efficiencies at the back end, leveraging what is already in place, such as the postal system, to deliver this value at minimal cost.

'When I use Amazon, it "knows" me,' says Thompson, 'and is able to proactively propose things I might like. It offers me a range of options 24/7 and it lets me rate those who provide them so others can see what I think of their service. It can quickly combine an electronic storefront with payment, logistics and feedback about me, and deliver something very specific to my needs, in my home, at a time of my choosing. And it does this cheaply and in ways that are wildly popular with everyone.'

There is absolutely no reason why many public services could not be run in the same way. And yet they're just not. Public service providers do not typically 'know' us and cannot generally propose services that are configured to our needs. We cannot choose between different service providers and there are limited availability times. We cannot usually rate their services in real time, and neither can the services constantly improve through the use of such data.

An example of these inadequacies of public services are the multiple silos around health and social care in the UK, and the failure to configure these services around patients.[12] On the one hand, it is widely recognised that good social care can prevent ill health and speed up hospital discharges and that the health and social care sectors should be integrated to provide people with joined-up, efficient care. On the other hand, the sectors differ hugely in how they are structured and funded. Healthcare is commissioned and provided by the NHS and is largely free at the point of use. In contrast, social care is commissioned by local authorities from a range of mainly private providers, with most people paying for some or all their care. The two types of care are governed by very different legislation, and operate under very different regimes of decision-making and accountability. As a result, an overall strategy to integrate the two sectors is lacking, and people do not get the coordinated care they need, leading to poorer outcomes.

In contrast, as consumers, we struggle *not* to use Amazon because its services are so disturbingly personalised and joined up. Like many of the digital giants, the company has, in an almost sinister way, applied a whole raft of principles of design – from hyper-convenience to feedback loops and instant gratification at an almost animal level – to drive our addiction to their service. 'When we get on the Amazon website,' says Thompson, 'it is like returning to an old friend who "knows" our deepest needs and desires, even better than we know them ourselves, and uses this knowledge to keep us coming back for more.'

Meanwhile, on the business side, Amazon's use of the internet has enabled the most terrifyingly efficient form of capital accrual in human history. 'No wonder Jeff Bezos is the world's richest man,' says Thompson. But what if, Thompson asks, public services could deliver the same value to citizens, while gaining similar efficiencies on the administrative side, and plough the savings back into the actual delivery of public service, to the people on the frontline? The consequences would be immense.

Consider Netflix and what its model offers governments. Unlike the Hollywood studios of old which 'owned' the whole chain of scriptwriters (set designers, composers, camera people, and editing suites right through to cinemas) Netflix, especially before it started making its own shows, merely assembled the work of others (content creators and managers, publishers and monetisers) and offered the end product to consumers in an easy, enjoyable and seamless way. As a result, the company was set up to focus on where it can create things that people value in the most efficient possible way. It didn't waste time and money building and maintaining its own version of things that others could produce better. By working like this, internet firms like Netflix avoid building and maintaining common functions over and over again, freeing them up to focus more efficiently on where they generate value.

Again, unfortunately, this is not how governments work. They typically do everything on their own and create a long and complex supply chain of intermediaries and middlemen. This not only creates inefficiencies but also adds distance between the state and its citizens, reducing the state's ability to sense and respond to citizens' needs.

For a long time, this was precisely the situation with the over 600 balkanised NHS Trusts in the UK, each doing recruitment on its own, through agencies acting as middlemen. Fixing this waste involved creating a single online platform for recruitment – NHS Jobs – the largest, mass-subscription, shared service in the UK. NHS Jobs is now the biggest single employer recruitment site in Europe, with a unique visit every 2 seconds and over 275,000 job applications per month. It has already generated savings of over £1 billion since its launch.[13]

Finally, consider Google. The search giant offers the same service to everyone, wherever they are in the world. Further, Google aggregates demand (by getting millions of us to use its ubiquitous search feature) while disaggregating supply, thus getting advertisers to bid for space on the Google website where they compete for our eyeballs.

Ideally, says Thompson, governments should do the same. Instead they do the opposite. They replicate everything and, in the process, offer idiosyncratic services everywhere: from city to city, council to council. Specifically, instead of aggregating the demand produced by their citizens, states disaggregate it and thus lose the benefits of integration. And instead of disaggregating supply and using their immense bargaining power to realise efficiencies, states allow a few large suppliers to do business with them again and

I don't see where this is going...

again, handing huge rewards over to them in the process, at the taxpayer's expense.

An outstanding example of this form of inefficiency is the government procurement of information technology (IT) for public services. Where IT is concerned, governments are typically over-reliant on a small oligopoly of large suppliers. Moreover, government departments, rather than pooling their purchasing to increase their bargaining power, contract with these suppliers in a piecemeal way, again and again, across departments. As a result, departments end up paying more for IT, resulting in a waste of public money.[14] Indeed, benchmarking studies have shown that government departments pay substantially more for IT when compared with commercial rates. Given pressures on government budgets, it is particularly egregious that some departments in the UK, for instance, spend an average of £3,500 on a desktop PC. Given that they buy in bulk, they should be spending far less than the average citizen does for such hardware. Instead, they spend more.

All this is made worse by the duplication of work. Thompson points out that the same tasks that public services everywhere must perform – case management, registration, identity checking, workflow and licensing – are duplicated time and again in councils everywhere, across services such as waste management, planning and transport. 'There are over 350 councils in England alone,' says Thompson. 'Each of these replicates all these routine tasks thousands of times, over and over again. Imagine the waste! And imagine the scope for improvement!'

So, what if public services could be more like the digital giants? What if they were more joined up and organised around the needs of citizens, rather than those of bureaucrats? What if they focused relentlessly on service outcomes, and then used technology to deliver these better and more economically?

For Thompson, these digitally savvy public services would be more open, auditable and transparent. They would be more flexible and responsive to feedback. They would focus their resources relentlessly on caring for people, rather than on bureaucratic processes. And they would achieve all this by making the best use of the technology to minimise administrative and managerial overheads, thus offering value for money.

As John Micklethwait and Adrian Wooldridge point out in *The Fourth Revolution*, a 2015 book about the future of government: the private sector has been convulsed by a decade of radical change and innovation and has learned to do more with less under the sheer dint of shareholder and competitive pressures. In the process the internet has reorganised everything from newspapers to music to travel to entertainment. So why not the state?[15]

It would appear that the time has come for governments to prove that the same radical transformation can also be achieved in the public realm. But then the questions arise: who will do it first, and how will it be done?

What Buurtzorg did right

'When I first read about Buurtzorg,' says Thompson, 'I nearly fell off my chair. Here finally was evidence that what the internet behemoths were doing in the private sector could be done with public services as well.'

What particularly excited Thompson was that Buurtzorg wasn't just about technology: it was first and foremost about organisation and people. He was struck by how the Dutch organisation, by placing patients and nurses at the heart of what it did, had managed to do two very different things at once: improve the quality of care while increasing the satisfaction of nurses. 'Typically, there is the sense that what is good for the customer must be bad for the provider. But Buurtzorg dispelled that myth.'

What also impressed Thompson was how Jos de Blok had found a way to create a back office that was light and nimble, thereby freeing up resources that could be applied towards expanding the number of nurses on the frontline. As he said:

> That ratio of 14,000 nurses to 50 administrators is akin to what we see in the world of the digital giants. It is similar to the way that companies like Amazon, Facebook and Google use the shared plumbing of the internet to create huge value for consumers while freeing up resources at the back end. All this made me wonder what the effect might be if the same approach was applied to the delivery of public services in the UK.

In a 2015 piece in *The Guardian*, Thompson speculated on the savings that the Buurtzorg approach could bring to the UK. An Ernst & Young audit of Buurtzorg had concluded that if all Dutch nursing organisations adopted the Buurtzorg model, the Netherlands could save about €2 billion a year. For the UK, given its larger population, Thompson concluded this would mean savings of about £6 billion a year in community nursing alone.[16]

But what if the approach were adopted across the *entire* National Health Service? The NHS has a budget of about £120 billion a year. While no one knows the precise figure, a conservative estimate is that 14 per cent of this budget goes on administration. Working with the assumption that about 40 per cent of that 14 per cent could be streamlined, that would lead to savings of about £7 billion a year. This could in turn pay for nearly 200,000 more junior doctors. (The gains in a far larger economy like the US would be even more eye-catching: the American healthcare sector spent over $3.5 trillion in 2018, and employed about 18 million workers, with the greatest growth being in administrative and management jobs.)

Thompson goes on to argue that if the Buurtzorg model were extended across the public sector more generally, the savings could be truly significant. The UK, he points out, has just over 5 million public sector workers, of which 1.5 million are in public administration. Given an average salary of about £24,000, these non-frontline workers cost the state about £36 billion a year. If the UK could adjust its ratio to fit the Dutch model of fifty back-office workers to 14,000 frontline staff, Thompson estimates that the country would need 'fewer than 23,000 back-office staff to support 5.3 million frontline workers'.[17] Reducing the number of back-office staff from 1.5 million to just 23,000 would generate salary savings of up to £35.5 billion. These savings could then be ploughed back into cash-starved frontline services.

While the precise numbers can be contested or may be unknowable, there is no doubt that the savings would be significant. Moreover, it is the qualitative principle of what is at stake that matters more than the quantitative figures as such. What Thompson is suggesting is nothing other than a reconfiguration of the public sector, away from management and bureaucracy and back to the public it serves.

This transformation will not be easy, of course.

Obstacles to change

All the technology needed to transform public services currently exists. The obstacles to change are not technological, therefore, but social and organisational.

First, the conversation about how to bring about this change is yet to enter the mainstream. Public discourse these days still veers between the old extremes of increasing taxes or reducing spending. Citizens themselves seem caught up in an endless cycle of attacking public services while resisting change. 'In our private lives,' notes Thompson, 'we use these new digital services like Amazon and Uber and love them dearly. But to even consider touching public services is taboo. Our politics are still stuck in old dichotomies of state versus market. All too often we wallow in dog whistle rhetoric and a religious commitment to preserving the status quo.'

The second challenge is the enormous transformation weariness that afflicts the public sector. Having been sold snake oil for so long by so many different consultants and academics, there is a legitimate fear among public servants that any new change will be just more top-down reorganisation that only benefits managers. 'There is a distrust of managerial language, mentality and solutions,' says Thompson. 'There is a weariness about previous changes that have gone nowhere.'

Third, there is the knotty problem of what to do with all those who will be made redundant by reorganisation and new technology. There are ways to address this, of course, but retraining, for instance, would be slow. 'These changes might take ten to fifteen years to achieve. And there is a question of how that change will be managed.'

Most of all, perhaps, government is stuck with massive legacy systems where administration and cost have grown at the expense of frontline staff. Prior attempts to change the old command and control, siloed structures have only resulted in still more layers of government, of further levels of compliance and governance that do not add value for citizens.

A way forward: starting with councils

Thompson recognises that, as with all 'legacy' organisations, efforts to reorganise government at scale will run up against inertia and entrenched interests. Instead of going at the problem head-on, with a grand plan that is implemented top down, he suggests starting small. He recommends starting with a pioneering set of public bodies that are keen to reform, or face a burning need to do so.

Indeed, such bottom-up change is already under way in the UK, the US, Canada, Spain and Bangladesh. Take the UK, for example. At first glance this may seem almost insignificant, but two progressive local bodies in West Sussex – Adur District Council and Worthing Borough Council – recently came together to transform their public services in a radical way. Led by an ambitious chief executive and an enlightened digital officer, the councils began by identifying twenty-two common service patterns and capabilities. They then cast about for digital tools to automate these processes. Keenly aware that the relevant technology might change again in two to three years' time, they followed the principle of identifying a commonly used cloud-based platform on which they could build and share capabilities across silos. Eventually they settled on the Salesforce platform, a customer relationship management system that provides an interface for case and task management, and for automatically routing and escalating important events to the relevant people. Importantly, the platform also allows customers the ability to track their own cases.

Although the Salesforce platform wasn't the cheapest, the team determined that it was the best technology to use at the time. Further, to save money in the long run, they ran the software in tandem with a low code platform: one that didn't need expensive Salesforce developers to use it. This combined solution allowed public servants to literally drag and drop elements and create new workflows without having to go in and recode everything afresh.

This is an example of what Thompson calls 'Lego government': a process of combining a standard set of building blocks to achieve different work functions such as licensing, booking, registration, payments and case management. [18] 'Public servants', he says, 'can make use of off-the-shelf "plug and play" systems that are increasingly available over the internet, rather than spend time and money to develop bespoke systems for each department.'

This approach, in addition to being flexible, is cheaper than hiring programmers. It is also more open. Not only does it allow government workers to create new workflows, but it also empowers citizens in the community, enabling them to use standard council capabilities to set up their own businesses or charities quickly.

Where the Adur and Worthing councils have led, many others, in sleepy places such as Cheltenham, Forest of Dean, Cirencester and Essex, are following. Thompson is hopeful that this is the start of a trend that will bring about a transformation from the bottom up. 'As more councils adopt these approaches,' he says, 'even more are likely to be inspired, learn and follow suit.'

User-centric design and the responsive state

In their quest to be more responsive to their people, governments have two broad options before them. They can move closer to citizens, or they can bring citizens closer to them, by creating and delivering solutions in partnership.

Buurtzorg is the embodiment of the first approach. The Dutch organisation came closer to its patients through organisational redesign (simplification and flattening) as well as by moving resources to the frontline and empowering nurses. At a higher level, governments can also move closer to their citizens by devolving power: from the centre to the provinces, and ultimately to cities and local councils. Such an approach towards devolution has been credited, for instance, with Germany's more effective response in tackling Covid-19 relative to France. Germany's federal system gives its sixteen partly sovereign states autonomy over their healthcare systems. As a result, German public health isn't driven by a central authority but by nearly 400 public health offices, controlled by the states and run by municipal and rural administrations. This allowed for a variety of laboratories to act independently of central control. As a result, very early in the pandemic, over 250 laboratories around the country were able to carry out between 300,000 and 500,000 tests for Covid-19 every week.[19] As Matthias Orth of the Institute of Laboratory Medicine at Stuttgart's Marienhospital put it: 'I don't have to wait to get a call from the health minister before I can go ahead with a test.' In contrast, France's more centralised system hindered local initiative and led to an amplification of bad decisions at the centre. The result was that France lagged Germany on testing and suffered far more deaths in the same time period. 'On testing,' says François Heisbourg of the Foundation for Strategic Research, 'we have seen a beautiful centralised system failing abjectly.'[20]

The worldwide trend towards empowering city mayors is a further example of devolving power away from the centre. There are several reasons why mayors are increasingly effective and popular around the world. At the level of the city, government is closer to the lives and problems of citizens. The nature of activity here is on a more human scale. This in turn reduces complexity and increases transparency and responsiveness. Mayors are often from the very communities they govern: this gives them unique insight and helps them build trust. They can move faster to identify problems, design and deliver solutions, and monitor progress. Because these solutions are likely to bear fruit in a short space of time, the typical tenure of a mayor is sufficient for changes to be made and results to be seen. And because of the relative lack of complexity, the causal chain between actions and consequences can be traced in a less contentious manner. Citizens can monitor success and failure in ways that they rarely can for politicians at the national level.

Finally, mayors are often less ideological and more independent; even when they come from established parties with established ideologies, they are frequently more pragmatic and can experiment with new ideas. As *The Economist* puts it: countries like Britain are prisoners 'of a cult of centralised government that was created in the age of mass production but is increasingly irrelevant in the age of tailoring and customisation'.[21] This cult, *The Economist* argues, is killing innovation. In contrast, many of the most interesting policy experiments – from using smartphones to coordinate ride-sharing to giving schools more freedom – seem to have come from American mayors.

This new crop of mayors is part of a global movement that has boasted figures such as Michael Bloomberg, the former mayor of New York City, and Park Won-soon, the former mayor of Seoul. Indeed, Bloomberg has been a part of this wider movement in his post-mayoral career. Along with Harvard University, he has funded the Bloomberg Harvard City Leadership Initiative, a training programme which in 2017 invited forty mayors from around the world to learn how to lead their communities better. As Bloomberg has put it, 'We provide world-class training to private sector CEOs. Shouldn't we do the same for elected mayors?'[22]

So, governments can come closer to their citizens or they can bring their citizens closer to them. Tim O'Reilly's notion of government as a platform is an embodiment of the second approach.[23] Bringing citizens closer to governments is often enabled by digital tools. These tools can be used to involve citizens themselves in creating and delivering public services and solutions. Examples abound. U-Report is a free, SMS-based system that empowers Ugandans to discuss what is happening in their communities and partner with others to bring about large-scale change.[24] Citizens register for free on their mobile phones and answer weekly polls on issues that affect them, such as healthcare, education and sanitation. The results of the polls are then announced in newspapers and on the radio and passed on to public officials. Many members of parliament in Uganda have voluntarily signed up to U-Report to monitor what people are saying in their constituencies. One MP, for instance, was galvanised into action when she learned through U-Report that the immunisation levels for children under five were extremely low in her district. Her reaction was to launch a much-needed public awareness campaign. U-Report is now being rolled out in other countries in Africa and elsewhere, including Rwanda, Burundi, the Democratic Republic of Congo, South Sudan and Mexico.

D-CENT (Decentralised Citizens ENgagement Technologies) is a Europe-wide project to create digital tools for direct democracy.[25] The tools notify citizens in real time about issues that matter to them and help them propose, draft and vote on local solutions collaboratively. The project's base code uses open standards and is released under an open-source licence. Launched in 2013 with funding from the European Union, the project has been applied in Spain, Finland and Iceland. In Barcelona and Madrid, the tools have been used to create digital platforms to involve citizens in defining, developing and implementing policies. In Helsinki, D-CENT tools have been used to inform citizens about municipal policy decisions. And in Reykjavik, D-CENT has helped build a participatory budgeting platform for the city: the Betri (Better) Reykjavik platform allows citizens to submit ideas on how to spend a part of the city budget in their neighbourhood.

The key to the success of both these approaches is that they place the citizen at the heart of everything they do. They see things from the citizen's perspective and then design solutions and organisations accordingly. Governments around the world are increasingly using such citizen-centricity to solve problems across departments, at different levels of the state.

In the US, for example, the Office of Personnel Management set up a lab in 2012 to apply human-centred design to solve problems from the point of view of the people who use a particular product or service. Known as the Lab at OPM, it works with federal agencies to improve the quality of their programmes and services. In 2015, the lab worked with the US Department of Agriculture (USDA) on the National School Lunch Program, a service that provides healthy and low-cost or free meals to more than 30 million children daily. The USDA's challenge was: 'How can we make it easier for families to provide accurate information about eligibility for the free and reduced lunch program?' The OPM lab team interviewed school officials and families, brainstormed solutions with them and redesigned the application

(handwritten margin note: Ou wait this is really cool!)

process accordingly. In keeping with the principles of human-centred design, the new process was tested with families before it was approved by school officials.

Across the Atlantic, the UK's Cabinet Office set up its own Policy Lab in 2014. Led by Beatrice Andrews and Andrea Siodmok, it is a creative space where teams develop policy in an open, data-driven way that puts the user at the heart of the process. Andrews and Siodmok say that the lab has worked on problems across government departments but has also received visitors from other countries keen to replicate the model at home. Indeed, policy labs are now sprouting up in governments around the world. NESTA, the think tank, estimates that there are over 100 such labs around the world, at the national, regional and city levels, with a new one being formed every month.

Public services and citizens' trust

New forms of organisation, enabled by digital technologies, have shown ordinary people what is possible in their lives. Companies like Amazon, Netflix and Google have made us impatient for similar levels of convenience and responsiveness from our governments and public services. As a result, citizens everywhere now expect more from their governments and are hankering for change. For instance, a 2019 Gallup poll found that, on average across OECD countries, 30 per cent of citizens were dissatisfied with healthcare in their area, 34 per cent with the education system and 44 per cent with the judicial system and the courts.[26]

This dissatisfaction is at the heart of declining levels of trust in public institutions. Our leaders seem remote and their elected representatives slow to respond to our needs. Since 2002, Edelman, a communications marketing firm, has been surveying people around the world on their trust in institutions. Richard Edelman, the head of the firm, believes that there is a growing divide between 'informed publics', namely 'those who have a college degree, regularly consume news media, and are in the top 25 per cent of household income' and the 'mass populations' who form the bulk of the rest.[27] The 2008 financial crisis, Edelman believes, produced widespread suspicion among mass populations that the elites only act in their own interests, not those of the people, and that experts don't necessarily have access to better information than the rest of the population.

According to Edelman, there is a 31-point gap in trust in institutions in the United States between the top 25 per cent and the bottom 25 per cent of income earners. This gap persists across countries facing varying degrees of economic difficulty: it is 29, 26, 22 and 19 points in France, Brazil, India and the UK, respectively. Edelman states that 'people tend to trust businesses more than governments, in part because "business gets stuff done" while government is seen as "incapable".'[28] People seem to trust technology companies in particular because 'they deliver value'.[29]

So: governments have their work cut out for them. Nevertheless, there are green shoots from various quarters, suggesting real change and involving real plans: devolution, the empowerment of mayors, the development of government as a platform, and organisations such as Buurtzorg springing up around the world. We have a rare chance, given the state of technology, to transform the way government works in order to shift resources to frontline services from massively duplicated back-office functions.

The question, then, is not if but when, and how quickly, this transformation will take place. The pressure on governments is particularly acute to take along citizens who have been left behind by globalisation and technological change. How can governments make their programmes more inclusive and serve the different groups whose lives (and livelihoods) will be even more profoundly disrupted in the years to come? We turn to that challenge next, in Chapter 5.

5

The inclusive state: serving many tribes

'I have a dream that one day this nation will rise up and
live out the true meaning of its creed: We hold these
truths to be self-evident, that all men are created equal.'

Martin Luther King Jr

'Where there is discord, may we bring harmony …
Where there is despair, may we bring hope.'

Margaret Thatcher

On 8 November 2016, the day that Donald Trump was elected
45th president of the United States, Michael Tubbs, a 27-year-
old African American, made history of his own by being elected
mayor of Stockton, California. Joined in electoral triumph, the
two victors could not have been more different. Trump was,
nominally at least, a Republican, while Tubbs was a Democrat.
At seventy, Trump became the oldest president on election in US
history. At twenty-seven, Tubbs was the youngest mayor in US
history of a city with a population of at least 100,000. Trump was
born to a millionaire father while Tubbs was raised by a single
mother who held several jobs to make ends meet.

As mayor, Tubbs would frame his programmes around
bridging divides and healing divisions: governing rich and poor,
employed and unemployed, men and women, majority and minority alike. And while Tubbs brought with him a whole litany of
firsts – youngest elected official in the city's history and Stockton's

first black mayor – he was at twenty-seven already an old hand. Indeed, it was almost as if he had been preparing for this job his whole life – quite literally from the day he was born.

Growing up in Stockton

Tubbs' mother, Racole Dixon, was poor and barely seventeen years old when she gave birth to him. His father, who was in juvenile detention at that time, then spent several years in and out of custody before receiving a 'third strike' life sentence. Tubbs would only meet his father on a few occasions and still doesn't know what the three strikes were that got him sent to California State Prison.

In the early years, to make ends meet, Tubbs's mother took on multiple jobs. Those were years of real poverty, of moving a lot, of living off food stamps and Women, Infants and Children (WIC) vouchers. Things only stabilised when Tubbs was ten or eleven, when his mother was able to buy a house with her meagre savings. Despite the poverty and the disruption, Tubbs describes those years as happy ones. 'There were many safety nets and things didn't feel so bad. I had an amazing aunt and grandma. There were after-school programs, Head Start and WIC. Beginnings are not destiny.'[1]

Tubbs says he was rebellious, but schooling never felt hard. He was protected by a sense of community. His childhood revolved around church, curfew and education. 'My brother Drevonte and I enjoyed it,' says Tubbs. 'Our mother and grandmother shielded us from the harsher realities of the neighbourhood.'[2]

The two women were loving but demanding. They expected straight As from Tubbs, and he provided them. 'I had my nose in books,' he says, 'but I also played basketball, and I thought I was cool. From time to time I got kicked out of school for being defiant and disrespectful. I thought the teachers were making an example of me, to punish me. Be quiet, don't question – but that's not who I am.'

Tubbs visited his father in prison only once, when he was about twelve, and didn't like the way the guards treated him. 'The visit was formative for me. I knew I didn't want to be caged.' It was a 'weird situation' but Tubbs remains almost grateful for everything. 'All that has shaped who I am and my priorities. It has given me a real sense of the opportunity structure in this country, of the criminal justice system and poverty.'[3]

Preparing for office

Tubbs was a top student at Franklin High, a local state school in Stockton. Despite his rebellious nature, he worked hard: he saved up to buy books to prepare for the SATs, chaired a youth advisory panel and served as student council president. In 2008 he graduated with an international baccalaureate diploma and won a needs-based scholarship to Stanford. Over the next few years, he worked on a bachelor's degree in comparative studies and ethnicity and a master's in policy, leadership and organisation studies. On top of coursework, he took up internships at Google and the Obama White House. University could have been a ticket out of Stockton for him. He could have used his degrees and experience to become a lawyer, like his mother had hoped, or worked for Google, or any number of highly remunerative start-ups in Silicon Valley.

But fate would intervene in all these plans.

One day in November 2010, while he was at the White House, hard at work as an intern in the West Wing, his mother called to tell him that his cousin, Donnell James II, seven months older and living a parallel life, had been shot dead at a Halloween party.

Tubbs speaks about his cousin in wistful terms. James's mother and father had separated while he was growing up but they had remained in his life. His father was a construction worker and his mother worked in healthcare. Like Tubbs, James's teenage world had revolved around church, family and basketball. The boys had had sleepovers together. Like a lot of young people in Stockton, James didn't particularly connect with school. 'He had one foot in school and one on the streets,' says Tubbs. 'He wasn't a gang member, but he had relationships with people in gangs.'[4]

By October 2010, James found himself at a loose end. 'He was just hanging out,' says Tubbs, 'but he seemed to be doing fine. He had some good friends, some bad. He had a serious girlfriend.' On Halloween that year, James was at a house party when he became involved in an altercation and was shot. 'When my mom called me and said he had been murdered, I was like: what? I was at the White House then, six hours from home, trying to make my country better, but powerless to help when a member of my family was dying.'[5]

The shock made Tubbs think hard about what he wanted to do next. He began to ask himself how he could play a part in addressing the issues that affected the people he most cared about. He shared these thoughts with David Agnew, his immediate boss at the White House. Agnew was deputy assistant to the president and director of intergovernmental affairs. In this role, he oversaw the Obama administration's relationship with state, city, county and tribal elected officials across the country. Agnew predicted that Tubbs would run for office and told him so. But Tubbs said he wasn't ready. 'Maybe one day, maybe in 2024 at the earliest,' he said to Agnew. But Agnew held his ground: 'You are going to run for office in 2012.'[6]

In 2011, while back in Stockton for a winter break, Tubbs met a community activist he was close to. The activist asked Tubbs what he was planning to do when he graduated. When Tubbs said he wasn't sure, the activist asked him, 'How many people have to die before you feel ready to come back?'

The following week Tubbs decided to return to Stockton and

run for public office. He began living at home and commuting to Stanford, giving up all his other plans for the rest of his senior year. To beat traffic, he would leave home at 4.30 am and would return no later than 2 pm, or else at 8 or 9 at night. 'I wanted to get the pulse of the community. Even the summer before, I had spent time in Stockton rather than work at Google. Imagine: I turned down Google to live in Stockton and work with 50 kids!'[7]

This direct experience of working in his home town changed him profoundly. Now, instead of writing academic papers about its problems – the troubled education system, violent crime and imminent bankruptcy – he shifted his focus to what he could actually *do* to change things.

Eventually, as Agnew had predicted, Tubbs decided to run for city council in 2012.

'Your own circumstances are important,' says Tubbs. 'My father was in prison with 25 years to life. I still don't know what each of the three strikes was. What happened to my cousin changed me too.'

Oprah, becoming councillor, and then mayor

In April 2012, a few months before he ran for council, Tubbs had a significant encounter at Stanford. Oprah Winfrey, the talk show host, was visiting with a group of students from the African Leadership Academy, a secondary school in Johannesburg dedicated to developing the next generation of African leaders. Tubbs was invited to the dean's luncheon for Winfrey and the students, partly because he had worked in South Africa the previous winter. Determined not to embarrass Winfrey by trying to buttonhole her, Tubbs spent the time talking to the African students, attempting to convince them to study at Stanford. When the formal introductions began, Tubbs said he was from Stockton but didn't say anything about running for city council. 'I didn't want her to think it was a set-up, so I just said, "I'm from Stockton". But then the dean stepped in.'[8]

When she heard about Tubbs's plans, Winfrey's ears pricked up immediately. She began to bombard Tubbs with questions. Who supports you? What is your vision? Why Stockton? And crucially: How much have you raised so far?

To the last question, Tubbs responded: '$10,000'.

Winfrey then said: 'You know I helped Obama get elected? Where do I send a check?'

Two weeks later, there was a cheque in the mail from Ms. Winfrey. She had exactly matched the $10,000 Tubbs had told her he had raised.

Soon after the meeting with Winfrey, Tubbs formally announced his candidacy for Stockton Council District 6, against the incumbent Dale Fritchen. He went on to win the election, with 61.7 per cent of the vote, and took office in January 2013 at the age of twenty-two. That made him the youngest council member in Stockton's history and one of the youngest elected officials in the United States.

Then, on 2 September 2015, he announced his candidacy for mayor, running against the incumbent Anthony Silva in the 2016 general election. Less than a week before the election, Tubbs received an endorsement from President Barack Obama. He went on to win, with 70.6 per cent of the vote.

Shortly after he was elected mayor, his father sent him a letter from prison to congratulate him. His father said he had heard he was engaged and added that he was looking forward to having beautiful grandchildren.[9]

Tubbs's mother, for her part, had continued to hope that after his stint as councillor, he would get a good job and leave Stockton. When he told her he was going to run for mayor, she said: 'I guess you only have two terms, so you still have time!'

The problems of Stockton

The financial crisis of 2008 had hit Stockton hard. But its problems had even earlier roots. Following stock market gains in the 1990s, city officials had gone on a spending spree in the early 2000s and had approved several large infrastructure projects to raise the city's profile. In 2004, for instance, they had issued a $47 million bond towards the construction of a sports and concert arena in downtown Stockton. Another $100 million was then spent on revitalising the city's riverfront. The city offered its firefighters and public officials generous pension deals and early retirement. Homebuilding went into overdrive, catering to buyers from San Francisco's Bay Area.

Then came 2008 and the housing crash. Median house prices fell to $110,000 in 2009 from a high of $400,000 in 2006.[10] With the bust came foreclosures and tumbling revenues from property tax. Debt service ballooned to $17.2 million a year, from $3 million just six years before. Stockton defaulted on its bond payments. In 2012, the city filed for bankruptcy, becoming the largest US city to do so.

This was the crisis that Tubbs walked into when he became councillor.

Reflecting on what had gone wrong, he says: 'The entire political conversation had been driven by two groups – the developers and the city employees – who had acted in their own self-interest. There was no one else at the decision-making table.' The emphasis had been on building infrastructure – the marina and the promenade – without thinking about people. 'What we needed was an array of voices. I didn't know anyone who owned a yacht and parked it at the marina.'[11]

As with many cities around the world, the emphasis in Stockton had been on creating an image of the city built around hard infrastructure. After all, that was where the big money was. Vanity projects like sports arenas get noticed, and immediately. Investing in people, on the other hand, and in soft infrastructure like education and healthcare, takes a back seat. It is harder to show progress and the dividends come years, even decades, later.

When Tubbs took over as mayor, he had a sense of the problems of the city. After all, he had experienced its divisions first hand. 'City government', he says, 'may not be the best equipped to do it, and therefore not the only entity to do so, but it must focus on issues such as generational poverty and educational attainment.'

'The status quo', he adds, 'was unacceptable. I didn't get elected mayor to be liked. I got elected to do things that actually make a difference. To bridge the gap between the haves and have nots.'

Seized by a sense of urgency, Tubbs and his colleagues in the city council launched multiple programmes on multiple fronts. They used their contacts and experience from elsewhere to do so. Tubbs drew on his time at Stanford and the White House. He engaged external sources of money and expertise, from foundations and think tanks across the US. But the team also built on what was available locally. Drawing on their local knowledge, community participation became central to their approach.

Social inclusion: the role of education and justice

In many societies, divisions between various groups turn on the availability of opportunities for improvement and advancement. Indeed, the challenge for governments is not so much about ensuring equality per se, but about providing access to opportunities for all. Equality, on the other hand, is a far more demanding objective for governments to hold. There is always the question of 'equality of what?', and this is invariably politically charged. Inclusion, by contrast, is a more minimal aspiration and an altogether more reasonable objective. At the heart of such inclusion are education and justice.

'Education is a great equaliser,' says Tubbs, a view that is rooted in his biography. His ambition as mayor has been to provide a good education for every child in Stockton. 'This is what every parent wants,' he says. 'So many in the city are working class people, immigrants from elsewhere, for whom the US is the land of opportunity. Schools are the best conduit for their aspirations. It should be as if our own kids are going to these schools.'[12]

But Tubbs and his administration had their work cut out for them. When he became mayor, four out of five in the Stockton school district came from high-risk groups in terms of income, language needs or unstable homes. And only one in four left high school with the credits needed to get into a public university in California.

One of Tubbs's first moves was to launch the Stockton Schools Initiative, a coalition of students, community members and families, designed to improve educational opportunities for all. A related programme was Stockton Scholars. Funded by an anonymous donor to the tune of $20 million, the aim of the programme was to make college education accessible to students in the Stockton Unified School District who have difficulty paying their way. A third initiative promoted student internships in local government and was designed to give students the opportunity to have their voices heard in policymaking.

Tubbs was joined in these efforts by his wife, Anna Nti-Asare-Tubbs, whom he met at Stanford and who has a background in anthropology, sociology and education. When he decided to run for mayor, she joined him on the campaign trail, knocking on doors and switching from English to Spanish when needed. Like her husband, Nti-Asare-Tubbs is a big believer in education. For her, education 'is the avenue through which we can either teach kids to repeat the cycle they are a part of or where we can help them to change their lives and change the world.'[13]

Tubbs and his team also pushed for changes to the city's approach to crime and criminal justice more generally. As with education, the administration worked closely with local communities as well as with external partners to develop and deliver these programmes.

Locally, the city engaged with community leaders to get feedback on social issues such as community policing. Much of the inspiration came from local events and individuals. For instance, both Tubbs's cousin Donnell James II and Brandon Harrison – a young community organiser who was shot in October 2017 – inspired the city council's new public safety policies.

The city's external partner on criminal justice was Advance Peace, an anti-violence programme that provides fellowship opportunities for young men affected by crime. Founded in 2016 by DeVone Boggan, the Advance Peace model was first implemented in Richmond, California, where Boggan was the founding director of Richmond's Office of Neighborhood Safety from 2007 to 2016. The objective of the organisation is to 'interrupt gun violence in US urban neighborhoods by providing transformational opportunities to young men involved in lethal firearm offenses and placing them in a high-touch, personalized fellowship'.[14] It does this by identifying those who are most likely to commit gun violence, but whom the police have been unable to arrest. It then pairs these men with mentors – typically reformed felons with a similar background – for an intensive 18-month programme designed to provide alternatives to a criminal lifestyle. Some fellows of the programme may also qualify for a stipend of up to $9,000 for meeting goals such as obtaining a General Education Diploma or completing parenting classes.

The whole approach, including the money involved, was part of an experimental attempt to tackle crime in ways that hadn't been tried before. Only time and careful evaluation will, of course, prove whether it worked or not. But, as Tubbs points out, without trying, one will never know.

Economic inclusion: jobs, skills and wages

Perhaps the most eye-catching of Tubbs's programmes was one designed to provide Stocktonians with a Universal Basic Income (UBI). This programme, too, was at an experimental stage at the time of writing. Unlike other such attempts in California that are more ambitious, Stockton's plans were fairly humble. The business incubator Y Combinator, for instance, has funded a larger programme involving over 1,000 people in Oakland, California. In Stockton the city provided 130 residents with $500 a month over an 18-month period, with the aim of increasing the number of beneficiaries over time.[15]

Dubbed the Stockton Economic Empowerment Demonstration project, or SEED, the programme was the nation's first-ever city-led guaranteed income demonstration. The project was entirely philanthropically funded: no tax dollars were used for it. The main partner was the Economic Security Project (ESP), a network committed to advancing the debate on cash transfers and a guaranteed income in the United States. ESP contributed $1 million to the initiative and hoped that doing so would inform the debate and inspire the public's imagination about universal basic income.[16] A second partner was the Goldhirsh Foundation, which was committed to matching up to $250,000 in donations to SEED with the aim of galvanising others to support the exploration of a guaranteed income.

Speaking about how the partnership with ESP came about, Tubbs says: 'ESP was looking for a city to pilot what a basic income scheme would look like. They wanted to know what it would do for people's lives. As soon as I heard about what they were proposing, I jumped at the opportunity.'[17]

Tubbs's motives in supporting the project were many. On the one hand, he was aware of the disruptive effects of new technologies on employment. As robots and artificial intelligence begin to replace humans in the workforce, it will be increasingly necessary to provide a basic income to support those who are left out. On the other hand, before worrying about the threat of automation, Tubbs believes that we need to 'look at the economic structure of the country as it is now'. At present, one in two Californians can afford no more than one $400 emergency. And work involves finding and holding down multiple, low-paying jobs without benefits. All this is stress-inducing and a strain on mental and physical health. Tubbs knows from the experience of his own mother that an additional $500 a month can be very useful to those on a low income. He is aware that in Stockton there are many mothers who have two or three jobs, but still don't get a wage commensurate with their efforts. Tubbs also recognises that a basic income might benefit those in more risky lines of work like the creative industries and entrepreneurship.

The SEED team worked with a project designer to think carefully about how to pick the first 130 residents who would get the basic income, so as to make the scheme universal. 'We don't just want to reach those who now qualify for government assistance,' says Tubbs. Accordingly, the team also looked to include those earning one standard deviation above the median household income, and worked with the community to make this selection.

SEED is not without its detractors. To some on the right it sounds like communism in a different guise: an extension of expensive government programmes like Medicare and social security, and yet another excuse to hand out taxpayers' money. These critics have described SEED as 'free money', leading to a tweet from the mayor's account, in February 2018, about the projected economic benefits of the programme. Tubbs also responded to these critics by pointing out that only private money – from the Economic Security Project and the Goldhirsh Foundation – was used to fund the programme. After all, the city was nearly bankrupt. 'We have to secure our fiscal future,' he said. 'We are now the second most disciplined city in the state.'

All this, however, feeds into the fears of those on the left who worry that opening up to private money might mark the beginning of a creeping privatisation of government services. They also worry about corporations getting involved in and eventually taking over the government.

In response to all these critics Tubbs says: 'I'm a millennial. Left and right are not that important to me. What matters is forward.'

Indeed, some form of a basic income has enjoyed support from across the political spectrum going back decades. In the 1960s, both Milton Friedman and Martin Luther King Jr advocated for a guaranteed income. In the 1970s, Daniel Patrick Moynihan, a Democrat, and Richard Nixon, a Republican, jointly proposed an income floor that came close to being approved by Congress. And since 1982, the entire state of Alaska has distributed an annual dividend to every citizen.

Tubbs is aware of this history. But for now, SEED remains an experiment funded by philanthropy. The idea was to show proof of concept, how it might fit in with other priorities, and how private capital might work with state programmes. Hector Lara, the executive director of the Reinvent South Stockton Coalition, says: 'We really hope that through this implementation we can learn ... that it may shape future policy ... [and how to generate] future ideas for where this funding may come from.'[18]

Stockton is in many ways a microcosm of the United States: a city with a challenging past and an uncertain future. As elsewhere in the US, the city faces major shifts in its economy such as wage stagnation and inequality that have made it difficult for working people to make ends meet. What works in Stockton might just work elsewhere.

Indeed, interest in a universal basic income is increasingly global. In Europe, for instance, Finland began experimenting with the UBI in 2017. But the roots of the approach lie in an even older tradition in northern Europe, one that goes back almost a century, and which has come to be known as 'flexicurity'.

The Danes and flexicurity

The question of safety nets and employment has vexed governments around the world for well over a century. At least since the Great Depression, the welfare state has been central to mitigating the vagaries of the business cycle and the problems of mass unemployment. When economies grind to a halt and businesses are no longer hiring, what are the unemployed to do? Who takes care of them and how? And when people are in employment, how are they to be protected from potential exploitation by their employers?

Throughout the twentieth century, but especially since the Second World War, states in the industrial West have responded to these questions with laws to protect labour rights when people have jobs and provide them social security when they don't. But these efforts have had to contend with a whole new set of problems over time. [As entitlements and social security programmes have expanded, and as life expectancy has gone up – thus increasing the number who cannot work – the fiscal burden on the state has risen too.] And as protections for those in work have grown, making it harder for firms to fire (and hence also hire) workers, economies have, from time to time, lost their dynamism and ground to a halt. This has resulted in, for instance, insider/outsider economies, where those in work are protected by the law but those outside work are doomed to a life of insecure contracts, part-time, low-paid work, and the stigma of chronic unemployment.

And so: governments have had to grapple with, on the one hand, ensuring the dynamism of the economy while, on the other, protecting those who suffer from the ups and downs of the business cycle. How to provide flexibility to firms and those seeking employment while ensuring that those without work have a safety net to fall back on?

To achieve this balance, many countries have gone back and forth between the two extremes of unfettered markets versus giving people security and protecting those without employment. Only a few countries have found a pragmatic middle ground.

None of these is more exemplary, it would seem, than Denmark. In fact, so successful has the country been at striking this balance that economists and policymakers have even coined a term to describe its model: flexicurity, to indicate both flexibility in the labour market and security to workers.

Flexicurity made its debut in Denmark in the early 1990s when the government, led by Prime Minister Poul Nyrup Rasmussen, introduced a series of landmark labour market reforms. The idea was to balance easy hiring and firing (i.e. flexibility for employers) with generous benefits for the unemployed (i.e. security for workers). The impetus came from a need to break the unemployment trends of the time and use active labour market policy to reduce structural unemployment.

Per Kongshøj Madsen, emeritus professor of political science at Aalborg University, has spent much of his career studying the flexicurity model. Indeed, Madsen was one of the first to popularise the term. He recounts a trip in the mid-1990s, when he was first researching the phenomenon, to see a Danish civil servant who told him that the model really had three elements, not two. On the whiteboard in the civil servant's office was a diagram depicting the Danish 'golden triangle of flexibility, security, and active labour market policy', the third element including strong (re)training and education policies.[19]

The flexicurity 'golden triangle' was soon recognised by the OECD and the European Union as being closely associated with the strong performance of the Danish economy relative to its OECD and EU peers. The model reached its high point in the mid-2000s as the then centre-right government presided over a five-year boom. By 2007, unemployment in Denmark was at its lowest in over thirty years at 4.5 per cent; growth was faster than the EU average, while inflation was lower; and the budget was running a surplus of 3.9 per cent of GDP. Between 2004 and 2007, the Danes shaved 1 per cent off the public payroll and boosted private sector employment by 3.7 per cent. The country succeeded in creating 34,000 private sector jobs in 2006 alone. Hiring and firing could happen from one day to the next, giving Danish companies a competitive edge over their German and Swedish counterparts. About a fifth of Danish workers might lose their jobs but most would find a new one soon after. Things were so good that the Danish finance minister, Thor Pedersen, boasted: 'We'll end up owning the whole world!'[20]

But then came the financial crisis of 2008 and flexicurity suddenly lost its shine. The Danish labour market was hit hard by the downturn. 'If it is easy to dismiss employees,' says Madsen, 'employers will do just that.' Denmark experienced a bigger drop in employment than other EU economies, and EU officials championing the Danish model began to melt away. The trade unions had, in any case, been somewhat sceptical. They viewed the model as a Trojan horse that was really about flexibility rather than security. With the crisis, it became unpopular to talk about flexibility when workers were being dismissed. Plus the approach was expensive and public spending was already unsustainably high in many European countries.

But was this loss of faith in flexicurity premature? Madsen's research, and that of others, shows that, while in the short term the Danish model took a bigger hit than other EU countries, Denmark was quicker to bounce back in the long run. Thus, between 2007 and 2012, the country saw long-term unemployment as a share of total unemployment increase from 16.1 per cent to 28 per cent. In contrast, in the same period, in the remaining EU countries, the long-term unemployment rate increased from a higher initial level but at a lower rate – from 42.6 per cent to 44.3 per cent. Since 2012, however, long-term unemployment has declined in Denmark from 28 per cent to 22.3 per cent while it has continued to increase in the EU-27.[21] Thus, despite the sharp *initial* increase in unemployment, Denmark eventually went back to having the lowest unemployment rate of all EU countries. Importantly, job creation rates and mobility have remained high, while marginalisation and long-term unemployment have stayed low.

Madsen believes that flexicurity makes for a more inclusive economy and labour market. The model ensures low levels of long-term unemployment even during economic crises, lower unemployment among those with special needs, and a less segmented, insider/outsider labour market than in other countries. There is income security for those who lose jobs, and there is a lower probability of citizens ending up in poverty. For instance, a recent EU survey found that the share of people who couldn't pay their bills in the previous twelve months was 8 per cent in Denmark, compared with other countries such as Greece where it was nearly 50 per cent.[22]

But flexicurity is not without its limits. For one thing, while the model is much admired, it is not easy to copy. Madsen points out that in Denmark it is rooted in a century-long tradition of cooperation and dialogue between employers and labour unions. Such cooperation and dialogue cannot easily be replicated overnight.

Further, the unemployment benefits and training that the approach provides come at a cost: a higher tax burden on those who earn more. Flexicurity may therefore favour those on low-to-moderate incomes. On the plus side, the higher tax burden is offset by the country's relatively high growth together with low levels of unemployment and social exclusion. As Madsen puts it: 'Although we may pay higher taxes, we also get benefits for schooling, healthcare, training, and income support. As a result, there is very little tax resistance in Denmark. No party really attacks the welfare state.'[23] Perhaps as a result – and despite its weather – Denmark consistently ranks among the happiest nations on earth.

Overall, though, flexicurity may be best suited to small, relatively equal, well-established economies like Denmark. In *Small States in World Markets,* the political scientist Peter Katzenstein explains how the economically vulnerable Nordics, along with the Netherlands, Belgium, Switzerland and Austria, have over the last few decades achieved a higher standard of living than far bigger countries like the United States. Katzenstein locates the reasons for this in their ability to respond rapidly and flexibly to market opportunity and their 'democratic corporatism' – a mixture of 'ideological consensus, centralized politics, and complex bargains among politicians, interest groups, and bureaucrats'.[24] He maintains that such democratic corporatism is an effective way of coping with a rapidly changing world, a more effective one than several large industrial countries have been able to produce.

Madsen concurs. 'Small states like Denmark', he says, 'have a more cooperative tradition between government and social groups to make deals and compromises.'[25]

But even in small countries like Denmark there are those who believe that flexicurity has its limits. Erik Christensen, a colleague of Madsen's at Aalborg, argues that 'the welfare model we have realized contains some unfortunate features of the two ideological systems that our system consists of, liberalism and socialism'.[26] Flexicurity, for Christensen, [contains both too much government and bureaucracy (an unfortunate feature of socialism) and too little social security (an unfortunate feature of liberalism).] He argues that it is possible instead to create a system in which liberals can have less government and bureaucracy (and hence greater flexibility) while socialists can have more social security. This system would, however, involve a bold new approach as a new cross-political project. It would require nothing short of a universal basic income (UBI).

The UBI: smart investment or profligate handout?

Denmark may have pioneered flexicurity, but Finland beat it to experimenting with the UBI. In January 2017, the Nordic nation began paying €560 a month to a random sample of 2,000 unemployed people between the ages of 25 and 58.[27]

Initiated by a centre-right government grappling with

austerity, the project was intended to help both the government and its beneficiaries. Beneficiaries would be under no obligation to seek or find a job during the two years of the trial, and they would continue to get their cheques even if they did find work. The government, for its part, hoped to bring down a stubborn unemployment rate of 8 per cent while reducing bureaucracy and social security spending.

In terms of unemployment, the expectation was that a basic, unconditional income might provide an incentive for people to take up paid work. This was mainly because, if it was set at a level that was only just liveable, people would want to supplement it through additional work. And as in Stockton, there was also the hope that such an income would make it easier to negotiate a brave new world of casual, short-term work: it would obviate the need for citizens to reapply for benefits every time a short-term contract came to an end.

In terms of bureaucracy, the hope was that the basic income would simplify an increasingly complex social security system and thus reduce spending. The current system, for instance, offered more than forty different means-tested benefits, largely to deal with a contemporary labour market of part-timers, short-term contracts and entrepreneurs driving start-ups.[28]

Indeed, a growing problem in many advanced economies is not the lack of jobs per se but rather jobs that are insecure, low paying and contractual. Guy Standing, a British economist, uses the term 'precariat' to describe the class of people employed in this gig economy. In his 2011 book, *The Precariat: The New Dangerous Class*, Standing argues that members of this group – which includes immigrants, the industrial working class and the educated young – suffer not only from job insecurity but also from identity insecurity and loss of control over their time.

Many of these problems, Standing believes, are due to globalisation, but existing social policies make them worse. To address this, Standing urges radical reforms that will enshrine financial security as a right. A key aspect of these reforms would involve introducing an unconditional basic income. Such a move, he argues, would not only increase job security but would also unleash pent-up entrepreneurial energy and drive economic growth. 'In every industrialised country,' he writes, 'we currently apply means-tested benefits. That means you're targeting the poor ... The old system has broken. Wages will continue to decline. Insecurity will continue to grow. That is a recipe for economic instability.'[29]

Standing is hardly an isolated voice. The universal basic income now has widespread and growing support from both ends of the political spectrum. On the left, its champions, such as Bernie Sanders and assorted trade unionists, believe it can cut poverty and inequality. On the right, its supporters, such as the Adam Smith Institute and assorted libertarian billionaires, believe it could lead to a leaner, less bureaucratic welfare system, and free people to be risk-taking entrepreneurs. And it appeals to those such as Bill Gates and Elon Musk who worry that automation could replace a third of jobs in the west by 2040.

But the UBI also has its critics. Ian Goldin, professor of globalisation and development at the University of Oxford, identifies at least three big drawbacks. First, the UBI would be financially irresponsible. Because it is universal, even if the basic income is set at a modest level, paying everyone would be 'unaffordable and lead to ballooning deficits'.[30] To afford it, governments would have to raise taxes or cut spending on education and health. Second, the approach could actually lead to *greater* inequality while *reducing* social cohesion. Because the basic income would replace existing unemployment benefits, the most deserving would potentially get less financial support while 'billionaires would get a little more'.[31] And because people work, not only to earn an income, but also for 'meaning, status, skills, networks and friendships',[32] delinking income and work by potentially 'rewarding people for staying at home'[33] could drive up crime and drug use and lead to family break-up. Third, and perhaps most damningly, a universal basic

→ how can we expect everyone to work enough? it's not realistic

income could undermine the incentive to work. Goldin argues that social security should be designed to get 'individuals and families to participate in society, overcome unemployment and find work, retrain, move cities'.[34] Safety nets should not lead to a lifetime of dependence, but a universal basic income might do precisely this.

Goldin fears that the attention that the UBI is getting is distracting governments from looking for more creative solutions. These potential solutions, he believes, must include 'part-time work, shorter weeks, and rewards for home work, creative industries and social and individual care'.[35] To reverse rising inequality and social dislocation, 'we need to radically change the way we think about income and work'. Per Madsen agrees. 'If you have a basic income at a reasonable level it would be expensive. What we need to do is train people to qualify for new jobs. The state should only be there for people who cannot support themselves, not for those who can.'[36]

yes... but also recognize that not everyone can be productive

Sadly, the same Finnish government that initiated Europe's first national experiment with the UBI also decided, two years after its creation, to shut the project down. In April 2018, the government turned down a request for extra funding from the Finnish social security agency to expand the pilot; all payments to participants came to an end in January 2019. Olli Kangas, an expert involved in the trial, says: 'Two years is too short a period to be able to draw extensive conclusions from such a big experiment. We should have had extra time and more money to achieve reliable results.'[37]

All these debates about whether a universal basic income works or not suggest the need for more experiments, not less, and more data rather than more a priori arguments. Fortunately, we may soon have just such a body of evidence as basic income schemes continue to proliferate around the world. In addition to Stockton, California, similar schemes have been (or are being) run in rural India and Kenya, and in cities from Macau to Hamilton, and Glasgow to Barcelona.

The UBI raises all sorts of questions about its actual

implementation. Who exactly gets the money and how? And how is the effectiveness of the policy to be assessed? In Italy, a universal income was a key electoral promise of Italy's left–right coalition that came to power in 2018. Once in government, implementing its promise meant facing all sorts of practical questions that go beyond politics. Diego Piacentini, hired in August 2016 by Italy's then centre-left prime minister to lead a digital transformation of government, soon found himself at the heart of these new challenges. For Piacentini, however, government digitisation has 'no political colour'. The aim, even with the new, ideologically very different government, remains to develop digital platforms that underpin efficient services and encourage 'the whole of government to use them'. Addressing questions of how to make the UBI work will not only enable the current government to deliver on its promises, but will also help future governments better provide financial support to their citizens. 'Governments give money to people in one form or another, [so] let's make it efficient and measurable,' says Piacentini.[38]

Including the excluded in solving their problems

Hilary Cottam, social activist and author, argues that the time has come to completely rethink the welfare state. In her 2018 book, *Radical Help: How We Can Remake the Relationships between us and Revolutionise the Welfare State*, Cottam outlines how the state might reinvent itself around voluntary action and human connection in communities. 'When people feel supported by strong relationships, change happens. And when we make collaboration and connection feel simple and easy, people want to join in.'[39] She fears that the welfare state currently fails to connect people to one another, despite the abundant potential that such relationships offer. Most of its services for young and old people alike are 'aimed at managing risk and getting by'.

How, then, to bring communities and volunteers back in? How to include the excluded in creating and delivering their own welfare policies and plans? Inspiration here comes from an unlikely quarter: developing countries like Bangladesh that have pursued such community-led development for decades.

When it was formed in 1971, Bangladesh was one of the poorest countries on earth. To make matters worse, the fledgling nation was reeling from the aftermath of a civil war that had led to its split from West Pakistan as well as a cyclone in 1970 that killed over 450,000 people. Healthcare and education were poor. Infant and child mortality was high and literacy was low. The newly formed government – impoverished, disorganised – was simply unable to meet the many demands of the young nation. Into the breach stepped a few remarkable non-governmental organisations (NGOs) and the people who founded them. Over the next few years, these organisations would perfect a model of community-led development that transformed Bangladesh and countries like it.

The most impressive of these organisations was BRAC and its founder Fazle Hasan Abed. Now the world's largest NGO, BRAC has shown how non-governmental actors working with communities can create inclusive social programmes that benefit millions.

One of the first problems addressed by the fledgling NGO was child mortality. In the 1970s, a quarter of all children in Bangladesh died before they reached the age of five. A major cause of death was dehydration from diarrhoea or dysentery. Selling manufactured oral rehydration packets wasn't an option: at 8 cents a packet, they were too expensive for the typical Bangladeshi. Equally, subsidising the packs on a national scale was beyond the budget of the impoverished government. In any case, there was the challenge of setting up a supply chain to distribute the packs to over 75,000 villages in the country. It soon became clear to Fazle Hasan Abed that the best solution was to select and train local women who would in turn teach rural mothers to make their own oral rehydration solution at home using boiled water, sugar and salt. During a decade of experimentation and continuous learning, BRAC refined and extended this programme to reach 12 million households across practically every village in Bangladesh. By 1990, the NGO had helped save millions of lives and, in the process, built an army of thousands of local health volunteers across the country.[40] BRAC then trained these health volunteers to act as midwives and paramedics who treated illnesses and provided family planning at the village level. This community-based care not only resulted in dramatic improvements in human development indicators across the country, but also empowered poor rural women in turn. The health volunteers, or *shastho shebikas*, became important figures in their communities who, in addition to gaining an extra income from the modest fees they could charge, went on to become political figures who contested and won local elections.

As with healthcare, so too with finance. Along with other NGOs, such as the Grameen Bank, BRAC pioneered a model of microfinance that brought cheap credit and savings to rural populations, particularly women. The microfinance model, too, was built around community participation: intended beneficiaries were intimately involved in the delivery of the solution to their problems. At the heart of the model is the self-help group – a set of ten women who pool their often meagre assets to form a joint liability group. The group not only provides its members with collateral against which they can take out loans from microfinance institutions, but also ensures a mechanism that enables them together to repay loans that individual members take out. The loans are then typically put towards the purchase of income-bearing assets such as cattle or goats; the returns from these help repay the loans and also help educate children and improve livelihoods, offering a long-term solution to poverty and exclusion.

Hilary Cottam believes that such community-led welfare can work in the West. Take the UK's National Health Service. As the system struggles to deal with an ageing population, statists think that only more money can address the problem. Cottam disagrees. 'More money', she argues, 'will not fix our broken welfare state. We need to reinvent it.'[41] The trouble with the current model – as in India before Aadhaar or Brazil before Bolsa Familia – is that it is fundamentally paternalistic and disenfranchising, rather than empowering, quite apart from being financially and organisationally unviable. What the system needs is creative reorganisation that gives a greater role to local communities. This will require devolving more power to local levels of organisation as well as involving end users in the design and delivery of public services. Doing so will result in more effective and timely solutions to local problems, and engage people rather than alienate them from the communities they live in.

Indeed, the NHS has long depended on local volunteers. A 2016 British Social Attitudes survey estimates that there are now about 1.7 million volunteers in health and care.[42] The Department of Health and Social Care puts the number even higher at 3 million. Given the pressures on the system, the role of such volunteers continues to expand. According to Catherine Johnstone, Chief Executive of the Royal Voluntary Service, a charity set up in 1938, about 5,000 of the charity's 25,000 volunteers now help in hospitals. 'Take mobilising patients,' says Johnstone. 'If you're working on rehabilitation for older people, we know there is a big issue with getting people signed fit for discharge.'[43] Volunteers can help with this by teaching patients chair-based exercises or getting them out of bed for lunch. They can also help with patient transport and ward trolley services. Outside hospitals, a fifth of GPs' time is spent addressing non-medical issues to do with work, housing and relationships. Here, too, volunteers can help by providing support and advice.

Local volunteers play a particularly important role during times of crisis. During the Covid-19 pandemic of 2020, more than 500,000 people signed up to support vulnerable people unable to leave their homes because of the lockdown. Soon after Matt

Hancock, the health secretary, called for volunteers to bolster the NHS, nearly five people per second were enlisting in response.[44]

But the needs of the welfare system extend well beyond providing health, education or employment. Often, a whole network of issues needs to be addressed in a holistic fashion. The charity sector provides precisely such a holistic approach. In the US, for instance, the Ford Foundation set up the Local Initiatives Support Corporation (LISC) in 1979 as a non-profit to support community development in both urban and rural areas. A major pillar of the LISC's approach is its financial opportunity centres (FOCs), where coaches help 'overlooked talent to prepare them for quality, living-wage jobs, while becoming resilient to financial shock'. Maurice Jones, LISC's national CEO, says the goal is to help participants of the programme become 'net cash positive' and develop a life plan that is 'inspiring to them'.[45]

Kansas City is one of the many urban areas where LISC operates. The city is booming, but Sly James, mayor from 2011 to 2019, is disappointed that it has failed the African Americans who account for 30 per cent of its population. 'The impact of all things racial', says James, 'has left neighborhoods divided and segregated and that leads to a perpetuation of things like poverty and lack of opportunity.'[46] James adds that the link between structural racism and inequality, especially in education, 'impedes [African Americans'] ability to be employed in gainful employment that provides a living wage or even decent wage' and 'stifles hope' for them.

This is where the LISC's financial opportunity centres help fill the gaps left by the state. In Kansas City, their mentoring, training and financial aid have helped African Americans like Carl, who has a criminal record and collects social security after an accident on a construction site left him unemployed. Or Shellie, who combines part-time jobs with public benefits to feed her child. LISC's financial opportunity centres help such marginal citizens help themselves, not only by showing them how to access income

[margin note, left: community involvement]

[margin note, left: FINALLY we bring structural racism]

[margin note, right: are we going to talk about corporate responsibility for this?]

support but also by teaching them how to manage their finances better. As Shellie puts it: 'Everybody falls … But when a person falls, you need a little cushion so you can get yourself back up.'[47]

Stockton and elsewhere

In March 2020, as the Covid-19 pandemic began to spread across the world, Mayor Michael Tubbs, Stockton, and the universal basic income, were back in the news again. Indeed, governments in many countries had begun planning bailouts to the soon-to-be unemployed. In the US, for instance, the Senate passed legislation that would give the poorest families, who had no taxable income, $600 each while middle-income Americans would get a single payment of $1,200 plus $500 for each child.[48] Tubbs found this focus on direct cash assistance 'heartening' in principle even as he questioned some of the detail. Meanwhile, other Democrats called for larger, recurring cash payments, ranging from $1,000 to $6,000 per month.[49]

Early results from Stockton's experiment with the UBI suggested that there was merit in providing direct cash payments to citizens. Such payments were 'more flexible than a one-size-fits-all government programme' and allowed people to 'adapt to changing needs and new crises'. 'Everyone we talked to,' said Tubbs, 'there was a different way they would use $500, and they all made sense. There was no way, as a government official, I would be smart enough to think of all that.'[50]

Around the world, in places like Stockton, people are looking to create a new type of government: one that fosters an inclusive, diverse society and reforms and rebuilds the institutions needed to make such societies thrive. These attempts have been made more pressing by the Covid-19 pandemic and its aftermath. To achieve their aims, politicians and their teams have had to experiment: in areas such as jobs, income and productivity; training, skills and education; healthcare; women's empowerment; and criminal justice. And a key area for experimentation has been the UBI.

Nevertheless, the debate continues about the effectiveness of the UBI relative to other approaches to social security reform. Some champion a negative income tax (NIT) where, if your income falls below a certain threshold, the tax authorities pay you; but, as your income increases, you start to pay tax, thus tapering your income. Another contender is the Universal Credit system: an attempt to reform older approaches to social security by merging several different working-age benefits into one. Many now argue that the future lies with Universal Credit and variants of the NIT. And yet, in many parts of the world, UBI remains in the limelight. In the US, for instance, Andrew Yang, a 2020 Democratic Party presidential aspirant, ran on a universal basic income platform. In the UK, Rebecca Long-Bailey, a candidate for leader of the Labour party in 2020, advocated for it. In India, the Congress party included a variant of the UBI in its 2019 election manifesto.

The question, therefore, remains: how do we know whether schemes like the UBI, the NIT and Universal Credit work? Under what circumstances, and for what types of people? How can we compare these variants with each other and choose the best? And even if some of these approaches look good on paper, how easy or hard are they to implement?

We cannot know the precise answers to these questions until we experiment, collect the evidence and weigh up the pros and cons – before scaling a solution that is most likely to work. Indeed, as is often the case with government schemes, a great idea on paper may not work in practice. Implementation is key, as is learning about what works. And as with social security, so too with many other areas of government policy such as education and health. Hence the need for an experimental state, one that is constantly trying out new ideas and approaches, testing them against the evidence, and then dropping them or taking them forward at scale. We turn to this subject next, in Chapter 6.

6

The experimental state: let a thousand flowers bloom, then pick the best

'The country demands bold, persistent experimentation.
It is common sense to take a method and try it: If it
fails, admit it frankly and try another. But above all, try
something.'

Franklin D. Roosevelt

Shortly after midnight on 12 May 2010, the UK got its first coalition government since the Second World War. The Liberal Democrats, with 57 seats in the House of Commons, emerged from a meeting in the early hours to announce that they had found a way to work with the Conservatives who, with 307 seats, needed their support to form a government. Later that day, the two parties published a coalition agreement which set out the terms of their deal. David Cameron, the leader of the Conservatives, would become prime minister, while Nick Clegg, the leader of the Liberal Democrats, would be his deputy.

Coalition governments are far from stable and many did not expect this particular one to last long. To make matters worse, the UK was still suffering from the aftermath of the financial crisis of 2008. Despite the best efforts of the Labour government under Gordon Brown, the coffers of the state were bare. Almost as if to rub it in, Liam Byrne, the outgoing chief secretary to the treasury, had left a note for his successor that read: 'I'm afraid there is no money!'[1]

And yet the demands on the state were as severe as ever. Immigration had been a flashpoint during the campaign and the Conservatives had promised to create a national border force to deal with the issue. Tighter budgets meant that the number of police officers would fall by thousands in the next few years, but the jails were full, and the Prison Officers' Association was warning of an overcrowded and dangerous prison system. An ageing population was putting a strain on the pension system and the National Health Service was as embattled as ever. Somehow the new government had to find a way to do more and better with less, and do it soon.

In the great drama of democracy, new governments often bring with them fresh ideas and energy. This government was no different. David Cameron had been preparing for his turn in power ever since he had become leader of the Conservatives in 2005. First he had set about modernising his party. Then, as the 2010 election neared, he turned his attention to the big ideas he might apply while in government. In the first flush of his tenure as prime minister, there were many such ideas vying for attention. There was a push, for example, for smarter, more digitally savvy governance. There was an emphasis on less government and helping people help themselves: 'Big Society, Small Government' being the motto. And there would be greater devolution of power, away from London to the regions and cities. The Liberal Democrats, for their part, found themselves in sync with much of this. As Cameron and Clegg put it in their Coalition Agreement: 'There has been the assumption that central government can only change people's behaviour through rules and regulations. Our government will be a much smarter one, shunning the bureaucratic levers of the past and finding intelligent ways to encourage, support and enable people to make better choices for themselves.'[2]

But of all these transformative ideas, perhaps the only one that would outlast the Coalition's five-year term was the creation of the world's first Behavioural Insights Team – the Nudge Unit, as it would be dubbed – a small but powerful team designed to bring the tools of behavioural science into the heart of government. No longer would policy be made as it had been since time immemorial, by mandarins on top of the food chain who made sweeping assumptions about what made people tick and who used the heavy-handed levers of power to manipulate the masses. Instead, the state would acknowledge the complexity of human motivations and behaviour and, through engagement with citizens, test what worked before rolling out its plans. Policy would be driven by evidence and not mere appeals to authority and instinct. And at the core of this new approach was the experimental method, now brought into the heart of government, to be embedded there.

The messy realities of human behaviour

Two people were crucial to this new turn in government: Steve Hilton and Rohan Silva. Hilton had been a close friend of Cameron's for several years: the two were contemporaries and had worked together in politics since their early twenties. A colourful figure who was the antithesis of a traditional Conservative, Hilton was a 'big picture' man and a political animal.

Silva, on the other hand, had begun his career as a fast-track civil servant in the Treasury. The bureaucracy had frustrated him, and so, when an opportunity came in 2006 to work for George Osborne, a close ally of Cameron's, Silva took it. Soon he was organising reading groups and workshops to bring fresh ideas into the Conservative Party to help it find its way back into power.

In contrast to career politicians, Silva found being in opposition exhilarating. 'It was strange to me', he says 'that politicians get depressed when they are in opposition. In reality, for most citizens, local councils are a protest vote against the party in government. So, while Labour was in power in Westminster, the Tories were in power in the councils. I felt we could implement policy within the councils.'³ For Silva, being in opposition came with the excitement of being in a 'start-up in a garage'.⁴ There were no civil servants to stall ideas, and the Tory-dominated councils were 'laboratories in which to conduct policy experiments'.⁵

But first the Conservatives needed ideas to test: ideas that they could use to critique the Labour government and show why and how things could be done better. So Silva began to invite academics and writers to speak to a group of people like himself from within the party. Among the first to be invited was Robert Cialdini, a psychologist who had studied how social norms could be used to drive people towards socially useful behaviour such as recycling. Others followed, such as Daniel Kahneman, the Israeli psychologist and Nobel laureate, and Nassim Nicholas Taleb, the author of *The Black Swan*, which warned about the impact of unpredictable events on people who were ill equipped to predict or respond to them. But perhaps the most eventful encounter was with Richard Thaler, an American academic who had pioneered the field of behavioural economics.

Thaler had spent his career pushing against the mainstream of his profession. Most economists build their models on a view of humans as self-interested, rational beings who make decisions that maximise their pleasure (or utility) while minimising their pain. Drawing on the work of pioneering psychologists like Amos Tversky and Kahneman, Thaler had argued for a more nuanced view of how humans think and behave. He had shown that people are prone to systematic deviations from rationality which account for important economic phenomena such as stock market bubbles and overbidding in auctions. Thaler had also shown how an understanding of these deviations could lead to improved policymaking. For instance, pension plans would be more effective if people were required to opt out of rather than into them. In 2008, he published *Nudge: Improving Decisions about Health, Wealth and Happiness* with Cass Sunstein, a colleague from the University of Chicago. In the book the two argued that government policymaking and regulation could be greatly improved if they were behaviourally informed. Such a psychologically nuanced view could be used to drive a form of regulation and policymaking that balanced two hitherto opposing approaches to government: the libertarian and the paternalistic. Instead of being either too laissez-faire or too heavy-handed, governments could 'nudge' people into being healthier, happier and wealthier. Importantly, these approaches were simple and cheap.

Silva, always on the lookout for interesting ideas, invited Thaler to speak to his reading group in London. At the meeting were Steve Hilton, Greg Clark – a shadow government minister with a PhD in behavioural economics – and Oliver Letwin, a major figure in developing policy for the party. Thaler argued that the policymaker's view of human behaviour was often limited and driven by utopian ideology rather than empirical substance. People were not as simple, predictable and rational as assumed, and if policy were to get better, it would have to be rooted in the messy realities of actual human behaviour. This view sat well with those around the table, not only because it helped with policymaking, but also because it gave them a tool with which to criticise the Labour government in Westminster.

Soon after the meeting with Thaler, Silva wrote an article for George Osborne in *The Guardian* newspaper. Titled 'Nudge, nudge, win, win', the article set out why the Tories were getting behind a new behavioural or 'nudge' agenda.[6] Then, having set out their stall, Silva and his colleagues began implementing some of these ideas in local councils run by the Conservatives.

They started in the Royal Borough of Windsor and Maidenhead. Recycling was an important issue in the council and the councillors were grappling with how to get residents to do more of it. A recent study had found that people responded asymmetrically to incentives versus disincentives, and that carrots often worked better than sticks. And yet, the tendency of government was to prefer sticks to carrots. Silva then came across an American company called Recyclebank which paid people to recycle. This approach had worked well in the US. Would it also work in the UK where norms and mores might be different? 'I liked their approach,' Silva says. 'Plus, I was thinking about Gordon Brown and UK politics. The Labour government had an unpopular policy of fining people for not recycling. I said, let's bring Recyclebank to Windsor and Maidenhead and see if paying works better than fining.'[7]

The experiment worked. 'It was about policy,' says Silva, 'but it was also about politics: about making a point against the Labour government.' The experiment also got a lot of media attention, and this was important. 'When you're trying to get big ideas in, you've got to have wins along the way,' says Silva. 'These wins create a positive feedback loop: success with citizens, media coverage and political utility, all working in tandem to get you support. So we spent the next three years, from 2007 to 2009, doing more of this.'[8]

Another experiment came with the financial crisis. There were growing concerns about the huge levels of debt that people in the UK were groaning under. Thaler's work had identified 'hot' moments – times when people are in psychologically heightened moods – and how these affect spending behaviour. So Silva and his team began to look at the issue of store cards. Enticed by something they wanted to buy, and told they could get 20 per cent off with a store card, many people were making purchases they could not afford, and ending up with debts they couldn't service. Store cards were a terribly expensive form of borrowing for people, and one they used when they were most emotionally aroused or vulnerable. So the Conservatives introduced rules about a cooling-off period. If you wanted to sign up to a store card, it wouldn't kick in for a week. This would give you a chance to consider other types of better value credit, or whether you needed the purchase at all.

Back in the US, the nudge approach got a big boost in 2009 when Thaler's co-author Cass Sunstein, a legal scholar at the

University of Chicago, was appointed by Barack Obama to head the White House Office of Information and Regulatory Affairs. The task of the office was to ensure the design of good government regulations, and Sunstein immediately set about applying behavioural ideas to the job. He got several government agencies to use behavioural tools, in a whole host of areas from healthy eating and energy efficiency to financial and healthcare reform. Realising that this would resonate with Cameron and Osborne, Silva and Hilton went to Washington in 2009 to meet Sunstein. Over dinner they compared notes, and were encouraged by the progress that Sunstein was making. They also noted that his moves had attracted the ire of politicians on the right, for whom all this was more evidence of the nanny state, with Sunstein being the nanny-in-chief. This struck Hilton and Silva as ironic: back in the UK, nudge approaches were being attacked by Labour and the left as too weak!

Not long after their visit, the UK went to the polls, and the Conservatives soon found themselves in government with the Liberal Democrats. It was crunch time for Silva and Hilton, and the big ideas they had absorbed from the likes of Cialdini, Sunstein and Thaler. A window had opened up for nudge to find its way into government. The approach had helped them win the election. Could it help them win while *in* government?

Mr Thaler goes to Whitehall

In the early summer of 2010, shortly after the Coalition took over, Richard Thaler crossed the pond to meet Hilton and Silva and plot how to properly bring the nudge approach into government. They were joined in the tiny courtyard of 10 Downing Street by Oliver Letwin and David Halpern. Letwin was now the minister of state for government policy, a key player in the Cabinet Office who worked closely with the prime minister. Halpern was the director of the Institute for Government, a think tank set up to engage with members of parliament and civil servants to conduct research on public administration and government.

The first question was what to call the new team. The government had made it a point not to set up a whole lot of new units. So 'unit' was out, and anyway the word 'team' sounded better. But what sort of team would it be? 'Behavioural economics' was the term that Thaler, an economist, had popularised through his work. But this term annoyed influential psychologists like Daniel Kahneman who felt that it was just more evidence of the hegemony of economics in universities and elsewhere. 'Behavioural insights' sounded better to everyone. So the Behavioural Insights Team was what they settled on, though Silva quipped that it would probably just end up being called the Nudge Unit anyway, which is indeed what happened.

It was also Silva's idea that the team should be set up like a 'skunk works': it would be scrappy and lean and move fast, like start-ups in Silicon Valley. Cameron was clear that his office in Number 10 was not going to be big. His government was going to be about devolving power, not concentrating it. He wanted the departments to have the freedom to do their own thing and not be driven by an overbearing centre. Plus, the whole point of nudge was to be experimental, to see what worked, and if it didn't work, then to move on. So the team would set itself a target of two years to prove itself, or it would be dissolved.

There was one final issue to settle: who would lead the group?

'The civil service', Silva says, 'would typically decide this. But they aren't usually great at hiring.'[9]

Sure enough, the civil servants ended up proposing someone with no knowledge of behavioural economics or social psychology to be the head. They did, however, recommend David Halpern – who did know a great deal about the subject – to be his deputy.

'I thought this was mad,' says Silva. 'David was clearly the more appropriate person to lead. But we were new in government and I didn't want to over-rule the civil servants. I knew I needed some cover for this and that's where Steve came in.'

Silva knew that Hilton was close to Cameron. If Hilton agreed that Halpern should run the team, he could get the PM to over-rule the civil servants. So Silva worked on Hilton, who eventually spoke to the PM, and Halpern became the top choice to lead the new team.

'That's how the Behavioural Insights Team came to be,' says Silva. 'It was fascinating. It could so easily have gone the other way. My role was to get it going, to get the right people on it, with the right support to move forward. Once I did that, the Nudge Unit was on its way.'

Bringing rigour to government

David Halpern wryly describes himself as a recovering academic. After a first degree in experimental psychology and a PhD in social and political sciences from Cambridge, he became a research fellow at Oxford and then a lecturer in social and political sciences at Cambridge. Even as a junior academic, he had what his colleagues regarded as an unhealthy interest in the 'outside world'. This included a course he taught on how psychology could address policy challenges and develop creative solutions to address these challenges. But teaching and research were a pale substitute for the real thing, and so in 2001, when the opportunity presented itself, Halpern went to work in Prime Minister Tony Blair's Strategy Unit.

Blair had set up the unit to be a source of strategic advice and policy analysis on the key priorities of his government. According to Blair, the unit would 'look ahead at the way policy would develop' and examine 'fresh challenges and new ideas to meet them'. Right away Halpern was struck by how un-rigorous the unit's approach was, how aloof it was from the realities of people's lives and the psychological forces that drove their behaviour. 'The unit would do these grand sweep reviews,' says Halpern, 'but no one had access to journals. And for their reviews, there was no evidence that they really used. There might be some internal data but even this was surprisingly thin.'[10]

In 2004, Halpern produced a paper that examined the link between personal responsibility and behavioural change. Someone leaked the paper and the press pounced on a one-line reference to financial incentives and their use to discourage unhealthy eating. This turned into headlines in all the newspapers about what came to be dubbed the 'fat tax'. 'Anything linked to Number 10 attracts political interest,' says Halpern. 'In the context of a centre-left government, this was deemed as interventionist in policy, and evidence of a super nanny state. And so the PM felt compelled to say we will never do anything like this again.'[11]

Chastened by this experience, the unit supressed the empirical, behavioural approach for a bit, though Halpern continued to look for ways to bring it into government. In common with most politicians, Tony Blair was a lawyer by profession. 'He didn't really do what we would call experimentation,' says Halpern. 'Even though the government talked about evidenced-based policy, it was almost unheard of that people would think about policy in an experimental way.'

On another occasion Halpern would conduct a massive review of education with Paul Johnson, then chief economist at the Department for Education and now head of the influential Institute for Fiscal Studies. Wouldn't it be better, they asked, to systematically look at what would later be called What Works in government? 'We can look at everything that has been done on education, for instance, such as whether school grades are a good predictor of later performance. We can take interventions at various stages and see what effects these have had, and so on.'[12] So Johnson and Halpern looked at all the evaluations that the government had ever supported in education and found something in the range of seventy such studies. They looked at what the interventions had done; how good the method of evaluation had been; and what the size of the impact was. They then applied the criteria that one might use to assess rigorous experiments and found that a mere two out of seventy met them.

'This was truly shocking,' says Halpern. 'One was a study of playing for success, about an intervention where disadvantaged kids were taught maths in the local football club. That study had a proper experimental design with a control group and so on. But that was about it. To do things in that haphazard way was normal. That's how government was and had always been: un-rigorous.'[13]

And so, when Hilton and Silva conspired to have him lead the newly created Nudge Unit, Halpern knew that his moment had come. This would be his big chance to place behavioural science and the experimental method right at the heart of government for years to come. He could see no other choice but to seize it.

Get nudging

When it first got going, the Nudge Unit was a team of Halpern and six others. The founding seven gave themselves three objectives to start with: to achieve a ten-fold return on the cost of the team; to spread an understanding of behavioural approaches across government; and to have a major impact on at least two key areas of policy. Ranged against them were all manner of foes: complex coalition politics; a civil service that was largely uncomprehending of their new ideas; and a sceptical, even hostile, press.

Budgetary pressures had forced the unit to focus on being able to show value for money. 'Our performance targets and sunset clause', says Halpern 'had an interesting kicker. They were a major reason why we had to use the experimental approach. If we were going to answer the claim: how did you have a ten-fold impact, we had to show how our approach did relative to a comparable group that didn't benefit from it.'[14]

Interestingly, most government policy doesn't typically answer the question of impact in a compelling way, even though this is a profound issue in many parliaments. 'Politicians talk about accountability,' says Halpern, 'but what exactly does that mean? They can give you a narrative and maybe tell you where the money went. But they are usually pretty poor at answering: did it work?'

And so the Nudge Unit had rigour built into everything it did from the very start. It helped that many in the team had a background in psychology and the experimental method. For them, the core of the experimental method was the classic randomised controlled trial. In such a trial, the intervention – that is, a new way of doing something – is administered to a randomly selected group of people. The impact of the intervention on that group is then compared with outcomes for a similarly chosen control group that does not receive the intervention. Randomisation ensures that the two groups are representative of the population at large as well as similar to each other in all respects except that one group receives the treatment while the other does not. Any difference in the outcomes can then be attributed with confidence to the intervention rather than to any of a whole host of other possible causes.

Over the first two years of its existence, the Behavioural Insights Team would conduct dozens of such randomised controlled trials – experiments, in the rigorous sense of the word – across key areas of government, including tax, education, health, energy and employment. It was the ability of these experiments to show clearly and conclusively what worked that ensured not only the survival but also the success of the team.

Taxes: not as inevitable as death

One of the first experiments the Nudge Unit ran was with the UK tax and revenue authority (HMRC). Here the team had some good luck: the initial impetus for the trial came from HMRC itself. Nick Down, a civil servant in the department, had already begun to apply behavioural approaches to recovering a large sum of money – £600 million to be precise – from a group of late taxpayers. Inspired by the notion that people are often motivated by social norms ('good citizens pay their taxes on time'), Down had sent out thousands of letters to late payers telling them the truth: namely that nine out of ten people pay their taxes on time.[15] His trial had shown some promise, but it hadn't been done as a clean, randomised controlled trial. And so it wasn't possible to say exactly what effect the norm-based approach had had on getting people to pay their overdue taxes.

Working with Down, the Behavioural Insights Team designed a more rigorous trial that would systematically test the idea. Together, the group cleaned up the intervention and came up with further variations to make sure they could quantify the effect and say exactly how much money was being brought in.

But then they hit an organisational barrier. The tax system was (and remains) resistant to outsiders. The powers that be are rightly concerned about doing anything that interferes with the smooth running of government. So Halpern did a deal with the head of HMRC, the permanent secretary. 'I will find a good person,' Halpern promised him, 'who you can employ directly. That person will help run the experiment, answer to you and stay in-house.' This reassured the department about confidentiality and control and they agreed to proceed with the trial.

The person they tapped for the job – Michael Hallsworth – was a young behavioural researcher who was seconded to the tax department, where he performed his duties under the watchful gaze of the civil servants in the department. Hallsworth's role was not only to conduct the experiment but also to educate others in the department about how to do so. This included handling the massive machines that printed out tax letters; pulling out standard letters and manually replacing them with new variations; repeating this process thousands of times; and generally motivating a lot of hard-pressed junior HMRC staff to believe all this was worth the hassle.

Eventually, HMRC ran the trial and was able to show conclusively that simply adding the single, truthful line that 'nine out of ten taxpayers pay on time' resulted in a 4.5 per cent increase in the payment rate. Given that millions of pounds of unpaid tax were involved, this amounted to a considerable sum of increased revenue for the government. What's more, the cost of the intervention (rewording the letter) was practically zero.[16]

Buoyed by this success, and having found a systematic way to do such trials, the joint team went on to carry out a subsequent, more ambitious trial.

As in many countries, in the UK public professionals like doctors earn both a salary from their hospital and an income from private work. The salary is taxed at source, but it is up to the doctors to declare and pay tax on their private income. For various reasons, they don't often do so.

Working with HMRC, the Nudge Unit came up with four different versions of letters to send to randomly chosen groups of doctors.[17] The first version was a generic letter that anyone, regardless of their profession, would receive; this letter simply reminded the doctors that they should declare their extra earnings. The second version made specific reference to 'doctors and medics' (the relevant 'reference group' for the social norm to kick in) and noted that doctors and medics often had extra earnings that they needed to declare. The third version made specific mention of doctors and medics ('we know that many doctors receive extra income') but also noted that HMRC took doctors' prior lack of response to be an 'oversight'. It then went on to say that if they ignored this letter that would be taken as an active choice on their part. The fourth version was identical to the third but contained an additional moral message which pointed to a recent poll showing that most people trusted their doctor to tell the truth.

'The beauty of tax collection', says Halpern, 'is that you sit back and wait for the results to roll in and then you compare the effectiveness of the different letters.' What they found surprised even them: the generic letter led to a 4 per cent increase in response; the second version to a 21 per cent increase (a five-fold increase over the generic letter); and the third and fourth to a whopping 35 per cent increase in response (a nine-fold increase over the generic letter).[18] Interestingly, there was no difference in the impact of adding the moral message: the response to the fourth version of the letter was the same as that to the third. (Doctors, it would seem, are immune to news that people trust them to tell the truth.)

Importantly, all this was done without an extra penny being spent.

Into the dragon's den: meeting with the heads of department

A key moment came when the new head of the UK's civil service, Sir Jeremy Heywood, invited Halpern to present the Nudge Unit's findings to the permanent secretaries: the heads of the various civil service departments.

The crucial meeting was held in Whitehall, at the heart of the UK government. Twenty months had gone by since the founding of the Behavioural Insights Team, and Halpern had plenty of results to draw on.

He began by showing the heads the results of the tax trials with HMRC, and how a single sentence like 'most people pay their tax on time' had helped increase repayment rates and brought forward millions of pounds in late or unpaid tax.

He then presented results from a trial designed to get people to insulate their lofts and make energy savings. The Department of Energy and Climate Change (as it was then called) had thought that greater subsidies for insulation would do the trick, but the Behavioural Insights Team had found that the bigger issue for most people was the hassle of clearing out their lofts in the first place, rather than the cost of insulating them. Halpern presented results that showed how sending leaflets to households offering extra discounts for insulation was less effective than sending leaflets that offered a loft-clearance service that households had to *pay* for. Indeed, the loft clearance approach, even though it cost households more, was three times more effective than the subsidies approach, which would have cost the *government* more.[19]

Then there were the motoring fines. Halpern showed how adding a photograph of the owner's car, as it was caught by a roadside camera, made people more likely to pay their car tax. And as with the cars, so too with the courts. Sending text messages to those who owed fines – informing them that the bailiffs would collect in ten days – doubled payment rates, boosting revenues and saving the cost and human misery of having bailiffs actually show up.[20]

And so it went: more tax revenues, more insulated homes, more fines paid, and all at little or no extra cost to the government.

On seeing these examples, the heads of department seemed pleased, though in many cases they were only dimly aware of this work going on beneath their noses. Suma Chakrabarti, the head of the Ministry of Justice, was one of the first to comment. 'David,' he said, 'this is interesting. Have you shown the results to my minster?' David wasn't sure. He and his team had conducted the study out in the field, far from the gaze of the higher-ups. It was very likely the minister didn't know anything about any of this, and the Nudge Unit certainly hadn't discussed it with Chakrabarti before.

'At that moment,' Halpern said, 'my heart sank. I had a

sudden fear we were about to be ripped to shreds for not getting the proper permission from his department for conducting the trial. I could see the whole thing falling apart as others jumped in to question the very principle of conducting trials at all.'[21]

Instead, Chakrabarti smiled and asked for more details to be sent to him so he could brief his minister accordingly. He thought the minister would be impressed.

The tribulations of trials

There are many aspects of the experimental approach that make it a powerful tool for government. Governance and policymaking tend to be part of a monolithic system that often treats all citizens as similar and driven by similar motivations. The experimental approach, when combined with behavioural insights, recognises that people are different and driven by a whole range of motivations.

[Typical policymaking makes assumptions about human behaviour and then devises a priori solutions that tend to use broad-brush, blunt instruments to make change happen.]A good example of this was the plan by the UK's Department of Energy and Climate Change to get citizens to insulate their homes. The department simply assumed, consistent with standard economic theory, that as 'rational economic agents', citizens would seek to minimise the cost of insulating their homes. To mitigate these costs, the department set about spending huge amounts on subsidising installation schemes. And then, when many people still made no attempt to insulate their homes, the department threw even larger subsidies at the problem.[22]

In contrast, the Nudge Unit recognised that there are many situations when we cannot know a priori what will and will not work. And so, when it was brought in to address the insulation issue, the team took time to understand the problem from the citizen's perspective. Sure enough, it soon became clear to them that people didn't insulate their lofts not because of the financial cost but because of the hassle of clearing the piles of junk to enable the process of insulation. As Halpern puts it: 'When you helped people clear their loft – even though they had to pay for the service – there was a 4.8-fold increase in uptake.'[23] The presumption in the Department of Energy and Climate Change had been that you just had to make the subsidy bigger. But in practice, that didn't work; indeed, it was counterproductive.

Further, typical policymaking is concerned about effectiveness, but it has no obvious way of testing the impact of a policy. Even when it can test the impact, it can only do so after the fact, by which time any unanticipated damage has already been done, and done at scale. The experimental approach helps to reduce such risks in policymaking by testing new ideas in small doses before implementing those that work on a larger scale. Importantly, measuring and evaluating the impact of new ideas is built into the design of such experiments from the start.

Ironically, several arms of government such as tax and revenue are uniquely built to use the experimental approach. These departments have management information systems in place that track behaviour and collect data on large numbers of people at the individual level over time. They also have the means to try out variations: the letters sent to citizens being a classic example of a tool that can be used to test a whole host of variations at little or no extra cost.

So the question arises: if the method is so powerful and so relatively easy for government to implement, why isn't it more widely used? Why has it only been so recently that countries like the US and UK have even begun experimenting with experiments?

'It's a whole new paradigm,' says Halpern, 'a completely different way of thinking. Plus, change is hard, especially in large, monolithic systems.'[24]

Take tax, which in the UK is part of a massive and highly

conservative department of over 100,000 people, gathering billions in revenue. 'If we go to them', says Halpern, 'and say: we just want to make this little change in your massive machine, well, their response is that your little change is grit in the cogs of their machine. Downing Street may support it now, but if tax collection doesn't go according to plan, the whole government, which relies on this machine to work, will come to a standstill. And all because of our experiment.'[25]

Rohan Silva has a similar take. 'In the UK,' he says, 'the civil service is supposed to be independent. But civil servants are human, and loss aversion is a strong human tendency.'[26]

The behavioural agenda – when it was first introduced – was alien to most civil servants. Other than the people at the very top, like the cabinet secretary Gus O'Donnell and his successor Jeremy Heywood, almost everyone else had initially thought the approach trivial or irrelevant. 'And this was even after the PM', says Silva, 'had made speeches about it. Even after the civil service had received a mandate to proceed, it had failed to engage.'

But it isn't only civil servants who are resistant to change. Politicians, for their part, aren't keen on small-scale studies designed to see what works either. As Silva puts it:

> Their careers are short and they're constantly thinking of how to make a big splash with the press and the public. They want to make impressive announcements and leave a legacy. They don't want to show up in some remote corner of the country and say: 'Hi, I'm here to do a pilot study covering three streets in Wolverhampton and if it turns out well, we'll maybe expand it to the whole council.'[27]

Then there's the aversion to risk. 'As soon as something goes wrong,' Silva says, 'the press, select committees and the audit office are ready to beat the crap out of you. They don't want to see headlines that read "Government wastes millions on a programme found to be ineffective". The confluence of factors at the start of the Coalition government was a rare occurrence, Silva adds: 'Cameron and Osborne felt they had a five-year term; they could take some risks at beginning. But sadly this is a very rare thing in politics.'[28]

The challenges the Nudge Unit faced included convincing sceptical politicians, training recalcitrant civil servants, and changing mindsets. And so, in the first couple of years, it did quite a bit of flying below the radar. The team would get nominal permission, at best, from the top, and then it would find someone close enough to the operational detail and skip over the layers in between. As Halpern puts it: 'The question for us was: could we turn that process from something accidental and ad hoc into an innovation machine that could operate routinely across the whole system?'[29]

Eventually, the challenge became: could the method that the Nudge Unit had pioneered be rolled out throughout government and not just in one or two departments? Could it be institutionalised right across the public sector?

What Works centres and the experimental method

Long before Cass Sunstein had brought nudging to the White House and the Behavioural Insights Team had brought the experimental method to the UK, there had been an important area of the British public sector where such approaches had been institutionalised. That area was medicine and healthcare. And behind that revolution had been a Scottish physician, Archie Cochrane: the progenitor of evidence-based medicine in the modern era.

During the Second World War, Cochrane, a medic in the British army, had been captured and sent to the Elsterhorst prisoner-of-war camp in Germany. There he was put in charge of treating soldiers who had contracted tuberculosis. Unhappy with the existing treatments, and not knowing how to choose between them anyway, he began experimenting with food supplements and was able to show that these had a positive effect on the sick soldiers. Struck by this experience, and convinced of the importance of experiments, after the war Cochrane worked tirelessly to make randomised controlled trials (RCTs) a part of the standard practice of the medical profession. Throughout the 1950s, 1960s and 1970s, he and his colleagues conducted tests on a large number of medical practices involving, for instance, pregnancy and childbirth, and even the effectiveness of removing tonsils. Often, these experiments were met with hostility from others in the profession: some deemed them unnecessary, while others even saw them as unethical. But Cochrane and his colleagues persisted.

In 1972, Cochrane published *Effectiveness and Efficiency: Random Reflections on Health Services.*[30] In the monograph, he criticised the lack of evidence behind many healthcare practices of the time and advocated the use of RCTs to make medicine more effective and efficient. A review of the book in the *British Medical Journal* concluded that 'the hero of the book is the randomised control trial, and the villains are the clinicians in the "care" part of the National Health Service (NHS) who either fail to carry out such trials or succeed in ignoring the results if they do not fit in with their own preconceived ideas.'[31]

Eventually, Cochrane's insistence on the experimental approach had a profound influence on saving lives, in many countries around the world. In 1993, the Cochrane Collaboration (subsequently shortened to Cochrane) was set up to 'facilitate evidence-based choices about health interventions faced by health professionals, patients, and policymakers' through a network of collaborators from over 120 countries. Then, in 1999, the UK government created the National Institute for Health and Care Excellence (NICE) to focus entirely on collating and disseminating evidence on the effectiveness of medical treatments and drugs within the UK and the NHS. Indeed, the Labour Party had run on the platform 'what matters is what works'. The idea was to replace ideology-driven politics with a more pragmatic approach to policymaking and free it from the everyday pressures of politics.

And yet the success of the method did not spread to other parts of the public sector: whole areas of government remained immune. Until, that is, Halpern and his team brought experiments and evidence back into the heart of government. Buoyed by the success of the Nudge Unit, between 2011 and 2015 the UK government set up several What Works centres to cover broad areas such as education, wellbeing, ageing and crime reduction with the goal of 'collating and building evidence of what works' and 'putting this evidence into the hands of practitioners'.[32] As autonomous units, these centres were the logical follow-up to the Behavioural Insights Team. Halpern, who had been instrumental in making the case for them, became the What Works national adviser, thus cementing links between the two initiatives.

Since then, the most successful of the What Works centres has been one focused on education. In 2010, the UK's Department for Education was facing the unusual situation of having unspent money to the tune of £100 million at the end of the financial year. In a time of austerity, the last thing any minister wants to do is to give money back to the Treasury. And so it was with Michael Gove, the secretary of state for education at the time. Further, because of the Coalition's focus on smart government, there was an added pressure to do 'something empirical'. So Gove and the department decided to put the whole sum into creating an independent organisation dedicated to evidence-based policy in the field of education.[33] Called the Education Endowment Foundation, the new body would address the question of what works in education: it would look at existing evidence, but would also run new experiments and fund them. The larger objective was to make the education profession informed and empirical, as the medical profession before it had become.

What Works in education?

Kevan Collins began his professional life as a primary school teacher in East London in the 1980s before going on to run schools and work for the central government as national director of the Primary Literacy Strategy. He then went back to East London as director of children's services in Tower Hamlets, one of the UK's most deprived communities, before becoming chief executive of the Tower Hamlets council from 2009 to 2011. 'At the council,' Collins says, 'I was struck by the large number of decisions in a whole array of public services that we had to make without really having a clear set of rigorous options in front of us. People did put forward options, but they were ideas rather than evidenced choices.'[34]

Earlier in his career, Collins had completed a PhD involving a quantitative study of bilingualism and literacy. This experience exposed him to the power of using data to test hypotheses and assemble evidence for what works and what doesn't. Without such data and testing, he realised, on the basis of theory alone, it was hard to decide whether bilingualism (for instance) was a good or bad thing for educational outcomes, and whether it was therefore something that policymakers should encourage or not. So, when the government announced a competition to allocate £125 million to support efforts to improve outcomes for disadvantaged children in English schools, he took immediate notice. 'Traditionally,' he says, 'this money would have been spent on people with an idea constructing a strategy and then going out and doing it. But I put in a proposal not to do that but to use evidence instead to inform the decision-making.'

Collins became involved in the conversation and this eventually led to him becoming the first CEO of the Education Endowment Foundation.

'Our proposition was that, in England, similar schools with similar children and similar resources experience a huge variation in outcomes. We know that this is because different people make different decisions. But how then can we know what is effective and collect that information in ways that others can verify and use?' So, this was what Collins and his team set out to do. The idea was to go from compliance and uninformed professionalism to informed professionalism. Surprisingly, this had not been the tradition in education until then. 'Education had not been scientific or rigorous,' says Collins.

The Education Endowment Foundation (EEF) is a small organisation of twenty-five people that does three things, all in partnership with others. First, it maintains a toolkit that synthesises evidence of what works in education worldwide in terms of teaching 5- to 16-year-olds. The toolkit covers thirty or so key themes, including the impact of homework, one-to-one tuition and parental involvement. It uses a simple scale to summarise the cost of each activity, the strength of evidence regarding its effectiveness, and its impact on learning outcomes in terms of a common metric: the number of additional months of progress that it gives children. The toolkit is digital and interactive and gives teachers access to the findings of over 13,000 studies completed since 1980 that underpin the evidence. A team of social scientists from Durham University has the responsibility of confirming that the studies are rigorous and meet certain criteria, such as whether they are based on experimental designs, whether the studies have passed peer evaluation, and so on. As new studies come in, the evidence and toolkit are updated: items are added and dropped. 'The entire process is dynamic and iterative,' says Collins. 'And the toolkit has proven popular with schools. About 67 per cent of headteachers in England now use it to make decisions in their schools.'

The Education Endowment Foundation is also a fund: it gives money to those with ideas for how to innovate in schools. Anyone from the public or private sector with a new way to make a difference to disadvantaged students can apply for support. If the foundation likes the idea, it sets up a panel of independent evaluators who decide on how to find evidence that the new approach works. The panel makes sure that the developer is clear about the logic of their model, and sets out the parameters for testing it: 'to get such and such statistical certainty, you will need so many schools, teachers and students, and so on'. The protocol and design are then made public, the project is funded, and the developer recruits schools that are willing to participate, with about ninety schools as a minimum. The foundation then randomly assigns some schools to the intervention while others are kept in a control group which only receives the intervention the following year. If the efficacy trial works well, the developer is given an opportunity to scale the project and run an effectiveness trial. 'We check to see, for instance, if what works in Newcastle also works in Cornwall,' Collins says. 'We need reliable practices that we can use everywhere and put them to work.'

A final objective of the foundation is to encourage the teaching profession to be more evidence based. To this end, it disseminates and mobilises knowledge, not only about the outcomes of the trials, but also the process. For instance, UK schools employ an army of teaching assistants to help in classrooms. Research finds that, on average, teaching assistants don't have a huge impact on improving educational outcomes, but teachers and schools are reluctant to drop them. 'So we say to them,' Collins says, 'that if you do use teaching assistants, then here are some ways you can use them better.' Drawing on key lessons from the evidence, the foundation shows teachers how to use a programme, and encourages them to see links to the evidence. There is no coercive pressure put on teachers to use these resources. 'We don't tell them what to do,' says Collins. 'We nudge them to adopt and adapt intelligently to their own context. Our goal is to more actively involve teachers in their own learning about learning.' The emphasis is on gentle persuasion through ongoing engagement with headteachers and the clever use of funding.

Collins provides an example of how the EEF approach works. In 2014 there was a proposal to feed breakfast to disadvantaged kids as a way of boosting their performance in school. 'The proposal sounded intuitively correct but how could anyone know for sure? And what might the precise effect be?' So the foundation launched a large-scale randomised controlled trial to see what the evidence said. 'We recruited 10,000 families from all over the country,' says Collins, 'from within a set of schools. We did an independent pre-test on the attainment of children in these schools in English and Mathematics. Then, one year after the breakfast programme had begun, we did a post-test on the attainment levels of these children.'

In the schools where kids had been fed breakfast, the outcome was two months more progress than in the control schools where there had been no breakfast programme. This was the headline finding. But the process study revealed something even more interesting. In the first set of schools, even the children who didn't get breakfast made progress: the disruption caused by hungry children went down in those classes and behaviour as a whole improved. The government liked the finding so much that it created a £26 million fund to make breakfast free in hundreds of disadvantage schools around the country.

Does What Works really work?

The What Works approach – and evidence-based policy more generally – is not without its critics. A common objection is that the approach, in the context of education, puts even more pressure on already harried and overworked teachers. But Collins says that there is absolutely no obligation for teachers to work with the foundation. 'At the very outset,' says Collins, 'we deliberately decided we didn't want to be part of a compliance framework.' When a school joins up to do a trial, it does so out of curiosity and a desire to do better rather than through compulsion. 'Plus,' says Collins, 'it is not only about new things to do, it is also about providing insights about what schools and teachers shouldn't be doing, about things that are a waste of time.'

Take marking a child's work, for example. There is little research on this but teachers do a lot of marking nonetheless. 'In education, you get these moments when there is a firestorm: every child's work should be marked three times! So schools were doing this. But we said, stop: there's no evidence that this works. We said to teachers, mark less but mark better. This has reduced the burden on them.'

Another criticism is that the evidence-based approach pretends that policymaking is cool and rational, when it is actually all about values and ideology. This view is powerfully expressed by Paul Cairney, a professor of politics at the University of Stirling, who says that 'the biggest misconception is that evidence could ever be used at the heart of policymaking' and that evidence-based policymaking is itself a kind of a political slogan.[35] Given the pressures of time, Cairney argues, policymakers are forced to choose what evidence they use, and this is where values creep in.

Collins responds by saying that the evidence-based approach, rather than stalling questions of value, actually provides a surer footing on which to ask them. Indeed, experimental data makes it hard for teachers to shy away from the big questions.

> After one has controlled for everything that might account for school performance – prior attainment, English language, wealth – why is it that some schools do so much better than others? Teachers have an obligation to think about what they are doing in their schools. Of course, there are a whole set of big questions about wealth. So let's have that conversation.

Take, for instance, the vexed issue of streaming children according to their abilities. The evidence shows that putting the best kids in one class and the worst in another ensures that the brighter kids will do better than if they were in a mixed ability group, while the kids who didn't do well will do worse. 'Now you are left with a values question,' says Collins. 'No one can tell you what to do. You have to work out what you want as a school. But the evidence is there to help you with that decision. You are now informed. You cannot then say, oh we didn't know that.'

How about the difficulty of replication and the criticism that what works in one country or region might not work in another? Collins admits that it can be hard sometimes to replicate results. But this doesn't mean that one shouldn't even try to find out what replicates and what doesn't. The aim is to improve the performance of a control group over time. 'Different countries have different educational systems. In the US, children spend more time writing than in England, but oracy is better in England. So, if you replicate a US programme around oracy in England, you won't see the same effects because the baseline here is already better.' But again, Collins argues, this is precisely why teachers need to know how to use evidence, how to adopt and adapt it to their circumstances. Knowing that something has worked in hundreds of other schools is only a starting point. 'In the end,' he says, 'you have to evaluate what works in your school. You must understand the evidence to know which features should be in place, and be thoughtful about implementation.'

Finally, there is the view that the world is awash with evidence, too much, in fact, for anyone to pay any proper attention to it. Cairney, in *The Politics of Evidence-Based Policymaking*, states that there's just too much evidence for anyone to consider, and that policymakers often resort to shortcuts, basing things on one piece of research or one consultant's advice, which negates the whole attempt at achieving balance.[36] The problem therefore is not the lack of evidence. Rather, it is how one chooses from the plethora of findings out there, some of which contradict each other.

This is a fair point, Collins agrees. 'But that's why our toolkit is so interesting. Our guidance isn't based on only a single study.' Knowledge, Collins points out, is iterative, and so it is necessary to build knowledge banks that give teachers a better understanding of what matters.

This is why we also include a 'strength of evidence' column in the toolkit to remind them of this. We say: be sceptical about the guidance, think about what it costs, as well as the strength of evidence it is based on. There is certainly no doubt that we don't know enough. But that shouldn't stop us from constantly trying to find out.

The UK, through the Education Endowment Foundation, spends about £12 million per annum on studies of what works in education. This is quite possibly the largest amount spent by any country in the world. And yet the UK spends 3,000 times more – over £37 billion a year – on education as a whole. 'What major industry', asks Collins, 'would put R&D and learning at such a small ratio? Shouldn't education be the most important industry in any nation?'

Governments have so much more nudging to do

By the end of 2013, the Behavioural Insights Team was at a cross-roads. It had had many successes at the heart of government, across several departments. Halpern and his team had more than survived their initial two-year sunset clause. But now the team encountered a fresh set of challenges. There was only so much that seven people could achieve. Even hiring another member, in a time of austerity, required ministerial approval. Plus, other governments had come asking for help. Even though these clients were willing to pay, taking up such work was bureaucratically difficult. Extending nudge to other UK departments or helping the Australians apply it was proving almost impossible. 'We were trapped by being inside government,' says Halpern. 'What had been an asset – being based in Number 10 – was now also a constraint.'

And so, in 2014, with the support of the prime minister, the

Behavioural Insights Team was hived off. It became a 'social purpose company', part-owned by the government, part-owned by NESTA – a public policy think tank – and part-owned by the employees themselves. Halpern explains:

> In government, you get promoted by going to another job. After 18 months in one post, you go to another department. This helps spread ideas but deep knowledge is never built. We wanted to encourage wider adoption but also give opportunities to our people so they didn't feel they had to leave. All those things came together, prompting us to spin off.

In 2017, Richard Thaler was awarded the Nobel Prize in economics for his contributions to behavioural economics. His empirical findings and theoretical insights, the citation said, had been instrumental in creating a new and rapidly expanding field which had had a 'profound impact on many areas of economic research and policy'. In his acceptance speech, Thaler acknowledged the work that Halpern and the Behavioural Insights Team had done in making nudge a part of a government's toolkit.

By 2020, the team was over 200 people strong. It had grown to twenty times its original size, had opened offices in five different countries, and run projects in over thirty. In February 2020, during the early stages of the Covid-19 pandemic, the UK government's advice to citizens was heavily focused on nudges such as 'wash your hands, don't touch your face, don't shake hands with others, stay at home if you feel ill, and self-isolate if you have a continuous cough'.[37] Even when lockdown was imposed towards the end of March, nudges remained important as a way to ensure people complied with the potentially hard-to-follow guidance around isolation and social distancing.

Canada, too, now has its own Nudge Unit. In Australia, the New South Wales Department of Premier and Cabinet has set up its own Behavioural Insights Unit with help from Halpern's team. And in the US, the White House Office of Science and Technology Policy has a Social and Behavioral Sciences Initiative whose mission is to translate 'academic research findings into improvements in federal program performance and efficiency using rigorous evaluation methods'. In September 2015, President Obama had formally created this initiative to direct government agencies to use behavioural insights in improving the effectiveness and efficiency of government work.

As with behavioural insights, so with the What Works centres and approach. By 2020, these centres were responsible for billions of pounds in funding decisions in the UK, across several important areas, including education, health, ageing, wellbeing, crime reduction and local economic growth. And in the US, from 2016 more than a hundred cities also committed to using evidence and data to improve their policymaking under the slogan 'What works'. The experimental approach, it would seem, had become embedded within government and the public sector in many countries around the world.

And yet: even though we have known about 'nudges' for over a decade, and the broader point about checking what works is almost obvious, the bald fact is that there is so much more that can and should be done in this space. These ideas haven't penetrated as far or stuck as well as they should have done. Hence the ongoing need for this approach to continue to be spread more widely across government.

Moreover, the experimental approach can be taken well beyond the public sector, into how governments work with others in the wider economy more generally. Indeed, an even more profound role for trials can come from how the state engages with new technologies and the companies that innovate around them, both in the regulation and the cultivation of such activity. In Chapter 7, we turn to the question of how governments can experiment with regulating new technologies in better ways.

7

The entrepreneurial state: regulating the economy

'Move fast and break things. Unless you are breaking
stuff, you are not moving fast enough.'

Mark Zuckerberg

'[Zuckerberg] … has created a leviathan that crowds out
entrepreneurship and restricts consumer choice. It's on
our government to ensure that we never lose the magic of
the invisible hand.'

Chris Hughes, co-founder of Facebook

Over two billion people around the world – a third of the globe's
population – live and work without access to formal banking.
Lacking the many benefits that banking brings – cheap credit, ways
to save, and insurance for families and businesses – these large
populations are left to the mercy of money lenders, who charge
extortionate rates of interest, and to the vagaries of earning and
spending on a daily basis. No access to formal banking means no
access to the formal economy. This in turn means no access to
improved livelihoods, increased productivity and prosperity. As
Milton Friedman put it: 'The poor stay poor not because they
are lazy, but because they have no access to capital.'[1] Unbanked
economies are doomed to a cycle of poverty.

Governments around the world know this well. They know
that financial inclusion is a key condition for growth. This is particularly true of governments in developing countries where the

vast majority of the world's unbanked live. With increased access to credit, their citizens could invest in their farms and small businesses, and pay for the education and training they need to improve their productivity. With more ways to save money securely, they could build the financial reserves they need to weather shocks in income and expenditure. And through insurance they could take on the risks they face as farmers or traders.

But despite their best efforts, the governments of many countries have struggled to drive financial inclusion. This is partly due to the costs of taking banking to the poor in remote places: the so-called 'last-mile problem' that dogs many developing countries with rural populations. India, for instance, has over 600,000 villages. To set up a branch in every village would literally break the bank. But regulators, too, have a role to play in the process, particularly the central bankers who regulate their economies and tend to be cautious in their approach to financial innovation.

Kenya in 2006 was a typical case. Only 18 per cent of Kenyans at that time had access to the formal banking system, while 35 per cent relied on informal financial services and another 38 per cent were totally excluded.[2] The entire country had only 450 bank branches: less than two branches per 100,000 people.[3] In contrast to the poor state of banking, however, mobile telephony was thriving. More than a third of the population used mobile phones, and SMS messaging was popular. For every Kenyan with access to a bank account, at least two had access to a mobile phone.

Noting these facts, Safaricom, the Kenyan subsidiary of the telecoms giant Vodafone, began several pilot projects in the slums of Nairobi in early 2006. The idea was to test for ways in which mobile phones could be used to enable the urban poor to perform financial transactions electronically. It soon became clear that there were many different uses for such a service, but a particularly handy one was 'texting' money to friends and family. Safaricom realised that there was a huge opportunity to extend such a mobile payments service to the whole of Kenya. By using its agents in corner shops in villages, the firm could enable mobile-based cash-in and cash-out and money transfer from cities to the countryside. Such a service would be particularly popular with urban migrants who frequently sent money home to their families using expensive, time-consuming and unsafe methods. The key proposition and advertising strapline of the new service would be Send Money Home.

To proceed, however, they needed the permission of the regulator. So in August 2006, Safaricom approached the Central Bank of Kenya with plans for what they called M-Pesa. *Pesa* is the Swahili word for money: the service literally meant mobile money.

Dial M-Pesa for money

Gerald Nyaoma has worked for the Central Bank of Kenya for over thirty years. The director of the bank supervision department, Nyaoma grew up in Nakuru town in the Rift Valley Province of Kenya and joined the Central Bank in 1988.

In 2006, when Safaricom first approached the Central Bank with its new idea, Nyaoma was one of the first to be involved. He remembers the visit well:

> It was my first stint as director of bank supervision. The CEO of Safaricom, Michael Joseph, and his CFO, asked to meet us to discuss a new idea they had. At the meeting Joseph and his team presented their findings of pilot tests they had done in Nairobi and made an informal request to be allowed to proceed with a commercial product based on them.[4]

But here a problem presented itself: neither Safaricom nor Vodafone had a banking licence. This meant that the legal and regulatory structure of the business would be a delicate matter.

The initial instinct of Nyaoma and his team was that this project was not for them.

'At that time,' says Nyaoma, 'our typical response to a firm like Safaricom would have been: you are not a commercial bank. You are not registered as a Central Bank partner. We can't deal with you.'

But something niggled at Nyaoma during the meeting:

As it happened, just a week before that meeting, my uncle who lives in my home town of Nakuru had asked me to send him 30,000 shillings via bank transfer. I had gone to a local commercial bank which promptly charged me 500 shillings for the favour. But this was not all. A few days later, my uncle called and said: You sent me less money! I didn't know what he meant until we both realised that he had been charged another 500 shillings from the other side as well.

It had cost Nyaoma 1,000 shillings to send 30,000 shillings.

With this in mind, Nyaoma asked Michael Joseph what it would cost customers to send money home through M-Pesa. Joseph replied that the cost would be between 100 and 200 shillings, a significant reduction.

This impressed Nyaoma. But something further weighed on his mind. At that time, the results of the FinAccess survey – the first major study of financial access in Kenya – had just been released.[5] The findings had been damning for the Central Bank and for the Kenyan government more generally.

'The survey made us acutely aware of the low reach of the traditional banking sector,' says Nyaoma. It revealed that barely 18 per cent of Kenyans had access to formal financial services through regulated banks and building societies. Another 35 per cent had access to informal services such as rotating savings and credit associations (ROSCAs) and Accumulating Savings and Credit Associations (ASCAs). But fully 38 per cent of Kenyans had no access whatsoever to financial services of any kind – formal or informal. In contrast, the report noted, over 30 per cent of Kenyans had access to mobile phones and their adoption was growing much faster than was formal banking.

'At that time there were only 2.5 million bank accounts in the country,' says Nyaoma. 'The vast majority of our 30 million citizens were unbanked. I had grown up in the Rift Valley and had family there. I knew that many people who left home to work in Nairobi would send money back regularly.'

Nyaoma knew that low-volume payments and internal remittances could play a vital role in extending financial services, especially to rural Kenyans. Remittances, in particular, were a big source of internal flows of money. But most existing practices were inefficient and risky. Urban migrants would typically send money home through their friends who were going there. Others would send it through the drivers of public transport or put the money in the post. In that context, M-Pesa made lot of sense. It would make remittances and payment services more efficient and secure.

Due diligence: refuse or engage?

What the Safaricom proposal was offering the Central Bank was a powerful solution to their problem. The growth of mobile telephony, Nyaoma and his team realised, could kick-start financial inclusion in Kenya. The challenge, however, was balancing the opportunity with the risks posed by a new and unproven technology. Moreover, the new technology was being introduced by a non-banking entity, typically overseen by the telecommunications regulator.

'We had two options,' says Nyaoma. 'We could simply wash our hands of the affair and refer Safaricom to the telecoms regulator. Or we could require the service to go through the banking system, so that it could be properly regulated by the Central Bank.'

Indeed, when faced with new technologies like M-Pesa, the typical response of regulators is to ensure 'proper sequencing': first to pass sweeping legislation and establish specific regulations before giving way to innovation.[6] This was the approach that central banks in countries such as India followed, slowing down, in the process, the onset of mobile banking. But Nyaoma and his team realised that they had an opportunity to do something different. In fact, doing something different was the need of the hour.

'Safaricom had not been in Kenya long,' says Nyaoma, 'but its parent company, Vodafone, was the biggest telecoms firm in the country. The company had a reputation for understanding technology well. Plus, it was partly owned by the government, which gave us comfort.'

And so Nyaoma and his colleagues decided to adopt a third way: a middle path between the two extremes of strict regulation and laissez-faire.

Soon after the first meeting with Safaricom, the Central Bank formed a team to review M-Pesa. Members of the team came from the national payments systems department, from the bank's legal services group, and from Nyaoma's department – the bank supervision group. Nyaoma was made head of the team in addition to his other duties.

Reviewing the situation, they realised that there were three major questions that had to be addressed: was M-Pesa a banking business or not?; what were the operational risks to consumers?; and could the product be abused by money launderers?[7] There followed several weeks of intense engagement between the Central Bank and Safaricom, as the bank deepened its understanding of the product and examined the potential risks it posed.

Of these, the trickiest was the issue of whether M-Pesa qualified as a banking service or not. If it did, then all bets were off. Legally, the Central Bank would be required to ask Safaricom to get a banking licence – an expensive and time-consuming process that would discourage the company and kill the product in its infancy. A major aspect of this was whether the deposit-taking activity that M-Pesa involved qualified as a banking service. After some discussion with internal and external legal experts, the team concluded that, because M-Pesa would not be paying consumers interest, any payment through the system need not be deemed a deposit.

Some of these definitional discussions involved a fair amount of creative interpretation. Nyaoma gives an example:

> Suppose you go to a shop and buy bread, and suppose you give the shopkeeper money before you get your bread: is the shopkeeper involved in deposit taking? Isn't he simply exchanging bread with you for value? In the same way, if you pay an M-Pesa agent money in exchange for 'e-money' that sits on your phone, well that's not deposit taking, is it? That's merely another form of exchange for value.

This line of reasoning reassured everyone on the team, including the legal experts. But the bank's legal counsel also had to study how the service was placed vis-à-vis Kenya's Banking Act. Did the service fall within the Central Bank's ambit and did it comply with the national payments system? After looking at these issues carefully, the legal counsel concluded that there were three reasons why Safaricom would not be entering into a banking business by offering M-Pesa: neither the customer nor Safaricom would be taking on any credit risk; the money received from customers would not be lent-on for any other business or to generate interest; and no interest was going to be paid on customer deposits.[8]

Next, there was the question of how secure the platform was and the risks it might pose to consumers. In early meetings, members of Nyaoma's team met Michael Joseph and the M-Pesa team to test the prototype and better understand how the funds transfer service would work. In one of the first meetings, the Safaricom team brought along M-Pesa-enabled phones and made a presentation to senior Central Bank managers, including the deputy governor. They examined the phones and saw how the prototype worked.

'We central bankers are naturally risk averse when it comes to new products,' says Nyaoma. 'We immediately think about consumer protection and product security. Playing with the phones ourselves gave us some comfort.'

But now the central bankers had further questions. They wanted to know: what happens to anyone who gets on the system? How will the firm train its agents to serve consumers? How will the agents do customer identification and how will the company maintain adequate float?

A mechanism to protect consumers soon presented itself. A trust account would be used to hold money in a commercial bank which would be reflected on the user's phone. The balance of e-money on the phone would be equivalent to real money in the bank. But this money would have to be ring-fenced; Safaricom would not be allowed to use it for its own business. And so it became important to know who would run the trust. Eventually it was decided that M-Pesa would be its holding company.

Nyaoma and his team then hired Consult Hyperion – an independent company that specialises in electronic transactions – to conduct a detailed audit of the robustness of the M-Pesa platform. The consultants tested the end-to-end encryption of M-Pesa's SIM card functionality, reviewed the hardware security of the company servers, and ensured that all business processes had live back-up and other security procedures embedded.[9] Because the service was digital, they ensured that all M-Pesa transactions could be monitored individually and collectively by both Safaricom and the Central Bank.

Consult Hyperion was also hired to address the final issue of money laundering. To do so, the consultants set up a dedicated team with the necessary expertise in the relevant international standards and laws. The team went about ensuring that the

M-Pesa system complied with the money laundering standards set by Vodafone, the Financial Action Task Force and the Kenyan Anti-Money Laundering Legislation.[10] This final check ensured that the Central Bank could request – and receive at short notice – accurate information about the system's audit trail, including its anti-money laundering procedures, its liquidity management and its clearing and settlements record.

Letter of no objection

After seven months of due diligence, Nyaoma and his team were satisfied that the M-Pesa project had passed all its legal and security hurdles. The acting governor of the Central Bank of Kenya then issued a letter of no objection to Safaricom in February 2007 which allowed the firm to launch M-Pesa in March 2007.

The Central Bank's engagement with Safaricom did not, however, end there. Nyaoma and his team continued to oversee and monitor M-Pesa's progress over the subsequent months. Three of the main conditions of the letter of no objection were that Safaricom would continue to take all appropriate measures to protect customers, that it would guard against money laundering, and that it would send regular reports to the regulatory authorities. In particular, the letter required Safaricom to prepare and send monthly returns to the Central Bank of Kenya, which enabled the supervisory team to track the volume and usage of the system carefully.

'When we gave Safaricom the letter of no objection,' says Nyaoma, 'we put conditions in place to protect consumers against fraud, maintain their privacy, guard against money laundering, and so on.' To limit the risk to consumers, the Central Bank set an initial transaction limit of 75,000 shillings (£500). They also made sure that Safaricom reported all transactions on the system. This helped them track where the transactions were coming from, ensure that they were below the transaction limit, monitor what the agents were doing, and see when the system went down and for how long.

This was relatively easy for Safaricom to report. As the system was essentially digital, it automatically collected and stored data that could be processed in a reportable form on a weekly basis.

Nyaoma's team also tracked the progress of the product in the marketplace through independent sources, including surveys of financial behaviour and inclusion. 'We were constantly checking to see what problems might come up. We would then send questions to Safaricom who would have to respond. We would ask them hard questions thinking they wouldn't come back. But they always came back with answers.'

Questions in parliament

M-Pesa soon proved a huge success with users. In 2009, a second FinAccess survey showed a dramatic increase in the use of mobile payments in Kenya. The survey estimated that, in the space of two years, 5.3 million Kenyans – roughly 25 per cent of the adult population – had become registered M-Pesa customers. Close to half these customers had been brought in from the informal economy, accounting for 85 per cent of the increase in people who had entered the formal economy since 2006 (when the previous FinAccess survey had been conducted).[11] The report concluded that the advent of mobile phone accounts was 'undoubtedly one of the most important developments' in Kenya since 2006 and that 'M-Pesa accounted for a lion's share of the growth in access to formal financial services'.

This very success, however, brought opposition from several quarters. Many banks, including those that were state owned, complained that Safaricom was engaged in banking without a proper licence and that the sector no longer enjoyed a level playing field. Zain, Kenya's second largest mobile network company, joined in the protests: the company claimed that the Central Bank had been partial to Safaricom because of its market dominance. Together these interests lobbied ministers and politicians with their grievances.

In late 2007, Kenyans went to the polls to elect a new president and national assembly. The elections were marred by controversy and there was ensuing violence. But by April 2008, the country was stable again with a new government in place and new ministers appointed to the departments of communications and finance. These ministers had had no involvement in M-Pesa's development and felt no stake in its success. As Parliament got down to business, questions were raised over how the Central Bank had allowed 'unregulated money transfer services' to operate in the country.[12]

In December 2008, the Kenyan Ministry of Finance publicly ordered the Central Bank to conduct an immediate risk audit. Nyaoma and his team were now forced to address the issue of whether or not they had functioned within the law and in the wider public interest. Given the very public nature of the call, they knew that they had to do more than simply respond to the finance minister alone.

'When we gave Safaricom the go-ahead in 2007,' Nyaoma says, 'we didn't know whether it would work.' The questions before the regulators were many. Would the product be sustainable? Would the system remain stable as more people joined it? Indeed, as the product gained in popularity and more people came on board, the anxiety of the Central Bank only increased. 'So when questions were raised in parliament,' says Nyaoma, 'and the finance minister asked us to get back to him, we decided to go public with details of the process of due diligence we had followed prior to the launch as well as all our continued scrutiny thereafter.'

Nyaoma and his team also drew on evidence from the independent FinAccess survey of 2009. The survey showed that M-Pesa had fulfilled major unmet needs in the Kenyan financial services sector and that it was popular with customers, especially the rural poor and urban migrants. But the team also acknowledged that a new payments services law was needed to fill the regulatory gap regarding mobile services. To maximise the impact of this statement, the Central Bank published a full-page advertisement in *The Daily Nation*, the leading Kenyan newspaper.

Eventually these actions succeeded in convincing the sceptics, both in government as well as in the state-owned banks, and M-Pesa was allowed to proceed unimpeded.

The many successes of M-Pesa

By 2020, new variants of M-Pesa had taken off in countries as disparate as Tanzania, Uganda, Afghanistan, Pakistan and Bangladesh. But Kenya remained the capital of mobile-driven financial inclusion. By 2019, the total value of M-Pesa transactions had exceeded $38 billion, more than 50 per cent of the country's GDP.[13] Kenya has more than 100,000 M-Pesa agents across the country serving more than 25 million accounts, equivalent to two-thirds of the entire population. No less than 95 per cent of small businesses in Kenya now state that they regularly use M-Pesa, including to pay wages. Schools accept fees and consumers make contributions to pension funds and pay insurance through M-Pesa accounts.

Indeed, as Nyaoma and his team had hoped, M-Pesa enabled a deepening of formal financial inclusion in the country. The first step on the ladder was mobile payments; on the back of that came access to other formal services such as savings and insurance. In January 2013, for instance, Safaricom entered into partnership with the Commercial Bank of Africa to launch M-Shwari, a product that gave Kenyans access to micro-savings and micro-credit straight from their phones. In barely a year, the service had over 9 million savings accounts and had disbursed

$20 million in loans to 3 million borrowers.[14] In 2013, only 19 per cent of M-Shwari users were below the national poverty line; this increased to 30 per cent by the end of 2014. The service has continued to grow in its reach since then.

All this was made possible by the approach that Nyaoma and his team had pursued. Instead of adopting a traditional, risk-averse approach, they engaged with the innovator and embarked on a rigorous but speedy process of due diligence that led to launch. Following the launch, they continued to monitor and manage the service. Specifically, the Central Bank authorities were willing to experiment and take a 'test and learn' approach rather than pre-judge matters and introduce draconian legislation.

As Nyaoma puts it: 'Looking back, when Safaricom came to us with M-Pesa, we could have said no, we're not going to look at this product. We could have passed the buck and said: you are regulated by the telecommunications authority, why don't you discuss it with them?' Alternatively, the team could have told Safaricom to come back with a banking partner. But that option would have taken time and added cost. And the banks would have wanted to maintain their margins, so the benefits of efficiency would not have accrued to customers. Such an approach would have made the process long drawn out, raising costs and dampening the enthusiasm of the innovator. Indeed, M-Pesa may never have got off the ground. In Egypt and India, for instance, a heavy-handed regulatory approach introduced delays and stunted the fledgling mobile payments industry.

Ironically, being *too* lax with regulation could also have stunted financial inclusion efforts. Something of the sort happened in India in 2010 when the country – and the state of Andhra Pradesh in particular – faced a microfinance boom and bust.[15] A lack of regulation in the microfinance industry there led to the absence of credit rating agencies in the sector as well as an influx of capital looking for quick returns. Microfinance organisations, for their part, looking to grow quickly, began to offer high-powered incentives to their sales agents. These agents, in turn, started offering loans to consumers whose credit-worthiness was far from certain, and who often used their loans to buy consumption assets like TVs rather than income-generating assets like cows and goats. Soon, indebted consumers began taking loans from one microfinance organisation to pay off another. But this was unsustainable, and consumers started failing to repay their loans. When sales agents began to use strong-arm tactics, even violence, to pressure them to do so, politicians intervened on the side of their constituents, even encouraging consumers not to repay their loans. Eventually, the market crashed, investors pulled out, and companies went bankrupt. It was only then that India's central bank, the Reserve Bank of India, intervened and introduced legislation requiring lending limits, credit checks and the entry of credit rating agencies into the sector. Unfortunately this came too late: the damage had been done in terms of the loss of consumer and investor trust, and the industry was set back several years.

M-Pesa, it would appear, is an all-too-rare case of regulators getting the timing and nature of their intervention right. More often than not, it is hard to assess the many pros and cons of new technologies a priori, *before* their effects have played out in society. As a result, governments either overestimate the downsides of a new technology and step in too early or underestimate them and step in too late. And so, as we shall see, they often end up over-regulating and even banning new technologies, setting them back considerably in the process.

Over-reacting, then over-regulating: psychedelics and GM crops

In 1938, the Swiss scientist Albert Hofmann, an employee at Sandoz in Basel, found a way to synthesise lysergic acid diethylamide

(LSD) in the lab. After an interlude of about five years, while re-synthesising LSD in 1943, Hofmann accidentally absorbed a small amount of the drug and immediately felt its effects. He described becoming restless and dizzy: 'At home I lay down and sank into a not unpleasant intoxicated [...] condition, characterized by an extremely stimulated imagination ... I perceived an uninterrupted stream of fantastic pictures, extraordinary shapes with intense, kaleidoscopic play of colors. After some two hours this condition faded away.'[16]

Three days later, Hofmann intentionally gave himself a dose of 250 micrograms of LSD and felt the drug's effects as he rode home on his bicycle. Throughout the rest of his life, Hofmann would take small doses of LSD, seeing it as almost sacred, and trying constantly to establish its beneficial uses. For him, the true importance of LSD lay 'in the possibility of providing material aid to meditation aimed at the mystical experience of a deeper, comprehensive reality'. 'It gave me an inner joy,' he said, 'an open mindedness, a gratefulness ... and an internal sensitivity for the miracles of creation ...'[17]

Hofmann's work with psychedelics didn't stop there. When he became director of the Sandoz natural products department, he went on to study hallucinogenic substances found in Mexican mushrooms and other plants used by aboriginal people. In 1957, he succeeded in isolating psilocybin, the active agent of many 'magic mushrooms'. As a result of his work, Sandoz began to sell psilocybin and LSD during the 1960s, for use in research and medical trials.

Meanwhile, a clinical psychologist at Harvard named Timothy Leary had begun experimenting with the new drugs under the Harvard Psilocybin Project. With his colleague, Richard Alpert, he began to take these drugs with his research subjects. This got the duo into trouble with the Harvard authorities who questioned the legitimacy and ethics of their approach and worried that they were pressuring students into taking psychedelics in their classes.

Eventually, in 1963, Leary and Alpert were fired from their posts. As a result of the national scandal that ensued, psychedelics achieved a sudden notoriety among the general public.

But being fired only freed Leary to be bolder in his support of the drugs. He became a vocal advocate for the use of LSD in psychiatry, and popularised the phrases 'turn on, tune in, drop out' and 'think for yourself and question authority'.[18] His efforts gained the support of young people and the counterculture across the US and elsewhere. But this use of psychedelic drugs by a growing number of young people began to spread moral panic among their parents and the establishment. During the 1960s and 1970s, Leary would be arrested several times, and no less a figure than President Nixon would describe him as 'the most dangerous man in America'.

The consequence of all this was that psychedelic substances were soon outlawed around the world. LSD was banned and psilocybin came to be listed in the most restricted category under the US 1970 Controlled Substances Act, the 1971 UK Misuse of Drugs Act and the UN Convention on Psychotropic Substances. Serious research into the therapeutic properties of psychedelics came to an abrupt halt and would not be resumed for decades.

Eventually, however, it proved hard to ignore the therapeutic potential of the drugs. In December 2007, the Swiss medical authorities gave permission to Peter Gasser, a psychotherapist, to use LSD in experiments on those suffering from terminal cancer and other fatal diseases. Completed in 2011, these were the first studies of the therapeutic effects of LSD on humans in nearly forty years.[19]

Then, in April 2019, the first formal centre for psychedelic research in the world was launched at Imperial College London. Led by Dr Robin Carhart-Harris, the focus was on the use of psychedelics in mental health and the study of consciousness.

At the time of its launch, the centre had already begun clinical trials into the use of psilocybin as a treatment for depression.

Why haven't we mentioned social justice + it's relation to politics/government?

How Should a Government Be?

David Nutt, a professor of neuropsychopharmacology who oversees the trials, believes that the ban on psychedelic drugs since the 1960s has propagated 'lies' about their risks and has hindered research into their medical potential. For him, the decision to outlaw the drugs was 'one of the most atrocious examples of the censorship of science and medicine in the history of the world'.[20]

Early results of the research at Imperial support the view that governments since the 1960s have failed to appreciate the benefits of psilocybin. Carhart-Harris believes that the drug offers a better treatment than current antidepressants, and that it is a powerful therapy for a host of other mental illnesses, including anxiety, food disorders, smoking and alcohol dependency. For instance, a 2016 Johns Hopkins University study of over fifty patients with cancer showed that high doses of psilocybin can help patients accept the prospect of death: the drug significantly reduced end-of-life depression and anxiety for six months in 80 per cent of cases.[21] A similar study at New York University in 2016 showed similar results.[22]

All this would have heartened Albert Hofmann, who died in 2008 at the age of 102. In an interview before his 100th birthday he called LSD 'medicine for the soul' and expressed deep frustration at its global prohibition. For Hofmann the drug had been used very successfully in psychoanalysis in its early days. However, its initial misuse by the counterculture of the 1960s had led to an over-reaction by the governments of the day and its eventual ban.

Something similar happened to genetically modified (GM) crops in Europe in the 1990s. Under pressure from international NGOs, European regulators banned GM foods, eventually inspiring counterparts in other parts of the world to do the same. It all began in March 1996 when European officials approved the first import from the US of a GM food: herbicide-tolerant soybeans. This decision incensed activists from Greenpeace, Friends of the Earth and the European Consumers Organisation (BEUC). These NGOs saw no benefits from GM foods that justified even a hypothetical safety risk, and so they began to warn citizens away from the foods on purely 'precautionary' grounds.[23] Moreover, efforts by European officials to reassure consumers about soybeans in particular had no impact. The activists, for their part, went into overdrive. They took to the streets and mobilised demonstrations to block the unloading of ships carrying GM soybeans. Supermarkets followed suit, removing GM products from their shelves rather than rile consumers and activists.

Nonetheless, public anxieties grew. Under pressure from activists and citizens, the EU decided in June 1997 that all GM food sold in Europe should carry an identifying label. But instead of reassuring consumers, this only fuelled the growing panic about GM foods. By 1998, political anxieties had become so intense that EU regulators placed a moratorium on any new approvals of GM crops.[24]

Robert Paarlberg, a political scientist at Wellesley College, Massachusetts and an expert on the politics of food, has argued that the victory of the NGOs in Europe then emboldened them to move to the global arena. First, they gained access to negotiations of the Cartagena Protocol, an international protocol governing the trans-boundary movement of living genetically modified organisms (GMOs). Once they had this access, Greenpeace, Friends of the Earth International and the Third World Network all advocated that the new protocol be modelled around a 1989 Basel Convention on the Control of Transboundary Movements of Hazardous Wastes and their Disposal. As a result, GMOs that had been developed at considerable expense and approved by regulators for safe use were suddenly compared to hazardous waste. According to Paarlberg, this was 'a bizarre and inappropriate framing, but it was accepted by the environmental advocates from Europe who dominated the protocol negotiation, and it was sold to Africans and to delegates from other developing countries as something the UN had to do in order to protect their rich biodiversity'.[25]

As a result, by 2000, the final Cartagena Protocol bore a strong resemblance to the Basel Convention. It required that anyone seeking to export GMO grain as living seeds had to provide warning labels. If the seeds were going to be planted rather than processed or consumed, the exporter would first have to 'secure the informed consent of an officially designated biosafety authority in the importing country'.[26]

All this effectively led to a worldwide blockage of GM foods. Moreover, as Paarlberg argues, this blockage did not reflect any malfunction of the seeds or the crops themselves. Critics had focused relentlessly on the risks but did not acknowledge that the national academies of science and medicine had found 'no new risks either to human health or the environment from any of the genetically engineered crops so far in existence'.[27] Indeed, this remains the official position of the British Medical Association, the Royal Society in London, the German Academies of Science and Humanities, and the French Academy of Sciences and Medicine. In 2010, the Research Directorate of the European Union (EU) stated that: 'biotechnology, and in particular GMOs, are not *per se* more risky than e.g. conventional plant breeding technologies'.[28]

And yet governments around the world have not eased their tight grip on the crops.

More often than not, governments over-react in response to moral panic or a backlash from a group of interested parties that the state feels it has to assuage following the arrival of a new technology. They over-react and then over-regulate, introducing draconian measures that set the new technology and its benefits back, often by decades.

But equally, governments often make the opposite mistake: they *under-react* and move too slowly. Or else, entrepreneurs 'move fast and break things' without any threat of restraint. Taken unawares by the speed of progress or lulled into a sense of complacency, governments under-react until something eventually *does* go wrong. Then they are forced to step in, but do so only to *over-regulate*, with negative consequences for many. Indeed, this seems to be precisely what is happening in the digital economy.

Under-reacting, then over-regulating: the digital giants

Increasingly, innovative firms move so fast and technologies evolve so quickly that regulators can barely keep up. Mark Zuckerberg famously wrote the code for Facebook while at Harvard in one month, in January 2004. Within a few weeks, more than half the undergraduates at the university had registered for the service. By March 2004, Facebook had expanded to Stanford, Columbia and Yale; by December 2005 it had 6 million users.[29] The arrival of smartphones further accelerated its adoption. By October 2011, over 350 million people worldwide accessed Facebook on their mobile phones, accounting for 33 per cent of all the site's traffic.[30] In 2012, Facebook crossed the 1 billion mark and by 2020 it had over 2.5 billion active global users, more than the population of any country on earth.[31]

Meanwhile, WhatsApp was created in 2009 by four men in a bedroom, in little over six months and with about $250,000 in funding.[32] By early 2011, WhatsApp was in the top 20 on Apple's US App Store. In February 2013, it had about 200 million active users worldwide. And by December 2013, this number was over 400 million. Then, in February 2014, Facebook bought WhatsApp for nearly $20 billion.

There is no doubt that Facebook, WhatsApp and firms like them have moved fast and broken a lot of things. There is also no doubt that, in the process, they have brought many benefits to a great number of people through increased communication and options for education and entertainment. But it is also true that these dazzling benefits have served to blind regulators and governments to several problems that have systemic repercussions. The lightning speed with which these companies have taken off has led to the failure of governments to understand them and regulate them properly, leading to many negative spill-overs and abuse on a grand scale.

Not a day goes by, it would seem, without some new downside of these digital platforms coming out into the open: the spread of fake news, the invasion of privacy, the manipulation of voter sentiment and elections, and the accretion of abusive monopoly power. These developments now threaten the social and political order in many countries, leading to unrest and violence, and a steady erosion of public trust.

Take the case of India. By April 2019, when it faced general elections, the country had over 300 million, 200 million and 250 million users on Facebook, WhatsApp and YouTube, respectively. A failure to control and regulate these platforms had resulted in the country being hit by a tsunami of doctored images, videos and text messages. Indeed, a 2019 study by Microsoft found that over 60 per cent of Indians had encountered fake news online, the highest among the twenty-two countries surveyed.[33]

Much of this fake news and disinformation was designed to influence political choice during the 2019 general elections. Some of the worst examples included a fake video of Rahul Gandhi, the Congress party president, stating that a machine could convert potatoes into gold, and a made-up BBC survey that predicted victory for the Bharatiya Janata Party.[34]

While many such stories were ludicrous, some had a decidedly deadly impact. For instance, six months before the 2014 general election, a fake video on WhatsApp whipped up sectarian passions, leading to over sixty deaths and 50,000 people displaced from their homes in the state of Uttar Pradesh.[35] In 2017, a rumour on social media about child kidnappers led to over thirty deaths in nearly seventy incidents of mob violence.[36] In both instances, the scale and speed of the underlying processes was so great that governments at local, state and federal levels were left flailing, and in perpetual fire-fighting mode. Their only option was to impose blanket bans, as the government did when it ordered Google and Apple to take down the Chinese-owned TikTok video app in April 2019.

Complicating everything is the fact that fake news is often spread by legions of online trolls, including professionals from other countries. The *New York Times*, in a survey of how social media platforms influenced the 2016 US elections, highlights the role of Russian agents in spreading disinformation.[37] According to the survey, Russian agents at the Internet Research Agency in Moscow act as trolls – humans who write social media posts – to push a particular agenda online. These trolls then create bots – short for robots – that make individual tweets popular by retweeting them automatically. The entire process is designed to heighten tribal fears and spread division, especially around sensitive topics such as immigration and gun violence.

Facebook was a major platform for Russian trolls and bots leading up to the 2016 US elections. It is estimated that ads on the platform created by Russian trolls were shown to over 125 million Americans before the election.[38] And while Facebook may be bad, YouTube is probably worse. Zeynep Tufekci, a sociologist and technology critic, argues that its 'search and recommender algorithms are misinformation engines'.[39] As with other technology companies, YouTube's algorithms are secret: proprietary software that only a few engineers have access to. Guillaume Chaslot, a software engineer who worked for several months with a YouTube team on its recommendation system, believes that the priorities YouTube gives its algorithms are dangerously skewed. 'The recommendation algorithm is not optimising for what is truthful, or balanced, or healthy for democracy,' says Chaslot. 'There are many ways YouTube can change its algorithms to suppress fake news and improve the quality and diversity of videos people see … I tried to change YouTube from the inside but it didn't work.'[40]

These are technical issues that politicians are only dimly aware of and don't know what to do about. As in India, so too in the US:

governments have been paralysed, both by the speed of change, as well as a lack of understanding, let alone knowledge of what to do about the change. This was on display for the world to see when Mark Zuckerberg was hauled up before the US Senate in April 2018, a full two years after his firm had been involved in the Cambridge Analytica data-sharing scandal. The ignorance of the senators was clear from their anodyne questioning. Thus, Senator Orrin Hatch asked: 'If [a version of Facebook will always be free], how do you sustain a business model in which users don't pay for your service?' Zuckerberg, unable to believe his luck, dead-panned: 'Senator, we run ads.'[41] Then Senator Brian Schatz asked: 'If I'm emailing within WhatsApp, does that ever inform your advertisers?'[42] This question was risible on a number of levels. Not only does one not send 'emails' over WhatsApp, the app is also encrypted end-to-end, meaning that the information sent within it cannot be accessed by third parties.

A further danger of the state's uncertain grip on new technology is the build-up of monopoly power that leads to anti-competitive behaviour. The dominance of the tech giants now threatens to destroy other businesses, leading to job losses and the crowding out of healthy competition and innovation. Google, for instance, made $4.7 billion in advertising from news content in 2018, only $400 million less than the $5.1 billion brought in by the *entire* US online news industry.[43] Further, this dominance of the media – both in the pricing and distribution of news – has come at breakneck speed. Thus, in 2009, CNN and the *New York Times* had 50 million unique visitors in the US compared with Google News's 24 million. By May 2018, Google had approximately 150 million unique monthly visitors in the US, almost double the number for CNN and the *New York Times* combined.[44]

George Soros, the billionaire philanthropist, argues that Facebook and Google are now a menace to society. Speaking in January 2018, he said: 'Mining and oil companies exploit the physical environment; social media companies exploit the social environment

… This is particularly nefarious because social media companies influence how people think and behave without them even being aware of it.'[45]

In these views, Soros has an unlikely ally in Rupert Murdoch, the owner of *Fox News* and the *Wall Street Journal*. Famously libertarian, Murdoch seems to have overcome his qualms about government intervention in calling for stronger regulation of the online giants. Even Facebook's co-founder, Chris Hughes, has argued that the company should be broken up over its 'unprecedented' power. 'I don't blame Mark [Zuckerberg]', says Hughes, 'for his quest for domination. Yet he has created a leviathan that crowds out entrepreneurship and restricts consumer choice. It's on our government to ensure that we never lose the magic of the invisible hand.'[46]

And yet governments have been unable to do much for some time now. In Europe, despite the introduction in May 2018 of strict General Data Protection Regulation (GDPR) laws about how businesses process and handle data, strong enforcement and big fines have largely been absent. Under-resourced European regulators have struggled to define their mission and have taken time to build investigations that will probably end up in court. Meanwhile, GDPR may in fact have strengthened the hand of the digital giants. Evidence suggests that Google, Amazon and Facebook have increased their market share of online advertising while smaller players, struggling to keep up with compliance costs, have seen their share shrink.[47] Indeed, smaller firms, whose fortunes were a major concern of EU planners, have suffered from the relatively high costs of compliance. Meanwhile, the digital giants have found new forms of data collection that are GDPR compliant: Google harvests information on third-party websites and Facebook has reintroduced facial recognition technology.

'Big companies like Facebook are ten steps ahead of everyone else, and a hundred steps ahead of regulators,' says Paul-Olivier Dehaye, a privacy expert who helped uncover Facebook's

Cambridge Analytica scandal. 'There are very big questions about what they're doing.'[48]

When regulators do catch up, however, they often over-regulate and introduce draconian forms of legislation, including implementing bans. This has negative consequences, not only for the firms involved, but also the many people who use their services. In the US, for example, antitrust agencies appear to be preparing to break up the big tech monopolies. The Federal Trade Commission is looking into Facebook and Amazon while the Department of Justice is planning an investigation of Google and Apple.[49] But if they do break up these giants in order to jump-start competition and innovation, that process will also disrupt the lives of the millions who use and benefit from the (often free) services of the digital giants. Regulations will have come too late and be too draconian in the process.

A case in point is that of Uber in London. Right from its launch in 2012, the company proved hugely popular with users, but faced ongoing clashes with the city's black cabs and growing concerns about how it screened and treated its drivers and managed customer safety. So much so that, when the firm's contract came up for renewal in September 2017, Transport for London stripped it of its licence citing 'public security and safety implications'. And though the decision was eventually reversed through the courts, the ban, while it lasted, caused a major upheaval in the lives of over 30,000 licensed Uber drivers and the 3.5 million Londoners who relied on them.

Indeed, this experience has been repeated across many other cities around the world. As Benjamin Edelman, a professor at the Harvard Business School, puts it: 'as Uber's problems worsen, regulators feel emboldened to proceed and ... sense that it's particularly urgent for them to do so'.[50]

The challenge for the regulators is acute, and real. As Sadiq Khan, the mayor of London, puts it:

I want London to be at the forefront of innovation and new technology and to be a natural home for exciting new companies that help Londoners by providing a better and more affordable service. However, all companies in London must play by the rules and adhere to the high standards we expect – particularly when it comes to the safety of customers.[51]

How, then, can governments keep up with rapid change and new technologies? How can they learn *with* innovative companies and users, not *after* them? And how can they use this proactive, real-time learning to formulate the right level of the right kind of regulation?

One way is to engage early, as the Kenyan Central Bank did with M-Pesa. In that case, however, the task was made relatively easy by the presence of a single actor – Safaricom – with whom the regulators had to engage. More often than not, however, new technologies involve a bewildering array of actors and interests.

Take the case of connected and autonomous vehicles. This growing sector involves not only large and small car companies but also software firms, insurance companies, legal agents, cities and states, universities and citizens at large. How can governments systematically engage such a broad spectrum of players, to manage and regulate the new technology early in the process, so as to realise its potential without endangering citizens and society?

Autonomous vehicles: who's in the driver's seat?

'The auto industry will change more in the next 5 to 10 years than it has in the last 50.'

Mary Barra, CEO of GM

A 2017 study by Cambridge Econometrics and Element Energy projects the global market for autonomous vehicles to be worth

£907 billion by 2035.[52] This equates to annual sales of roughly 8 million cars, vans, heavy goods vehicles and buses – about a quarter of the 32 million vehicles expected to be sold in that year. The same study suggests that the global market for related technologies such as software and systems, navigation, AI, sensors, cameras and maps will be worth a further £63 billion by then. These figures are backed up by Allied Market Research – it reports that the 2019 global market for autonomous vehicles was worth over $50 billion, increasing tenfold to over $500 billion by 2026.[53]

But the impact of these vehicles on our lives will far exceed their economic value. Autonomous and connected vehicles will profoundly change the way we work, live and travel. Many new cars are already equipped with technologies that enable them to be connected and semi-autonomous. For instance, GPS technologies allow drivers to track where they are going and be tracked by others. Many cars and larger vehicles already have technologies that enable then to brake independently of the driver or assist the driver with parking. It is expected, however, that by 2030 all new vehicles will be fully connected and autonomous. A combination of computers, sensors and data will allow these vehicles to communicate with each other and with infrastructure, and drive themselves by performing various tasks in various situations during entire journeys.

The impact on how we live will include the good and the bad. On the upside, it will mean dramatically fewer vehicles on our roads, as vehicles are shared across households. For instance, a 2018 UBS study suggests that the number of private cars worldwide will have dropped by 50 per cent from a global high of 1.2 billion in 2027 to little over half a billion in 2035.[54] This drop will be driven by the arrival of about 200 million 'robot taxis' on our streets and highways. The overall result will be far fewer cars on the road and thus far less congestion and pollution. City spaces – now taken up by parking – will be freed for housing, pedestrians, and beautification. Car accidents, a major source of fatalities, mostly because of human error, will be dramatically reduced. (In the US alone, nearly 40,000 people died in motor accidents in 2019.) Those who are unable to drive because of age or disability will have mobility. Any way we look at it, driverless vehicles could be ubiquitous by 2050 and will have radically changed how we live and work.

But none of this will happen on its own, as if by magic, or purely through the functioning of the market. On the contrary, for this vision to materialise, governments around the world will have to play a significant and proactive role. And it isn't only the upsides that governments will have to work towards. They will also have to find ways to reduce the negative consequences. For instance, autonomous vehicles are likely to bring with them the displacement of large numbers of people who are currently employed as drivers of taxis, buses and trucks. These jobs will have to be replaced by other sources of employment, but we don't yet know what these will be or how this change will happen. Governments will have to think of ways to encourage new types of jobs to be created around autonomous vehicles. And they will have to help retrain the workforce with the skills needed for the new market. All this will require early engagement and learning while doing so. And smart regulation will be key.

The Centre for Connected and Autonomous Vehicles

In 2014, the UK government set up a new centre precisely to stimulate the incipient market for autonomous vehicles. Named the Centre for Connected and Autonomous Vehicles, it was tasked with developing the necessary policy at a pace that the rapidly advancing technology required. The centre's major aim was to maximise the economic and social benefits of the new sector without compromising the safety, security and privacy of citizens.

As Michael Talbot, the former head of strategy at the centre, tells it:

> When the senior-most British civil servants formed a group to look at new technologies, they soon realised there was no way that regulation could keep ahead of the pace of change. The best we could hope for was regular dialogue with industry to monitor expectations and close that gap. We would have to engage early and constantly update our views.[55]

The UK government realised that, as regulators, they had to be aware of what was changing and then act quickly. They couldn't expect technologies and markets to wait for months or years while they sorted out how to regulate them. Further, they had to engage technical and regulatory experts to understand their position. 'What industry wants is certainty for investment,' says Talbot. 'It wants governments to be clear about their strategy and not change too often down the line.'

One of the decisions the senior civil servants made was to put the UK at the forefront of the AI and data revolution. And they realised that autonomous vehicles would be a big part of the revolution. 'We wanted to be a world leader in the way people, goods and services move,' says Talbot.

The size of the prize was significant. The hope was for the UK to gain a £50 billion share of the global market for connected and autonomous vehicles (CAVs) by 2035 and a further £5 billion from the market in auxiliary technologies like navigation, AI, sensors, cameras and maps. Success could mean up to 47,000 new jobs in the economy.

While the aims of the centre were ambitious, there was also clarity about what the government could not do. 'Our vision', says Talbot, 'is to make the UK the destination of choice in R&D for autonomous vehicle technology. But we know we can't lead in every area, so we focus on our strengths. We don't have vast amounts to spend.' Among the strengths of the UK that the centre hoped to build on were a track record of early investment in R&D and a good regulatory environment.

⌈A key feature of the centre was how it was set up. To break down government silos and to take a systemic view, the centre was planned from its inception as a joint initiative of the Department for Transport and the Department for Business, Industry and Skills.⌉The idea was to work across government to support the early market for connected and automated vehicles.

Talbot describes this as a pioneering effort to enable more creative policymaking in new, cross-cutting areas like autonomous vehicles. 'In the past, the government would have set up the centre within a department such as the Department for Transport. We would then invite representatives from other departments to our meetings and try to bend them to our view. But this wouldn't work because everyone would be pulling in different directions.'

Open regulatory approaches: the UK versus the US

A cornerstone of the approach of the Centre for Connected and Autonomous Vehicles is its open mindset: its stated objective is to create a welcoming and engaged regulatory environment.

Very early on, the centre devised a regulatory framework that made it easy for anyone to test their driverless cars in real-world conditions without needing special permits or surety bonds. This was exemplified by the code of practice it developed for anyone wishing to test autonomous vehicles on UK roads. Set out in 2015, the code has three clear rules that all testers must obey: test vehicles must be roadworthy; a suitably trained driver or operator must be ready, able and willing to take control; and appropriate insurance must be in place.[56] Further, although permission from the road owner is not required, testers must discuss plans with them and use a data recorder.

It is instructive to compare the British with the American approach. Given its federal nature, the US lacks a single centralised policy or agency to oversee the autonomous vehicles sector. Nevertheless, governments at both the federal and state level remain engaged in shaping it, to differing extents. Thus, at the federal level, the US Department of Transportation and the National Highway Traffic Safety Administration (NHTSA) provide broad guidelines for autonomous vehicles, which they periodically update, while the individual states debate and pass specific, relevant laws. Indeed, by May 2018, twenty-two states had passed laws concerning the operation of autonomous vehicles, ten had governors who had issued executive orders, a further ten had considered legislation, and eight had not considered any.[57] There is also considerable variation in these laws: some state governments are more proactive and permissive than others.

Such variation across the country could hinder progress in the short term but enable learning in the long term. For instance, in the short term, different rules of the road between US states means that firms wishing to carry out interstate testing face considerable obstacles. Thus, in order to drive coast to coast, firms have had to put together circuitous, complicated routes, because some states don't permit such tests while others require special insurance and permits. In the UK, on the other hand, because of the comprehensive code of practice, firms can drive their autonomous vehicles anywhere from Land's End to John O'Groats.

In the long run, though, different rules across US states mean more experimentation and data, with the potential for some states to learn from others. For instance, states differ on how they define a 'vehicle operator'. While Texas requires a 'natural person' riding in the vehicle, Georgia identifies the operator as the person who causes the autonomous driving system to engage: this person could therefore be remotely present in a vehicle fleet.[58] These differences are likely to influence how different states license human drivers and autonomous vehicles in the future.

Then, the rules with the best outcomes can be adopted by all the states.

States can also adjust their laws over time through the gathering of data. California, for instance, requires testing firms to report the number of miles driven as well as the number of disengagements, i.e. the number of times a human driver takes control of the autonomous system. This data provides regulators with insight into and confidence in the technology. Based on logs of over a million miles of autonomous driving, the California regulators know that the number of disengagements per mile fell from a peak of sixteen per 1,000 vehicle miles in 2014 to an average of five throughout 2016.[59] The stability in this figure for over a year gave the California Department of Transportation the confidence to relax its rules requiring firms to have a safety driver in the front seat of the test vehicle.

Relaxing the rules too early though, i.e. having too lax a regulatory regime, could backfire. On 19 March 2018, an Uber-owned Volvo in self-driving mode struck and killed 49-year-old cyclist Elaine Herzberg in Arizona. Governor Doug Ducey immediately directed Arizona's Department of Transportation to 'suspend Uber's ability to test and operate autonomous vehicles on Arizona's public roadways'.[60] As with LSD, psilocybin and GM foods, however, this could be an over-reaction, with the intervention coming too early and being too draconian. After all, self-driving cars could kill a lot of people and still be far safer than human drivers. Alternatively, the ban could end up being a temporary attempt to dampen public panic and prevent it from snowballing in unhelpful ways. Only time will tell, but the challenges for governments to get it right are real. And here, early engagement can help: working with different players, as the technology is evolving, enables the state to cope with the regulatory challenges in real time.

In the US, states can learn not only from each other but from foreign governments as well. Talbot describes how the approach of

Californian regulators has undergone a striking shift over the last few years. In 2015, at the annual Automated Vehicles Symposium in San Francisco, the California Department of Transportation laid out the ten things that firms would have to do to satisfy the regulators. This was in marked contrast to the UK's Centre for Connected and Autonomous Vehicles whose director spoke about how easy his country's code of practice made it for testers. 'Compared to California, the UK approach seemed less heavy-handed,' says Talbot. 'We offered some common-sense things you were expected to abide by but there was no great regulatory burden. The message to industry was clear: they don't really trust you in California, but we do, provided you behave responsibly.'

Seeing the effect their approach had had on industry, the Californian regulators quickly changed their stance. California is now on a par with the UK in terms of its code of practice, if not ahead. In response, the UK began to review its own code of practice to see what more it could do. Indeed, by the end of 2018, the Centre for Connected and Autonomous Vehicles was allowing developers to test without a human operator in the car. But testers had to earn this privilege first: they had to apply and there was a greater expectation for them to demonstrate the case for safety.

Governments should steer, not row

In the next few decades, the world will see the advent of many new technologies, including artificial intelligence, robotics, 3D printing, cryptocurrencies, driverless cars, quantum computing, genetic engineering and more. These technologies could transform the lives of citizens for the better, but they could also cause untold disruption and suffering. Moreover, many of these technologies are systemic in nature: their success or failure will depend on a number of disparate, previously unconnected players playing their part and interacting in hitherto unimaginable ways.

Who will ensure that the good outcomes materialise while mitigating the risks?

Only governments have the power, the remit and the means to perform this role. But to do so, they will need to step up their game. They will have to strike a balance between being too permissive and too heavy-handed. Excessive regulation, intended to protect consumers, could kill innovations before they have a chance to prove themselves. Overly permissive legislation, on the other hand, could result in an initial spurt of growth with an eventual backlash when some consumers suffer and resistance grows.

To strike such a balance and regulate in an intelligent way, governments will need explicit principles to guide them. They will need to engage early and proactively with all relevant actors, including those who do not belong to the same sector. And they will have to create the conditions that enable these actors to experiment with and test new technologies in order to identify early what the benefits and drawbacks are likely to be. This process of learning along with others will have to be backed by data and evidence and inform the setting of standards, responsibilities and protections. Such early collaboration and engagement with multiple stakeholders will, in turn, help governments assess and establish the relevant benefits and risks in a safe environment. Experiments and trials with others will also ensure that industry does the heavy lifting, while the regulators play the influential role of steering everyone along.

The role of governments in stimulating innovation and enterprise may start with smart regulation, but it doesn't stop there. Governments must also stimulate economic opportunities, enable the formation of new firms, and encourage innovation. Indeed, the state's role is not only to regulate economic activity but also to *cultivate* it. We turn to this subject next, in Chapter 8.

8

The entrepreneurial state: cultivating the economy

'... society at large, is not yearning for a five-year plan of
centrally delivered tractor quotas ... we prize individual
autonomy and freedom of expression, and expect
government to help us to achieve our goals, not set them.'
Ruth Davidson, former Scottish Conservative Party leader

In the realm of industrial activity, countries around the world
are in constant competition with one another. They compete to
attract investment; to capture new sources of employment; to lead
in technological innovation; and to create the firms that will dominate the markets of the future. Some countries, like Singapore, are
small and agile and can work by command and control. Others,
like the US, are large and diverse, and can experiment and learn;
they can leverage large internal markets and giant domestic firms
to dominate in the long run. Still others, that are mid-sized like
the UK, need to be flexible and leverage international and domestic investment and capability. In all three cases, governments have
an important, proactive role to play in driving the competitiveness
of their economies.

How should the state attract investment in R&D and manufacturing? How should it encourage innovation and improve
productivity? And how should it generate employment and ensure
a workforce that is fit for purpose? These questions all lie at the
heart of an old but still controversial role of government: its
industrial strategy.

The new industrial strategy

As the M-Pesa and autonomous vehicles cases show, in the new industrial policy the government has many roles to play in creating new markets and driving adoption. As we saw in Chapter 7, the state can facilitate innovation by identifying technologies that offer long-term value to the economy and then setting standards and formulating regulations in an agile yet rigorous way.

But the state can do even more. It can provide financial incentives to encourage firms to enter and partner with others in testing and in conducting R&D. It can help prepare the workforce with the necessary skills. And it can stimulate the adoption of new technology by creating a procurement environment that encourages big business to partner with smaller firms in bidding for public contracts.

Consider again the case of autonomous vehicles. The government's role in driving the sector isn't just limited to setting the rules of the game, to formulating and implementing regulations and laws. It also needs to stimulate investment, create new jobs and compete against other economies in the innovation race. Doing all this requires the state to convene firms across sectors and encourage collaboration and competition in R&D, testing and commercialisation: a new approach to industrial policy for the twenty-first century.

Take the state's convening role. As with many new technologies and emerging sectors, the issues with driverless cars are systemic. The UK's Centre for Connected and Autonomous Vehicles began by bringing together many different players to work on many different issues: insurance, vehicle roadworthiness and maintenance, traffic management, mapping, theft and cybersecurity, accident investigation, connectivity, international standards, product liability and owner responsibility.

The centre catalysed these collaborations by launching three driverless car projects in four cities in late 2014. The three trials, held in Greenwich, Bristol, Coventry and Milton Keynes, cost a total of £32 million, a little over half of which came from government funding.[1] Thus, the centre used its funding to gain leverage and influence over industry to achieve something that was world leading. The first on-the-road demonstrations began in 2016. During the trials, test cars were able to drive around these cities at any time as long as they followed the official code of practice. The idea was to understand what the technology could and couldn't do. Three different types of vehicles were involved: low-speed pods, cars and delivery vehicles. Each trial was a collaborative effort where partners amplified the capabilities of others. Each trial had to have an insurer, a local authority, a university, large car manufacturers, a mixture of small, medium and large businesses, and telecoms and law firms.

Next, consider the state's role as a coordinator of collaboration and competition among private actors. Side by side with its four city trials, the Centre for Connected and Autonomous Vehicles (CCAV) coordinated industry-wide R&D in autonomous vehicle technologies. Again, it did this in a consortium model with seed money from the government matched by industry. So much so that, by 2020, the centre had seeded over eighty collaborative R&D projects worth £250 million, with £170 million coming from government and the rest from industry. The matched funding proved that the state's industrial strategy wasn't only about money but also about the state showing commitment and building trust.

By 2020, over 200 companies were involved in the UK's autonomous vehicles' research and testing ecosystem. Some of these were large established companies like Ford, Nissan, Volvo and Jaguar Land Rover. But several were new firms that would not have existed without the collaborative approach required by the government. One such was Machines with Vision, an Edinburgh based start-up. Funded by the centre in 2016 to do a feasibility study, the firm had developed 'road fingerprinting' technology which maps travel surfaces to enable precise, dynamic vehicle positioning. The firm subsequently entered into a partnership with Jaguar Land Rover to improve this technology and then signed a deal with Deutsche Bahn to apply it to trains. Another collaborative project was led by Oxbotica, a software auto-control spin-out from Oxford University's Mobile Robotics Group. Oxbotica partnered with Caterpillar, the construction giant, to build an autonomous truck for off-road use in extreme environments such as mines. The belief was that its product could revolutionise the construction and mining industry in the years to come.

As Michael Talbot, the CCAV's former head of strategy, puts it: 'We reckoned that once we led with R&D, manufacturing could follow. And so we focused on securing R&D facilities and stimulating domestic and foreign direct investment. No one country, however large, and no single government, however efficient, can do the whole thing well.'

But there are also pitfalls in how the CCAV engages industry and drives industrial policy. The 200 companies that the centre has brought together comprise a large and self-sustaining group. Now that this 'ecosystem' has been created, the question for government becomes: is there a case to keep on spending? 'We can't create another thirty projects every year,' says Talbot. 'So we have experts to help us to ensure we spend well and fill the gaps that need filling.' In spending its money, he says, the state must also guard against the corporate equivalent of dependency on handouts. 'Our other question is funding junkies, companies that are living from grant to grant. We cannot create such dependency. Eventually, we need to stimulate banks and venture capital to enter and invest.'

The space race

Perhaps nowhere is the competition among nations more apparent than in space. Russia, China, India, the US, the EU and even

Israel all have space programmes and ambitions to colonise the moon and Mars. These programmes are not maintained merely for reasons of national pride. At bottom, the space race is about commercial opportunity: it is about technology development, employment, economic growth and access to resources.

This is even true of countries like China where government initiatives are more overtly about nation-building rather than simply commerce. As Namrata Goswami, a researcher at India's Institute for Defence Studies and Analyses, says: 'Given the vast economic potential that lies in outer space resources, China is already shifting a major part of its resources to invest in research on space-based solar power, asteroid mining and developing capacity for permanent presence in space.'[2]

In some ways the space race resembles the nineteenth-century settling of the American west. That process, too, involved a land grab that fuelled economic growth. Then, too, the government was involved in a big way: it provided cash subsidies and the US army led high-risk expeditions to secure territory and create the infrastructure that paved the way for private actors to follow. But, as *The Economist* puts it, it would be 'a mistake to promote space as a romanticised Wild West, an anarchic frontier where human-ity can throw off its fetters and rediscover its destiny. For space to fulfil its promise, governance is required.'[3]

Can the US repeat the trick in space in the twenty-first century? This time it has competition, not from the Soviet Union or Europe, but from China. Currently, the US would seem to be at a relative disadvantage to its new rival. In a democratic country, initiatives like space exploration require huge investments and considerable public buy-in. When it comes to funding, NASA often loses out to other more pressing concerns in Washington. In contrast, China's communist leaders have been very good at linking their earthly ambitions to their goals in space. In the US, space may seem passé as a national project, but in China the political rhetoric is full of phrases extolling the 'spirit of aerospace' and the 'space dream' as a way to rejuvenate the nation. Ye Peijian, the head of China's moon programme, has even compared space exploration to the country's designs on the islands in the South China Sea. 'The universe is an ocean', he has said, 'the moon is the Diaoyu Islands, Mars is Huangyan Island.'[4]

China's programmes are state driven, and the central government pumps huge amounts into its space programme. But even in this communist-controlled country, the state works actively with the private sector to achieve its goals. Liberal subsidies flow to commercial space companies, and the state is always at hand to help these firms attract international customers for their products and services, driving its own overall space programme in the process.

It is here, however, that the US might have the upper hand. Led by entrepreneurs like Elon Musk and Jeff Bezos, the private space industry in the US is now thriving. Thus, Musk's company SpaceX is developing rockets to send humans to Mars while Bezos' company Blue Origin has recently unveiled a lunar lander designed to reach the moon's south pole. Moreover, these are only two of many companies that aim to help NASA with its ambitions in space.

NASA has recognised this. Under its current administrator, Jim Bridenstine, the agency has become a gatekeeper that lays the groundwork and sets the rules for private enterprise to flourish. The core rocket for NASA's Space Launch System, for instance, was built by Boeing, while Lockheed Martin made the Orion crew exploration spacecraft. In 2011, when the space shuttle programme ended, the agency no longer had the means to achieve low Earth orbit. So it turned to SpaceX. 'It was something that could be turned over to the private sector, which invariably can do almost anything faster and cheaper than the government,' says Dale Ketcham, the chief of Strategic Alliances of Space Florida, the state's aerospace development agency.[5]

In 2014, NASA awarded SpaceX and Boeing a combined

$6.8 billion to build competing spacecraft to carry astronauts into orbit from the United States. The Americans are now developing two new crew modules – one by SpaceX called Dragon and another by Boeing called Starliner – both of which are being lined up for human spaceflight trials. In March 2019, SpaceX used its Falcon-9 rocket to launch the Crew Dragon: a reusable spacecraft capable of carrying up to seven astronauts.

In addition to bringing capital and ideas, the private sector also brings greater efficiency. According to NASA, it would have cost the agency $4 billion to develop the Falcon rockets; it cost SpaceX a tenth of that.

The agency now has many partnerships with the commercial space industry for its moon mission, and acts as an incubator of private ventures. An example is its Commercial Lunar Payload Services programme, which shares the cost of developing lunar landers with nine private companies to deliver supplies to the moon's surface. In the past, NASA would have acted as the sole developer of such a project. Now this approach should not only save NASA money but also enhance its ability to achieve its goals in time.

In Bridenstine's view, this new collaborative approach will change the human spaceflight programme. 'We're not purchasing, owning and operating the hardware,' he says. 'We're buying the service. We will invest in that hardware, but we expect [the private companies] to make investments in that hardware as well.'[6] The private firms, for their part, are making these investments because they know that there is a market for space travel that goes beyond NASA: there are international customers, foreign governments and even, eventually, tourists.

Charles Fishman, the author of *One Giant Leap: The Impossible Mission That Flew Us to the Moon* (2019), argues that in running this new space race, the US has learned many lessons from its Apollo missions.[7] First, it has learned that incentives matter. The race to the moon in the 1960s was led by national pride. As a result, everything was government driven, government directed and government funded. The new space race, in contrast, will encourage private entrepreneurs to do much of the heavy lifting and will be driven by a hard-nosed commercial calculus. Space entrepreneurs like Bezos and Musk won't operate space missions; instead, they will seek to make spaceflight economically viable. Their aim, says Fishman, will be to create 'a space economy – a zero gravity infrastructure'. This new space economy will be self-sustaining. Unlike Apollo, its growth will be organic: 'the way the digital economy has blossomed, and also reinvented itself, over the past 20 years'.[8]

Second, the state has learned that rivalry matters. But unlike the first race that was about rivalry between countries, the new space race is as much about rivalry between companies and entrepreneurs. According to Fishman: 'We already have the routine rivalry of capitalism in some parts of the emerging space economy, between companies contending to produce the best kinds of technology and services.'[9] This rivalry exists, for instance, at one end of the spectrum with small satellites; but it is also entering the other end with new rockets by Blue Origin and SpaceX. Just as we do not have one car or smartphone company, 'we won't have just one space company – nor should we'.

Finally, the state has learned that, while its agencies may be good at development, they are generally bad at operations. NASA may have helped invent space travel, but Apollo did not succeed in setting up routine passenger flights to a moon base. Private companies like Space X and Blue Origin are now stepping in to take over the operational elements of space towards precisely that objective. According to Fishman, in terms of human spaceflight, the Apollo example and the experience of the years since suggest that NASA 'should go back to being an advanced research and development agency and leave operational roles to companies and universities'.[10]

The entrepreneurial state?

In her 2013 book *The Entrepreneurial State*, Mariana Mazzucato attacks the libertarian view that the role of government in driving innovation is to get out of the way, regulate lightly, and let the private sector get on with it.[11] Instead, she argues for a strategic state that actively shapes markets and economies. In her view, the state is not a mere fixer of market failures, doomed only to intervene in the economy at times of crisis, or a passive investor in basic science, infrastructure and education. Rather it is a key player in the economic process of creative destruction: it is an entrepreneur, risk-taker and creator of markets. The state, according to Mazzucato, has a visionary and strategic role that libertarians only assign to entrepreneurs and the private sector. She goes on to argue that the internet, and breakthroughs in nanotechnology, biotechnology and green energy, did not occur 'because the private sector wanted something but could not find the resources to invest in it'.[12] Rather, these breakthroughs occurred because of a 'vision that the government had in an area that had not yet been fathomed by the private sector'.

There are elements of truth to Mazzucato's view. As the case of M-Pesa, autonomous vehicles and the space race show, the state can be an active shaper of markets especially in the early, uncertain stages of their evolution. In these stages, governments have a major role to play as conveners, coordinators, champions and more. Without the state's active and strategic engagement from the very start, many new sectors, innovations and markets would be stillborn or never even imagined, let alone brought to fruition.

Mazzucato, however, often frames her argument in adversarial terms. Innovation, for her, seems to be about the state *versus* the market; the public *versus* the private sector. And yet, as M-Pesa, autonomous vehicles and the space race show, the reality is somewhat less either/or. More often than not, innovation and market creation require the state *and* the market to work together. The state has to be proactive, without being dominant or smothering, but the private sector has a crucial role too. Indeed, it is far from clear that states can or should try to do all the heavy lifting on their own. They must spend, but not too much, and only then to encourage spending from industry too. They must engage with the private sector to leverage the energies, creativity and efficiency of the latter.

Take spending. As Michael Talbot of the UK's Centre for Connected and Autonomous Vehicles puts it: 'We knew we couldn't lead in every area, so we focused on our strengths. We didn't have vast amounts to spend.' The CCAV model therefore requires matched funding from industry partners for trials and R&D. And even then, it monitors this spending and what the taxpayer gets from it. As Talbot says: 'We constantly evaluate what our investments have got us. Are we getting a multiplier effect in terms of jobs and further investment? We need both qualitative and quantitative evidence of this.'

But even if governments had endless budgets with no limits on spending, there would still be a limit to what they could achieve on their own. Innovation is so complex now that it takes several different types of expertise to pull it off. M-Pesa required experts in mobile telephony, software and security, banking regulation and money laundering law to work together. Autonomous vehicles involve a bewildering array of specialists: car manufacturers, software companies, insurance, finance and law firms. Even the largest and most competent government agencies would struggle to comprehend, let alone master, all these areas and the issues they throw up. By definition, there will always be more experts outside government than within it. For the sake of effectiveness and efficiency it is crucial for government to partner: to steer and not to row. (Of course, the government must retain a certain amount of internal expertise. But this expertise need be no more than that required to make the right choices and avoid being taken for a ride by partners and advisers.)

Further, innovation isn't only about developing new

technology; it is also about commercialising it. Commercialising technology is often beyond the ambit of the state. Here the role of the private sector is crucial. In the 1970s, when it was at the height of its powers, the Soviet Union spent 4 per cent of its GDP on R&D, far more than countries like Japan, for example. And yet, without the help of a private sector to commercialise the breakthroughs that came from its defence and space programmes the Soviet economy stagnated and collapsed under the weight of its obligations. Japan, on the other hand, with a complete ecosystem of companies that were constantly learning from each other and from global competitors, became one of the most innovative and prosperous economies on the planet. Even if, as Mazzucato argues, a government agency like the Defense Advanced Research Projects Agency (DARPA) – the US body responsible for developing technologies for military use – did come up with GPS and the internet, the fact is that it took a Steve Jobs and an Apple to use these to create an iPhone.

Finally, there is the question of risk and how best to use public money. Governments and their agencies are under a legal obligation to make the best use of their resources. It is important for the state to take risk, but not too much. Contrary to Mazzucato's argument, a government's work is not all about spending or risk-taking in the sense of placing financial bets. Often, it is about *transferring* risk, especially when technologies move beyond testing to commercialisation. Equally often, it is about using regulation to maximise innovation while *reducing* risk, to society and to citizens in the first instance, but eventually to the government itself. As Talbot puts it: 'When testing infrastructure, we are very keen not to own any assets. This would be risky for government. We want industry to own that element. We are willing to address market failure and help industry get started and fill in the gaps. But it is better if industry owns and operates everything in the end.'

In 2012, after docking the Dragon Capsule to the International

Space Station, NASA awarded SpaceX a £1 billion contract to resupply the capsule on a regular basis. This contract proved mutually beneficial. While it helped SpaceX grow, it also helped NASA by 'pushing for fixed-price contracts to enable the federal government to change how it does business', according to Dale Ketcham of Space Florida.[13] NASA could then pay for milestones of achievement rather than pay through a traditional model that was based on upfront costs. This helped the agency keep its spending down while getting the private sector to invest its own capital and assume more of the risk.

Governments have to be careful not to overstep the mark. They should not put themselves in the business of placing bets on specific competitors. It is best to leave such gambles to the private sector. 'We are not about picking companies or specific products,' says Talbot. 'We are about creating an environment for successful companies to emerge – companies that may or may not be incumbents. We leave the job of picking winning areas of technology to them.' Thus, the Centre for Connected and Autonomous Vehicles does not favour specific technologies such as dedicated short-range communications or 5G because it does not know which will eventually be adopted and become a standard. And even when it does focus on broad sectors like autonomous vehicles, it is guided on why and how to do so by experts from universities, as well as consultants and trade bodies such as the Automotive Council.

Challenge-led innovation

The three issues of spending, looking outside for experts and managing risk are linked. Together they suggest that governments must find a way between the two extremes of libertarian laissez-faire on the one hand and draconian state control on the other. Ideally, states must find a way to steer rather than row when it comes to innovation and the economy. Mazzucato holds up DARPA as a paragon of state-led innovation. The agency, she points out, 'funded the formation of computer science departments, provided start-up firms with early research support, contributed to semiconductor research and support to human-computer interface research and oversaw the early stages of the Internet'.[14] Further, 'many of the technologies later incorporated in the design of the personal computer were developed by DARPA-funded researchers'.

All this is true. But the key word here is 'support'. Many of the experts responsible for the actual creation and conversion were outside the agency, in universities and companies. Indeed, the US agency is increasingly turning not only to large firms and start-ups but also to citizen-scientists and makers. Since 2004, for instance, DARPA has held several global competitions offering prize money to private parties that address the grand challenges it poses. By challenging others to do the creative work, DARPA puts its budgets to better use. Furthermore, the competitions aren't limited to the usual experts in a given field; they encourage broad participation from the general public. This stimulates out-of-the-box thinking, which in turn enables DARPA to pursue ambitious goals without having to predict who or which approach will eventually succeed. These challenges make economic sense too. DARPA only pays up if someone succeeds. Often, the amount of time and money spent by multiple teams exceeds the size of the prize itself. Nevertheless, even participants who do not win money report intangible benefits from their involvement in the process. These benefits include the intrinsic pleasure of working with others on solving systemic problems, a raising of their own profiles, the potential investment from other agencies, and access to new customers. Some competitions also offer non-monetary support to participants, including help with 'networking, mentoring, testing or access to legal and marketing support'.[15]

Thus, DARPA's first Grand Challenge in 2004 was a $1 million prize that was authorised by Congress to spur the development of autonomous vehicles. The general goal was to make one-third of ground military forces autonomous by 2015. The specific goal was to develop the technologies needed to create the first fully autonomous ground vehicles capable of completing a substantial off-road course within a limited time. In 2007, the follow-up DARPA Urban Challenge extended the competition to autonomous operation in a mock urban environment. And in 2012, the DARPA Robotics Challenge focused on autonomous emergency-maintenance robots.

Since then DARPA has launched several other challenges, including the Chikungunya Challenge to 'accelerate the development of new infectious disease forecasting methods'; the Cyber Grand Challenge to 'develop automatic defense systems that can discover, prove, and correct software flaws in real time'; and the Spectrum Collaboration Challenge to 'demonstrate a radio protocol that can best use a given communication channel in the presence of other dynamic users and interfering signals'.

NASA also works closely with partners in this way. In 2018, in one of his first speeches as administrator, Jim Bridenstine reassured Americans that forming a human colony on Mars remained on NASA's agenda. As part of this effort, the agency held a three-day summit with over 100 speakers from established firms, start-ups and the general public who presented ideas for how they could help NASA achieve a manned mission to Mars by 2033. These included plans for sustainable urban living on the planet, extreme greenhouse habitats, and self-cleaning Martian clothes made from pulverised starch polymer with 'a bacteria colony' to absorb sweat.

Thus, far from doing everything themselves, states and state agencies are increasingly working with others to drive industrial strategy and achieve their economic goals faster, better and cheaper. It is tempting to think that, in cultivating the economy, the state's main focus is or should be large corporations or high-tech start-ups. After all, it is these firms that either spend the most on

R&D or are the main progenitors of breakthrough technologies. The reality is that increasingly, states are not only engaging with corporations and hi-tech start-ups but are also cultivating citizen-led social enterprises. These social enterprises often adopt the new technologies and forms of organisations typically employed by businesses but apply them to solving local social, economic and environmental problems. Indeed, around the world, as the tools to create new hardware and software solutions for local problems quickly and affordably become ubiquitous, the barriers to entry for ordinary people to do what previously only large firms or the government could do are falling away. As a result, the means to innovate are increasingly democratised, and governments are learning to cultivate these trends.

Fab Lab Barcelona

Tomas Diez grew up in Venezuela, where he earned a bachelor's degree in urban planning at the Simón Bolívar University, Caracas. In 2006, he moved to Barcelona to pursue a master's at the Institute for Advanced Architecture of Catalonia (IAAC). Soon after, while he was working as an intern at the institute, one of his tutors invited him to lunch with the directors of the IAAC. Over lunch they told him of their plans to set up what they called a fabrication lab (Fab Lab) at the institute.

The idea was to change the way that cities like Barcelona were organised and run in the twenty-first century. In their vision, students and citizens would be more actively involved in finding solutions to problems in their communities. But they wouldn't merely theorise. Rather, digital tools and data would help them design and eventually make devices that brought change. Behind this idea was an even more striking one. Cities in the twenty-first century, they believed, could be increasingly self-sufficient hubs of production, employing local citizens in the making of the goods they consumed, and networked globally to other cities and their similarly empowered citizens. According to this vision, the twenty-first-century economy would be one of efficient and egalitarian networks of people connected by data and technology. The Fab Lab would be linked to the master's programme at IAAC but would also be part of a growing network of such labs around the world.

What the directors now needed was someone to set up the Fab Lab and lead a team to run it. They thought that Diez was just the person for the job.

Recalling that meeting, Diez says: 'I had been a tech freak since I was kid. But I knew very little about Fab Labs or how they were run. All I had to get going was a pile of papers and a book by a professor at MIT.'[16]

The professor turned out to be Neil Gershenfeld, an applied physicist and computer scientist who had pioneered, among other things, the area of personal fabrication. In 1998, Gershenfeld had developed a course at MIT called How to Make (Almost) Anything. Initially intended to teach students of technology about sophisticated industrial machines, the course soon attracted others without a technical background, including artists, designers and architects. Recognising that the course demanded a space where students could tinker, Gershenfeld and his colleagues set up a digital fabrication facility at MIT in 2001. The Fab Lab, as it was called, was equipped with various materials as well as computer-controlled tools such as laser cutters and 3D printers.[17]

Others who learned about the Fab Lab soon saw that there was a bigger idea lurking behind the merely technical one of helping people make 'almost anything'. One of these people was Melvin King, an African American politician and community organiser, who had also, since 1970, been adjunct professor of urban studies and planning at MIT. King had spent many years creating programmes and building institutions for low-income communities in Boston. This work had convinced him that behind the Fab

Labs was an idea with great social and economic potential; he saw how these spaces could be used to empower people to meet community needs that were not otherwise met. For King, the labs could be a way to provide opportunities for unemployed teens, for instance, and people left behind by racial segregation. Working with Gershenfeld, King applied to the National Science Foundation for a grant to set up the South End Technology Center in Boston: a collaborative venture between the Tent City Corporation and MIT. The purpose of the centre was to enable people to become producers of knowledge and sharers of ideas and information. It would provide free or low-cost access and training in most aspects of computer-related technology. The staff, mostly volunteers, would all have a background in computer technology and its applications. A key element of the centre was the presence at its heart of a Fab Lab.

Gershenfeld himself soon became a proponent of the idea of social transformation through Fab Labs, not only for communities near MIT but also for disadvantaged people in remote parts of the world. He began to travel – to Costa Rica, Norway, India – and set up Fab Labs in all those places. Soon people in those communities began to reward his faith in their creativity with fascinating solutions to their problems. In Pabal in rural India, locals developed a device in their Fab Lab to test the quality of milk so that dairy farmers could secure a fair price. In Norway, above the Arctic Circle, shepherds built radios to track their animals in the mountains. In the Boston Fab Lab, children made and sold antennae to set up neighbourhood wi-fi networks.

In Barcelona in 2007, Diez began preparing for his new role at IAAC by reading Gershenfeld's 2005 book *Fab: The Coming Revolution on Your Desktop – from Personal Computers to Personal Fabrication*. This process, says Diez, helped him to see how he could bring the vision of the IAAC directors to life in his adopted city.

I found the encounter with Gershenfeld's ideas exhilarating. As an urbanist, that was the first time I had made the link between the city and community spaces like Fab Labs. I came to see how, if we wanted to change the way that societies work, we needed to rethink how we use and transform resources in cities. Cities, after all, account for most of global consumption.

Now all that remained was to make the vision a reality.

The Smart Citizen kit

Once the Fab Lab at IAAC had been set up, Diez and his team began to cast around for concrete projects to work on. One of the most successful of these would be the Smart Citizen kit.

In searching for a local issue with global implications, the team had hit upon the problem of pollution: one that besets all cities wherever they might be. Typically, pollution is dealt with by city councils. As Diez describes it, councils will work with large companies like IBM or Cisco that produce bulky, pricey kits costing around £25,000 to monitor urban air pollution. A few of these kits are then placed in select locations around the city, typically near parks so that the councils can claim to meet the tough standards imposed by regulatory bodies such as the European Commission. But such an approach is not only expensive: it is also far from smart. As Diez puts it: 'Such centralised solutions are like reducing the brain to four or five neurons talking to each other. If this was a human body we were talking about, you wouldn't be able to move a finger.' And, cities are potentially more complex. 'What you need is a lot of cheap sensors all over town. A truly smart solution would be a decentralised, crowd-sensing system that captures, processes, monitors and responds in real time to pollution data.'

Driven by this idea, Diez and his colleagues began work on a Smart Citizen project as a bottom-up solution. In 2011, working in the Fab Lab at IAAC, they developed a rough prototype of a device that would enable citizens to collect and monitor pollution data from their homes. The device was based on cheap and widely available components such as the Arduino (an open-source, microcontroller-based kit for building digital devices) and interactive sensors that can record data and control objects. Then, in 2012, the team had a further idea: what if the data collected could be used not only for city planning but also to mobilise citizens? That way, the Smart Citizen kit could also become a social and political tool.

To raise money for the project, the team launched its first crowdfunding campaign in 2012, and came up with about £15,000. A second Kickstarter campaign followed in 2013 and raised a further £60,000. In 2014, the team set up a company in London to support the commercialisation of the kit. 'But we didn't go the venture capital route,' says Diez. 'Instead we joined an EU-funded project through which we could combine resources to develop the hardware and the approach.'

The team began to make the kits in the Fab Lab in Barcelona and sell them through the Smart Citizen website. Citizens could buy the kits for little more than £100 and install them in their homes after registering them on the website. One part of the kit – the sensor – would sit outside your window or on your balcony, where it would sense and collect data on air quality, sound levels, light intensity, temperature and humidity. The sensor would send this data wirelessly to the other part of the kit: a USB stick connected to your computer. The data would then travel via the internet to a central server that collated information from all users in this way. You would then receive regular reports based on the collated and processed data, giving you a clear picture of how your neighbourhood was performing on key indicators of air and noise pollution at different times of the day and different days of the week. Armed with this data, you could then lobby your local council to take appropriate action when needed. For instance, if you suffered from allergies or asthma you could more accurately track pollution levels where you lived, correlate these with your own health and use this evidence to push for improvements to air quality in your area.

In keeping with its public service ethos, the project was conceived as a social business: it was partly owned by the people who bought the kit and subscribed to the service. Every member of this community became part of the overall data-sharing solution. Each subscriber agreed to sell the data to the city council and share the revenues 20/80 with those who managed the system. The website, a hybrid between Facebook, Google Maps and Wikipedia, also helped to foster this community online. Members could comment on data from individual sensors and see what others in other locations were reporting. This was an unusual way of involving citizens in the running of their city while also bringing creative and productive work into local communities.

Once they had got the Smart Citizen kit to work in Barcelona, Diez and his team went on to sell the idea to other cities, working with the city councils there as their partners. In Amsterdam, for instance, the council bought 100 units of the Smart Citizen kit and gave them to citizens as a way to get them involved in city planning.

As Gershenfeld puts it: 'There's a new generation that's not waiting for top-down solutions. People starting Fab Labs and linking them are really ... creating a new notion of an economy. And it's a very different paradigm from the unemployed being an underclass that need to be given jobs, to empowering people to create jobs.'[18]

Mayors and Fab Cities

Around 2011, the mayor of Barcelona began to take notice of the IAAC Fab Lab. As luck would have it, some of the founding members of IAAC had become members of the mayor's office. This group set about expanding the initial Fab Lab vision to the rest of the city.

By 2014, the mayor's office was working with Diez and his team to set up a network of labs in Barcelona, with one planned for each of its ten districts. The idea was to create a new type of public service. Just as public bodies had created libraries in the nineteenth century to democratise books, and computer cafes in the twentieth century to democratise digital information, Fab Labs would bring digital fabrication to the people as a new type of public activity.

Working with the Barcelona city council and a team of architects, designers and programmers, Diez now led work on a number of projects that exemplified this vision. Two of these were architectural: the Fab Lab House (a computer-produced house that was customised and adapted to the environment), and the Hyper Habitat IAAC (a project that used information technology to rethink the 'habitability of the world'). The mayor's office also supported the launching of a broader, global Fab City mission. The idea was to use the global Fab Lab network to localise production in cities around the world and, in this way, bring production closer to consumption.

All this culminated in Barcelona hosting the 10th global Fab Lab conference in July 2014. Speaking at the conference, Barcelona's mayor Xavier Trias laid out the vision for the Fab City initiative in the Catalan capital and elsewhere. Cities were where most of the world's resources were consumed; for their growth to be sustainable, *they* needed to be sustainable. One way to make them so was to employ local citizens in the manufacture of many of the things they consumed. To make this vision a reality, Trias threw down a challenge to cities: to produce everything they consumed by 2054, giving them a forty-year window. This led to the launch of the global Fab City initiative. The idea was to drive a shift away from the industrial paradigm of product-in trash-out and towards a sustainable model of urban manufacturing supported by data. The initiative would comprise a network of cities and be governed by a foundation, working to make locally productive, globally connected citizens.

Sherry Lassiter, president and CEO of the Fab Foundation, is a vocal supporter of the plan. 'It takes the idea of a green footprint and sustainable city to a more interesting place. Rather than import and export goods, why not import and export data and manufacture locally? Rather than shipping materials and products all around the world, they're trying to do it all locally. That's a wonderful goal.'[19]

Boosted by Mayor Trias's public support and commitment, Diez and his team soon began receiving requests of interest from other cities around the world. An initial list of seven soon led to a further six. The Fab City movement has snowballed from there. As of 2020, over thirty-four cities have become part of the initiative. Some of these are from the rich world: Detroit, Paris, Sacramento and Oakland. But many are from the developing world, including Thimpu in Bhutan, Mexico City, Belo Horizonte in Brazil, and Ekurhuleni in South Africa. In each city, local actors and policymakers work together to make the Fab City vision a reality.

But in 2015, just as things were taking off elsewhere, the movement hit a roadblock in its home town of Barcelona. That year came the curse of all public supported programmes: a change of leadership at the top. In May the city elected a new mayor with a quite different agenda and background. Where Trias had been a member of the Catalan European Democratic Party, a centre-right party, the new mayor, Ada Colau, was a political activist who had founded the left-wing citizens' platform Barcelona en Comú in 2014. The first woman to hold the office of mayor, Colau's arrival marked a potentially revolutionary change.

Diez and his team now began to worry about the continuity of their project. They had suddenly lost their friends in government. 'New governments', says Diez, 'bring new leaders. And new leaders want to pursue new ideas. We thought that the new mayor might kill what we had begun.'

His fears would prove unfounded, however. Mayor Colau, seeing the importance of digital platforms in community life, soon appointed a chief technology officer, Francesca Bria, as well as a digital innovation director, Anna Majó Crespo. In Bria and Crespo, Diez and his team found like-minded allies. 'They understood technology and what we were trying to do,' says Diez. 'We were able to strike up a rapport with them that was independent of ideology.'

Colau then made a much-publicised visit to the IAAC Fab Lab. Following the visit, the original vision of setting up a Fab Lab network in Barcelona received a fresh impetus. By 2020, five labs were in place, with a further two to come and an eventual plan for sixteen in all. The labs will design and manufacture products using local materials in different fields, including furniture, clothing and housing.

'Our role at IAAC', says Diez, 'had been to get things started. And we had done that successfully. So, around 2015, we decided to hand everything over to the city council for them to run entirely.'

Launching the revamped plan with the council meant securing the future, not only of the Fab Labs in the Barcelona, but also the wider network of Fab Cities elsewhere. According to Diez:

> We now understood clearly that the Fab Labs needed to connect with neighbourhoods and communities. They were the Trojan horses, you might say, that could be used to ignite the innovation that would respond to the challenges that all cities face. Through them, cities and their citizens and councils could drive innovation around, for instance, climate change and social inclusion.

The maker movement: all the world's a workshop

In the fifteen or so years since their inception, Fab Labs have become a global phenomenon. As of 2020, there were over 1,750 in over 100 countries around the world, with the expectation that the number will continue to grow rapidly over the next few years.

To set up a Fab Lab requires an average investment of $100,000. The equipment costs between $25,000 and $65,000, while materials and consumables cost a further $15,000 to $40,000. Moreover, the Fab Lab approach encourages and thrives on the use of free, open-source software. This puts the labs within reach not only of universities but also many local governments, even in developing countries in Asia, Africa and Latin America. As Sherry Lassiter describes the process, the first Fab Lab in a community costs around $125,000. Subsequently, others can use that lab to set up others at a far cheaper rate. 'It's getting close to the point where a Fab Lab can self-reproduce at a tenth the price. If you're able to rapidly reproduce and prototype manufacturing machines, then your designs are not constrained by the tools that are out there. You just have to manufacture a machine that does what you want it to do.'[20]

Once it has raised the necessary funding, any group that wishes to set up a lab in its community can sign a contract with the Fab Foundation to ensure that it follows the Fab Lab Charter. In that sense, the network operates as a social franchise, with the potential to make growth easy and cost-effective. As a result, the foundation has helped democratise the use of digital technologies, not only to test and develop new solutions for local problems, but also to commercialise them in sustainable ways. As Zak Rosen, an American multimedia producer, points out, people around the world now work in Fab Labs to create 'bikes, houses, watches, forks, radios, cyborg hands' and much more for 'personal and community use, and for profit'.[21]

This variety and differentiation is important. As Lassiter puts it: 'Every Fab Lab in the world shares some of the same tools and processes, but they're each very different because they respond to their communities and what their needs and interests are.'[22] Some labs focus on technology and entrepreneurship, while others focus on addressing issues in the community such as improving education, conserving water or driving recycling.

Lassiter believes that these spaces can help promote a more equitable and sustainable world. 'We're about ... impacts,' she says, 'through both new economic opportunities and strong social networks ... Think about the digital revolution ... We made a small percentage of the population really rich and left many behind. Many in the world still don't have access to the internet. For them, trying to catch up economically is just not realistic. With the revolution in digital fabrication we have a chance to change that equation if we do it right – and now.'[23]

Gershenfeld agrees. He believes that digitally enabled personal fabrication is both a social and a technological change – a democratisation of 'the ability to manipulate matter, just as personal computers have democratised the ability to manipulate information'.[24] Fabricators, he believes, will move from factory floors into homes, just as computers morphed from filling rooms to sitting on laptops to fitting in the pockets of the billions who use them daily.

Indeed, the Fab Lab movement, successful as it has been, is merely part of a much larger transformation taking place around the world. More and more people are now empowered to do with ubiquitous resources what only large firms or governments could do in the past. Since the turn of the millennium, the spread of digital technologies and tools such as smartphones, cloud computing, 3D printers, crowdfunding and social media has given rise to a grassroots phenomenon that has come to be dubbed 'the maker movement'. A technology-based extension of the do-it-yourself and hacker cultures, the maker movement goes beyond building software to making physical objects and new electronic devices. Using open-source hardware, the movement combines electronics, robotics and 3D printing with wood- and metalworking and traditional arts and crafts. With the resources now available over the internet, virtually anyone can create simple devices, which are then, in some cases, widely adopted by others. There is a major focus on learning and sharing practical skills. In keeping with the open-source ethos, products created through the movement can be made by anyone through widely available documentation.

These makers can work in their homes or garages, but increasingly they also have access to formal 'maker spaces' of which the Fab Labs are only one type. Working in these spaces, like-minded individuals form communities in which they share ideas, tools and skillsets. While many of the progenitors of the movement came from universities and had a technical background, as the movement has spread maker spaces have become increasingly common in communities more generally. More often than not they are now set up, run and promoted by public bodies. In the US, for instance, the federal government has adopted the concept of fully open maker spaces within its agencies. The first of these – the SpaceShop Rapid Prototyping Lab – was set up at NASA's Ames Research Center in 2015. In Europe, such labs are even more prominent: there are now three times more maker spaces in Europe than in North America.

Outside the West, the maker culture is on the rise too, with maker spaces now becoming key drivers of entrepreneurial networks in several countries. In Singapore, HackerspaceSG has been set up by the team that runs the city's most successful entrepreneurial network. In Beirut, in a city fractured by ethnic and religious divisions, Lamba Labs is a maker space where people of all backgrounds can collaborate freely. And in Shanghai, China's first maker space, Xinchejian, enables innovation and collaboration in a country with strict internet censorship. By 2030, as cities begin to house over half of the world's people, hacker spaces, Fab Labs and maker spaces are likely to become key hubs for entrepreneurs to meet and collaborate, and develop local solutions to environmental, social and economic problems.

Side by side with the spread of maker spaces has come the popularity of Maker Faires. Since 2006, cities around the world have competed to host these events, which are often held in large exhibition areas, over several days, drawing in an excess of 100,000 attendees, including parents and children. Smaller, community-driven Mini Maker Faires are also increasingly common. And similar events, which use other brand names but follow the Maker Faire model, have sprung up across the globe.

The maker movement and the simultaneous explosion in entrepreneurship have shown what small groups, sometimes of students, can now achieve. For instance, as the Covid-19 pandemic began to spread in early 2020, there was a massive response from the world's maker communities. Armed with free, open-source hardware and working out of make spaces and Fab Labs, makers in towns and cities worldwide played an important role in the development of 'ventilators, face shields, face masks, diagnostics and other widgets' to tackle the spread and treatment of the coronavirus.[25]

Governments, for their part, have come to realise that they can tap into these trends to solve social problems, create employment, generate growth and develop creative communities in the process. For example, in recognition of the spread of the maker movement, President Barack Obama hosted a Maker Faire in the White House on 18 June 2014. Attended by over 100 entrepreneurs, engineers and students from more than twenty states, the event featured a '17-foot robotic giraffe; a 128-square-foot, portable "tiny house"; a 3D pancake printer; a giant red weather balloon; and more than 30 other inspiring and creative inventions of the makers'.[26]

The makers who attended the event demonstrated designs built with cutting-edge tools and technologies and shared stories about their motivations. Among them, Jane Chen exhibited 'Embrace', her low-cost baby-warmer which had helped save the lives of over

50,000 premature babies worldwide; and Mark Roth explained how he had used the skills developed at a TechShop (a type of maker space) in San Francisco to launch his own laser-cutting business and get homeless people like himself off the streets.

After viewing the exhibits, President Obama addressed the audience and announced several new measures his administration was taking to 'enable Americans from all backgrounds to launch businesses' and 'contribute to the renaissance in American manufacturing'.[27] Declaring 18 June 2014 a National Day of Making, Obama exhorted Americans to become producers and not just consumers of things, and promised to empower a new generation of pioneers in manufacturing and design. 'Our parents and our grandparents', he said, 'created the world's largest economy and strongest middle class not by buying stuff, but by building stuff – by making stuff, by tinkering and inventing and building; by making and selling things first in a growing national market and then in an international market – stuff "Made in America".'[28]

Building on the link between manufacturing and the maker movement, Obama painted a vision in which the latter became a means to revitalise cities that had been hollowed out by globalisation through the adoption of a new, high-value, environmentally and socially sustainable approach to industry. 'Your projects', he told those gathered there, 'are examples of a revolution that's taking place in American manufacturing – a revolution that can help us create new jobs and industries for decades to come.'[29]

Steering versus rowing: the challenge for governments

To drive economic growth, governments can now not only work with large firms and high-tech start-ups, but they can also stimulate grassroots innovation by citizens and social entrepreneurs. Despite these opportunities, however, governments face many problems in how they approach initiatives designed to solve the major issues in their societies. For instance, governments typically find it hard to go beyond broad policies to deal with climate change. They might formulate regulations, launch projects and hold press conferences to announce what they plan to do. But they then struggle with the actual implementation. As Diez puts it: 'Governments, including at the city level, struggle with on-the-ground action that actually addresses pressing challenges like climate change. They might at best have a plan. But executing the plan is a different matter.'

Even if some cities, like those in the global Fab City network, eventually manage to engage citizens in solving problems through collaboration, this change mostly comes from citizens themselves, bottom up. 'In about 70 per cent of cases,' says Diez, 'it is the local maker community that has lobbied the city government to create such spaces and foster such activity.' And even when the government does support such initiatives, there is often the problem of continuity. This was precisely the case with the Fab Labs in Barcelona: when Mayor Colau replaced Mayor Trias, the rupture halted and nearly ended all the progress that had been made in years before.

Further, governments tend to prefer working with large companies, in a top-down fashion, rather than with start-ups or citizens' groups, bottom up. This is partly driven by rational considerations of reliability and perceived value for money, and partly by the safety of working with known entities with established reputations. Sometimes, it is also a consequence of the dominant view that economic growth involves big projects and investment, and thus big companies. At other times, however, such a preference is driven by more dubious motives. Some critics argue that working with large corporations on big projects is evidence of corruption in government and an establishment stitch-up between the rich and the powerful. As Diez puts it: 'The race for smart cities is typically promoted by big companies. And governments gravitate to them for various reasons. Even though they can now tap into citizen activists and makers, governments tend not to build smart cities around open-source resources and communities.'

But perhaps the biggest challenge for governments is how to balance the need to empower others with the tendency to seek control. Diez has had ample experience of this, with the scars to show for his efforts. 'We survived governments 1 and 2 in Barcelona,' he says with a laugh, 'but now with the Fab Cities initiative we have to deal with another 33!' He is clear that councils and elected officials have a major role to play in supporting grassroots innovation in cities and countries. But he is also clear that, more often than not, their need for control gets in the way of progress. 'The common approach of governments often conflicts directly with the grassroots ethos which is all about open innovation,' he says. This conflict of values has, for instance, got in the way of the spread of public Fab Labs. In Barcelona, after the initial support from the mayor's office, the IAAC team had to force itself to fit into the logic of the public sector to grow.

> We were part of setting up the Fab Labs at first, but eventually we had to give way to the city government. When we did this, they then set up a couple of labs with non-expert, political appointees to run things. The labs then became part of a massive structure in government. Now, only some public servants really understand what we are trying to do and why.

It isn't all bad news, however. In some cities, things have worked better. In Yucatán, Mexico, there is a more fluid relationship between the city officials and the local ecosystem, although the risk of a change in government and hence in policy remains. 'If it only depends on political will,' says Diez, 'we advise cities to form a consortium with multiple stakeholders and create a legal structure with many actors participating and no single group controlling.' In Bhutan and Paris, too, the political will is aligned with the ethos of the citizens, and the city's role is more supportive. But in many other cases, 'when the city sees a good idea, they try to develop it themselves and end up leaving behind those who got it started in the first place. They see themselves as the only owner,' says Diez.

And so there is a constant tussle at the heart of government: between, on the one hand, the obvious benefits of engaging firms and citizens in industrial activity and, on the other hand, the need to control and own such programmes. In principle, the twentieth-century debate between libertarians and statists would appear to have resulted in a truce between the two. The state remains an important player in regulating and cultivating the economy, while typically stepping back from running and managing things itself: it steers but does not row. In practice, however, the instinct to control remains, and wanting to retain control often means that governments cannot resist doing more. This re-introduces into the proceedings the heavy hand of bureaucracy and what Diez calls the 'logic of the public sector'.

All this is further complicated by the fact that, even when the state's intention is to cultivate industrial activity in external players, it nevertheless retains primary responsibility for several important functions. With this responsibility comes the need for organisation and control. For instance, as in the case of M-Pesa, the state has to maintain teams – such as Gerald Nyaoma's in the Central Bank of Kenya – that set the rules of the game and then monitor and manage how the game is played. Or, as in the case of the Centre for Connected and Autonomous Vehicles, government bodies bear primary responsibility not only for setting the rules and managing the game but also for managing the process of funding, forming and maintaining collaborations between diverse external actors and state agencies. So, too, with the space race: NASA, as a government agency, remains a very significant organisation even as it increasingly works with external companies. It still needs to maintain (and constantly improve) its own organisational capacity to do what it alone can do as well as manage its external partners better.

Moreover, even in the most market-oriented nations, in many sectors, even if external players do the fuzzy front-end of experimenting with and proving solutions, it often falls to governments to adopt, adapt and scale these solutions. This is particularly true where public goods are concerned, as was the case with the Fab Labs in Barcelona. Although the initial impetus came from IAAC and MIT, eventually the council took over the running of the labs to ensure they could be expanded to the rest of the city. Similarly, in some sectors of the economy, governments still need to do much of the heavy lifting themselves. For instance, in most countries, governments are still responsible for the delivery of public services such as health and education. They need not only to deliver these services as they currently do, but also constantly to improve how they deliver them. Namely: they themselves need to innovate and find ways to do what they have to do faster, better and cheaper. This innovation comes in many guises. First, governments need to innovate around service delivery. How can they constantly make healthcare, for example, more efficient and effective? Second, they need to innovate around their internal processes. How can they improve how they organise and do their own work?

In both cases, even if the original ideas come from outside, government departments need to absorb these ideas and replicate them in-house. The question then becomes, as it does for any large organisation: how can the state do all the many things it must do without getting bogged down in the bureaucracy that makes innovating hard? This problem is especially knotty when, as with all large organisations, governments have structures, processes and cultures that constantly militate against change. How, in such situations, can they create a deep culture of innovation? We turn to this subject next, in Chapter 9.

9

The innovative state: making governments responsive to change all the way through

'Change, change, all this talk about change. Aren't things bad enough already?'

Lord Palmerston to Queen Victoria

'A state without the means of some change is without the means of conservation.'

Edmund Burke

Between 1993 and 2014, the civic life of Boston was dominated by its 53rd mayor Thomas Michael Menino. Re-elected four times, Menino 'presided over one of the most successful urban renaissances in modern American history'.[1] Looking back over his career, the *New York Times* would credit him with having transformed his city into 'a thriving economic and cultural center and a magnet for innovation'. Menino's legacy is writ large on the city's skyline, in South Boston and the downtown area, where abandoned warehouses and the once-decrepit waterfront have been transformed into stylish office blocks, condos and restaurants.

Strangely enough, at the start of his career Menino had been derided as an 'urban mechanic': one who was too focused on 'small problems' and the 'nuts and bolts' of city management.[2] Despite Boston's reputation for academic excellence, Menino had a disdain for visionaries: he dismissed them as people who didn't 'get things done'. His hands-on approach to governing showed up in the most concrete ways. Having been born in Boston's Hyde Park area, he never tired of visiting the city's neighbourhoods. As mayor, he could be seen walking the streets, talking to citizens and reporting local problems – broken streetlights, potholes – as he saw them. After the city got its first hotline for citizens' complaints, Menino became its most frequent user, calling in several times a day with requests. As mayor, he was said to have met more than half of Boston's half a million residents.

Along with his focus on the nuts and bolts came a suspicion of new technology. Even while he championed the city's high-tech innovation district, Menino developed a reputation as a technophobe. Once, he went so far as to ban voicemail at City Hall. And yet, even *he* could not resist the need for change and the use of technology to do so.

What Menino lacked in technical know-how, he made up for by surrounding himself with young people from Boston's world-class universities. One of these was Mitchell Weiss, a graduate of Harvard Business School, who would eventually become Menino's chief of staff and speechwriter. In December 2005, in a speech to the Boston Chamber of Commerce that Weiss had written for him, Menino announced that he was ready to move his practical, hands-on approach to city government into the digital era. He would hire a chief information officer (CIO) and create a fellowship to bring a generation of what he called 'new urban mechanics' into government.

True to his word, in 2006, Menino hired Bill Oates to be the city's first CIO. Oates set to work developing a new 24-hour hotline and back-end performance management system for making and processing municipal service requests. In this quest he was joined by Chris Osgood, another graduate of Harvard Business School, who worked in City Hall as a mayoral policy adviser. Together, the duo and their team launched the new system in 2008. With it, the time it took to replace burned-out streetlights fell by more than half while the delivery time for recycling bins fell by three-quarters.

In 2006, Menino's fellowship programme also attracted Nigel Jacob, another young graduate of the city's universities. Jacob, who had begun his career as a software engineer at IBM and had worked at a couple of start-ups, was then enrolled for a PhD in computer science at Tufts University. Attracted to the idea of applying technology to public services, he began his fellowship in the city's IT department. From there it was a matter of time before he teamed up with Osgood. 'Chris Osgood and I were doing complementary things,' says Jacob. 'Together, we began to think of ways to connect the city's government with its academics. We were surrounded by all these amazing institutions. It seemed crazy not to do more with MIT or Harvard or Boston University.'[3]

In 2007 came the launch of Apple's iPhone, and Jacob began to think about the civic applications of the new device. With Osgood, he set to work on building an app that would serve the same function as the city services hotline. To build the app, he consulted MIT's Media Lab, which in turn referred him to Connected Bits, a software firm. In late 2009, Jacob and his team launched Citizens Connect, an app that allowed users to report issues like potholes, graffiti and broken streetlamps with geo-tagged photos.[4] At a cost of just $25,000 in its launch year, the service was the first of its kind anywhere. Soon it would account for over a fifth of all city service requests, amounting to over 10,000 a year. Citizens Connect in turn led to the creation of Commonwealth Connect, a similar app that would eventually be used by over forty municipalities in Massachusetts.

Buoyed by this success, Osgood and Jacob teamed up with Mitchell Weiss to think of more systematic ways to bring innovation to City Hall. It soon became clear to them that what they needed was a dedicated team – an innovation unit – that could pioneer a model of 'peer-driven government' and change. But to do that they would first have to get Menino to agree to their plan.

Mayor's Office of New Urban Mechanics

In 2010, as he began his fifth and final term as mayor, Tom Menino responded to pressure from Weiss, Osgood and Jacob by creating an innovation unit within City Hall – the Mayor's Office of New Urban Mechanics (MONUM). Menino placed Jacob and Osgood at its head, but gave them no annual budget: they would have to manage with funds from the city's various departments. For Weiss – by now Menino's chief of staff, and the coiner of the term 'new urban mechanics' – MONUM would essentially formalise what Jacob and Osgood had been doing informally until then.

The idea was simple. MONUM would be a dedicated design studio or innovation engine within government. It would identify problems and develop solutions for Boston in an atmosphere that was as free as possible from bureaucratic constraints. The team would only take on projects with the potential to scale and have an impact on citizens' lives. It would avoid ideas that were too costly or time-consuming. Once a project had been chosen, MONUM would research it, design a prototype solution, test and evaluate it. If the solution proved to be a success, the team would hand it over to the relevant city department to scale. Otherwise they would call it a failure and move on.

From the beginning, the focus was on fostering small-scale initiatives – some of which might use technology and data – to draw citizens into what the founders called 'participatory urbanism'. 'Our starting point', says Jacob, 'was Menino's obsession with quality of life issues in Boston. We wanted to build on the social capital he had accumulated over fifteen years in office.' Weiss's idea was that the team would work on projects like Citizens Connect that they had been developing between 2006 and

2010, and create an 'innovation ecosystem' along with the citizens of Boston. 'We kept an open mind,' says Jacob. 'We didn't have a specific thing we would work on. Instead, we would build a lot of different things.'

But because the team aimed to connect with the innovation economy in the Boston area, it would first have to operate on the same timescale. 'We were a start-up *for* the government *in* the government,' says Jacob. 'That meant we had to be a responsive, nimble and small team.' Moreover, MONUM would not pretend to have the ideas. Citizens would provide the inspiration for projects: they would no longer be 'passive recipients of government services' but 'active makers of their own urban environment'. This made sense for another reason: the team's lack of internal resources. 'We've always been stretched thin,' says Jacob, 'and so citizen engagement has been a fundamental part of our strategy from the start.'

Over time, the team came to refine its approach. Jacob now describes the MONUM model as consisting of three stages: explore, experiment and evaluate. The first step is always to understand the universe of things the team should be doing: exploring problems and solutions with community groups, professors, conventional or social entrepreneurs, and people generally interested in improving life in Boston. Then comes the testing process and trial and error. 'We see ourselves as experimentalists in local government. We look for things we can try out, that we can kick the tyres on, things we can invest time and money on downstream.'

The basis for new initiatives always is: does it make life better for people? As the team tests whether a new solution works, evaluation becomes key. Because of its relationships with the research community, the team often engages academic teams in evaluating projects. Sometimes, however, it hires paid professionals to do the job. Each project determines what sort of evaluation is needed. The team takes a mixed approach to this: sometimes evaluations are in depth and longer term, while at other times they are more near-term. 'Evaluation takes time on a day-to-day basis,' explains Kris Carter, the co-chair of MONUM. 'We have to find a model that is appropriate to us. We think a lot about qualitative methods, using designers and design-based evaluation, rather than simply quantitative, outcome-based metrics.'[5]

After 'explore, experiment and evaluate' comes the crucial process of selling the solution to the relevant government department. The relevant department – transport, schools, planning or health – then looks to expand the solution. At that point MONUM's job shifts to helping the department with this expansion. Doing so could involve helping with staff training, writing requests for proposals if procurement is involved, and so on. 'We want to be in the trenches solving problems for the departments,' says Carter. 'Our business is to understand what their business is. Some departments care mainly about public reaction, so we have to make that part of what we're doing.'

Over time, Citizens Connect became a model for how MONUM could engage the city's talent to move quickly and develop solutions for Boston. In 2011, for instance, the office partnered with Code for America – a non-political organisation founded to promote the use of technology and design in the public sector – to build Discover BPS, an app that lets parents find out what state schools their children are eligible to attend.[6] The app was designed to make a once confusing and time-consuming process simple: all that parents needed to do was enter the relevant name, grade and address to get the data they needed. Other innovations in education soon followed. One card worked as a school ID, a library card, a community centre membership card, and a transit pass. Where's My School Bus let parents track how a child's trip was going; this proved particularly valuable when bus drivers went on strike. Boston Saves was a programme designed to help children in state school save for college.

In 2012, the office launched Street Bump, a mobile app that tracks users while they drive and collects data on the location of potholes. A prototype, which had been created some years earlier, had originally been tested on Mayor Menino's own vehicle. Because the mayor had developed a reputation for calling in a record number of potholes, the team had his SUV fitted with a gyrometer, an accelerometer and GPS to detect and report potholes automatically every time he drove over them. Later, as the iPhone became ubiquitous, the team realised that the sensors in it could be used to enable a large number of cars to detect and report potholes, and that this data could be crowdsourced. Drivers would only have to download the app and place their smartphone on the dashboard; the phone would then collect data on potholes and transmit it to City Hall. The team tested this new idea using a car from their press office, aiming for every pothole they could find while driving around Boston Common. 'We were all pretty sore by the end of the first day,' says Jacob. 'By the end of the week, the car was a wreck.'

But the app was eventually a winner. It got good reviews from the press and thousands of people downloaded and used it. The team was invited to Downing Street to explain how it worked to a group that included the UK prime minister. Indeed, the app had transformed the way Boston fixed its potholes. In the past, residents would have had to care enough to call and report potholes or the city would have had to send a crew out to look for them. This was inefficient. But along with Citizens Connect (which also allows users to manually report potholes), Street Bump helped Boston increase the proportion of pothole cases closed within two days from 48 per cent in February 2011 to 92 per cent by April 2014. Data from Street Bump also showed that sunk manhole covers were a bigger problem than potholes were, and the city ended up adjusting over 1,000 of these.

Trial and error

The MONUM team would have its fair share of failures, of course. Indeed, failing fast and early is part of the office's approach. For instance, a text version of Citizens Connect didn't work out the way the team had hoped. Other projects have had a less than impressive impact. Ed Glaeser, a professor of economics at Harvard University and an expert on cities, is sceptical, for instance, of Adopt a Hydrant, a programme which allows people to take responsibility for shovelling a hydrant clear after a snowstorm. For Glaeser, this programme requires 'a level of public spiritedness well beyond merely zapping in a complaint'.[7] Unsurprisingly, residents have been slow to take it up.

In launching MONUM, Mayor Menino had predicted that it would bring 'a wave of municipal innovation not seen since cities first brought water into people's homes'.[8] This claim now seems overblown. Some of MONUM's projects have been short-lived, and others appear gimmicky. Critics might regard getting citizens to register potholes and litter as unimportant, even futile, especially if the streets themselves are run down and infrastructure lacks investment. Jacob, however, believes that these small steps can build trust between the public and government, and create the foundation for tackling bigger issues.

Further, even though Citizens Connect, Discover BPS and Street Bump all involve technology, Jacob says that his team goes to 'great pains to separate innovation and technology' and ensure that 'innovation is about a better designed process or physical layout'. For Kris Carter, a great example of this is the housing work the team has been involved with for some time. A big issue here has been around the density of neighbourhoods: how the city can increase the volume of housing available by finding the minimum size of apartment that residents are comfortable with. Carter says that this was a hard conversation to have with any community. 'In the past, the city would have set up a series of community meetings where we would have said to residents: "We want to make apartments that are 380 square feet rather than 500 square feet, isn't that a great idea? Doing that will drive prices down hopefully, but we don't know.'"

In 2016, the team decided to go down a different route. 'Our take was, if we did have such a meeting, we would probably get the same twenty people who always show up to consultations like that. And some who came would probably oppose what we were proposing even without knowing what it was.' Instead, the first thing the team did was map out various square footages on a gym floor and then invite residents to try the space for themselves. 'People would stand in the space we had mapped out and try to imagine living in it. We would then ask them how it felt to them.'

But people still struggled to imagine what it would be like to actually *live* in such a space. 'They didn't really have a good feel for it,' says Carter. So the team went a step further and built a model house – an actual unit with the projected square footage – and put it on a trailer that could be driven around the city. 'We took the trailer to a dozen different neighbourhoods over three months and had people visit it like a showroom. They could pretend they were living there, having conversations, cooking something, or sleeping in the bedroom inside the space.' In this way, the team was able to broaden the conversation of what housing density would actually mean for citizens. They could observe the reactions of residents and draw insights about many different things. For instance, they soon learned that what they would have to do to keep millennials happy would have to be very different from what it would take to satisfy empty-nesters. They also discovered that residents, once they got into the space, quickly realised that it wasn't a tenement, and that it was both manageable and spacious.

Insights from the process then had a direct influence on policy enacted in the city, including moves that led to an increase in the minimum size of houses to be built in the future. 'A big question we ask ourselves', says Carter, 'is: how do we have better inter-actions with the citizens of Boston? Sometimes we have to use technology to do that. And sometimes we just have to build a model house.'

In this way, the team appears to have avoided the kind of criticism often levelled at innovation initiatives in cities elsewhere. For instance, the office has stayed lean, with only ten full-time staff in 2020, making good use of a regular flow of university fellows. MONUM's annual budget, says Jacob, has never exceeded $2 million, and much of that has come from philanthropic sources rather than public funds. For the most part, the city has been able to avoid the expensive fiascos that can occur when government bureaucracies procure technical solutions from corporate contractors.

The challenges of innovating in large organisations

To survive and prosper, all organisations need to be able to do two very different kinds of things: first, keep doing what they are doing now (namely, 'business as usual'); and second, change and improve (namely, 'innovation'). In the private sector, the pressures of competition are so intense that companies pay a lot of attention to how they organise for change and spend a great deal of money on it. Large firms typically have entire divisions that exclusively focus on innovation: on coming up with new things or improved ways of doing what they currently do. Many spend billions on such research and development. But doing the new while conducting business as usual is hard. Some experts describe this as like trying to change the tyres on a Formula 1 car while it is in the middle of a race. Others compare the process to refuelling a jet while it is in mid-air. The main body of the organisation cannot afford to slow down or halt business as usual while it experiments with the new.

Moreover, firms now also face pressures to change the way they change: they are innovating the very process of innovation. For much of the twentieth century, innovation used to be a long-term, structured, expensive process dominated by large companies with huge resources. The twenty-first century has, however, seen the rise of 'lean start-ups': agile firms with small teams that use ubiquitous technology in clever ways to get ahead of century-old behemoths. We can see this in sectors ranging from publishing to music, retail to travel, and transport to education. In this context, the big question for large organisations with significant current operations, products and customers is how, even while delivering in the present, to develop an engine for change that is constantly preparing for the future. This is a question to which many companies are applying themselves. And that is the very same challenge now preoccupying governments.

Government organisations may have a monopoly on what they do, but they too face pressures to change: to do new things and get better at what they already do. Governments also typically face serious constraints in terms of money, time and personnel. Indeed, one could argue that this has always been the case; that governments have always felt the pressure to reform. The city of Boston, for instance, has been at the forefront of change since 1799 when it created the first health department and carried out the first controlled experiments for a smallpox vaccine. Then again, in the mid-nineteenth century, Bostonians formed the American Association for the Promotion of Social Science, which pushed for free public libraries in their city and elsewhere. In due course, Boston would become the first city in the US to have a police department and a subway. So, governments have always had to reform. What is different today is the speed of change and the terminology used to describe it. In the twenty-first century, the clamour for reform has been replaced by the quest for innovation as a means to reinvent government. And linked to innovation in government are two broad approaches that often involve digital technology and the use of data.

The first is the 'smart city' model. Typically centralised and top down, it involves governments contracting with technology companies to wire up cities to monitor and automate the environment. A pioneer of this approach was South Korea which, in 2000, partnered with Cisco to build a smart city in Songdo, a new development on land reclaimed from the Yellow Sea. Computers were embedded in the buildings and streets and there were two-way screens everywhere. Residents could video-conference neighbours, control lighting and heating through control panels, and attend classes remotely. Data on traffic flow and energy was collected through ubiquitous sensors and used to notify citizens when a bus would arrive or alert the authorities when a crime had taken place.

A second, very different approach is the 'civic-hack' model. Typically decentralised and citizen-led, it involves governments using new technologies to facilitate 'self-help among citizens' and encourage 'community-reliance, rather than reliance on the state'.[9]

The MONUM approach is closer to the latter than the former. 'We are a civic innovation lab,' says Jacob, 'meaning that our job is to run experiments that push the envelope in terms of how services are delivered to residents.' Increasingly, those experiments are not high-tech. Moreover, MONUM has gone further than most governments by bringing the locus of innovation in-house rather than keeping it outside government in large corporations or citizens' groups. Doing this has meant that Boston can go beyond merely finding a mechanism and engine for innovation. It can actually tackle head-on some of the endemic impediments to systematic change that all organisations, but especially government bureaucracies, face. What MONUM has tried to do, in fact, is create an embedded culture of innovation to push against the inertia, risk aversion and distraction that afflict government bureaucracies everywhere.

A culture of innovation

In the private sector, firms have devised ever more ingenious ways to overcome these impediments and innovate even while conducting business as usual. In the jargon of organisation theory, firms have learned to be 'ambidextrous': to thrive in the present – by serving current customers with current products and services – even as they research new customers and technology, and test and deliver new products and ways of working. Many firms have created entirely new units – 'skunk works' – to emulate the agility of start-ups against which they increasingly compete. Freed from the bureaucracy and inertia of the parent organisation, and from the day-to-day pressures of serving current customers with current products, these lean units can focus entirely on identifying, testing and taking new ideas forward. Even Google succumbed to this trend when, in 2015, the top management split the company into two arms: Google (which focuses on the current business of search and advertising) and Alphabet (which focuses on riskier experiments – 'moonshots' – such as self-driving cars and the applications of AI to healthcare). Interestingly, the city of Boston and MONUM got there a full five years before Google.

One of the systematic problems that MONUM attempts to solve is the issue of risk. Government is traditionally cautious, but new ideas and new ways of doing things involve jeopardy. As Jacob puts it: 'Government's traditional response to dealing with risk is bureaucracy. Bureaucracy is designed to subject change, and any new idea, to a million tests and to slow the whole process down.' Governments are built to be deliberate for good reasons; in order to be accountable, they are slow and transparent. But this has repercussions. 'It means we can't typically be as responsive as our citizens want us to be,' says Jacob. And citizens are increasingly impatient. 'They can't understand why City Hall is so slow when the companies they do business with aren't.'

A big part of MONUM's job is to de-risk change so government can move fast. The unit acts as a 'risk aggregation function'.

When a particular government department, such as transportation or housing, wants to explore a new idea or approach, it will probably hesitate to do so if left to its own devices. It will hesitate to dedicate people or budgets to the new idea because it rightly worries about what will happen if the new idea fails. What if it makes the front page of the news? MONUM absorbs that risk. The unit also takes on the hassle of trying something new: it provides the personnel, the funding and the focus. Trying new things is its exclusive role. 'We don't run transport or schools, so, if we try something and it doesn't work, the lights don't go out. And we are able to learn why it does or doesn't work,' says Jacob.

Then there is the question of trust. Even if MONUM finds that something works in a trial, the team still has to convince the relevant government department to take it on and roll it out. The question then becomes: how to gain the trust of government employees, many of whom are taught to avoid risk? 'If departments don't trust you,' says Jacob, 'they're not going to listen to anything you say. You have to create the cultural context for this type of work, which is linked to building risk tolerance in government.'

This leads to the question of incentives. Departments may worry about having their name attached to something that might fail. Here, again, MONUM works to take the sting out of failure. 'If a new project tried by a department doesn't work, we try to absorb as much of the bad news as possible, so they can push all the negative publicity our way. If it does work, however, we try to give as much credit to these departments as possible.'[10]

Good news is spread out to other departments but also up to the mayor's office. 'We need to be smart enough to do those things that the mayor cares about,' says Jacob. 'If we're doing a project and the mayor has no idea what to say about it, that would not be good. We provide a steady stream of news for the mayor to report to the press. Those successes then buy us leeway for other things that may not succeed.'

What happens, then, when the mayor changes? Continuity is a problem that blights all organisations, including corporations. But governments may be particularly prone to this problem. Political leaders typically have limited terms. Even the legendary Tom Menino's five-time tenure came to an end eventually. When it did, with his death in 2014, it was far from guaranteed that MONUM would survive the transition. But giving the citizens of Boston solutions that they wanted had helped MONUM's cause. Between winning the election and then taking office in 2014, the new mayor Marty Walsh ran a series of community meetings with the residents of Boston. In these meetings, he asked which programmes he should keep and which he should kill. At each of these meetings, residents said he should not only keep MONUM but even consider expanding the programme. Immediately after his final meeting with residents, Walsh called the MONUM team and said, as Jacob tells it: 'I don't know who you are and what you do, but enough people have said that I should give you the runway to demonstrate your value, that I plan to do exactly that.'

Another key issue is leadership and the right personnel. Technologies like artificial intelligence and block chain promise to revolutionise how governments serve their people and do better with less. For instance, Sir Mark Walport, the UK's chief scientific adviser from 2013 to 2017, has argued that such technologies have the 'potential to redefine the relationship between government and the citizen in terms of data sharing, transparency and trust and make a leading contribution to the government's digital transformation plan'.[11] But these technologies, Walport also warns, create challenges, such as the need for the right kind of leadership and personnel.

In terms of leadership, many key decision-makers in government are typically at the top of the tree, only a few years from retirement. The sort of change they need to make is huge and takes time and effort. The tendency at the end of one's career is to kick the can down the road and leave the hard work to the next generation.

The technical capabilities of public servants are a further impediment. Many are not trained in technical subjects or engineering or design. And exacerbating this is the natural preference among those who choose to work in government to avoid risk and play it safe. To deal with these issues, MONUM actively hires people who are comfortable working within the rules that civil servants must follow, but who also have an entrepreneurial streak and are willing to push against limits. 'We try to hire hustlers,' says Jacob. 'We want people who are comfortable navigating big bureaucracies, but are still creative.'

Kris Carter says that other, softer skills are also relevant, such as the ability to communicate and tell a story about why change is needed. 'In Boston, we have a number of programmes going on at any given time. We don't just communicate that at work, but also through formal channels and the press. We need to put out stories to increase morale or communicate a specific strategy.' To do all that, MONUM needs a toolkit of communication. To push for change, people have to see change. And this means being able to tell stories. When new members join the team, they bring new skills with them in, say, writing or social media. 'I myself', says Carter, 'have experience making films and have found ways to use that skill to meet the needs of the team and the city.'

MONUM also recognises the need to identify 'hustlers' *elsewhere* in government. Accordingly, the team actively seeks out innovators and champions – early adopters of new ideas – across government departments in Boston. 'There are a small number of innovators', says Jacob, 'spread between departments that help us subvert bureaucracy. After all: bureaucracy is just people.'[12]

But MONUM doesn't stop there. The office also engages citizens themselves as champions and ambassadors of its solutions. The Citizens Connect app, for instance, relies on residents reporting problems to city officials: citizens are therefore at the very heart of the service. The Boston Saves programme, which gives children in nurseries $50 savings accounts to get them to save for university, was built in partnership with family members who, in turn, became champions of the idea. MONUM brought in members of the community to co-pilot and co-own the programme from the start. This got people talking about Boston Saves, and helped build trust with families.

Innovation at other levels of government

Since 2010, other cities have followed Boston in setting up innovation units to drive change within government. The idea is to bring an entrepreneurial spirit to bear on public problems and provide a structure for the messy business of experimenting with new ways of doing things. In 2012, for instance, Philadelphia started its own version of such an office. In 2014, a similar university-based collaborative was launched in Utah Valley. Such initiatives in the US have typically gained impetus from philanthropic money such as that provided by the Bloomberg Foundation. In Europe, meanwhile, the EU has pumped money into similar initiatives across its cities.

These initiatives at the level of cities have been matched or even preceded by similar developments at other levels of government. In the US, the Obama administration introduced several such federal-level programmes, some of which have been continued by the Trump administration. But Jacob says that these efforts tend to stop at the use of digital technology, even though there is considerable potential for innovation that goes beyond technology, as MONUM has shown.

North of the border, Canada's Treasury Board – the federal agency that reviews and approves government spending – set up the Innovation and Policy Services Branch in 2018 to be a special unit that focuses on innovation within the central government. Aleeya Velji, an analyst in the team, describes the unit as a start-up within government created by senior bureaucrats 'who understand that change needs to happen'.[13] To make that change happen, these leaders realised that they had to leave the Treasury Board itself – the helm of where policy is created – and create a new unit elsewhere. They chose the Canada School of Public Service, a branch of the federal government that was traditionally tasked with creating relevant intelligence and competency within the federal government.

Driven by leadership at the deputy minister level, the new branch has more leeway and space to drive systemic change. It also has several different sub-divisions, including a digital academy focused on capacity building, a research division, and a group that focuses on the applications of artificial intelligence. For senior leaders, the new branch is a way to infuse innovation as a core competency within the government at a high level: to 'rewire the brain of the organisation' and 'create the practical tools that people need to change'.

'People in government', says Velji, 'have grown up in a particular way. They tend to start young and stick with it. They need to be trained in how to be entrepreneurial.' The hope is that these new attitudes and capabilities will filter down to the various departments and functional communities within government. 'Analysts, grant writers, people in the passport office: each of these groups', says Velji, 'should be able to tailor this new mindset to their own situation. Given that their work is different, their specific innovations are also likely to differ.'

But the challenges of driving innovation in government at the federal level are considerable. Velji, who has been involved with innovation at three different levels of government – municipal, provincial and federal – has the experience to bear this out. 'At the federal level,' she says, 'government is so big and so remote from ordinary people that change from outside forces is hard to pull off. Unlike at the municipal or even the provincial level, external voices are rarely heard and find it harder to influence anything. So, change at the federal level must come from within.'

Velji points out that federal government is typically good at creating incentives, for instance, providing federal-level spending to stimulate others, such as social enterprises, to innovate. 'Most of the federal government's work is about distributing money to communities that can then go ahead and do the social innovation work.' But to accomplish things that are more hands-on is hard.

'As your scale gets bigger,' says Velji, 'and your money grows, it also becomes exponentially harder to make change because you move further away from people.' The federal government of Canada employs about 250,000 people and serves citizens around the country by distributing money through different channels, but it doesn't typically 'see' these people. To transform such a big, rambling organisation requires attracting the right talent and transforming the mindsets of those who already work in it: for example, to get them to work in more 'agile' or 'lean' ways. But the system is so structured, says Velji, so rigid in its initial design, that even though it logically makes sense to go from a pyramid to a horizontal, agile structure, such change is hard to make happen. 'Each department or ministry is like a business on its own, so scaling new services or approaches across several of these different departments is difficult.'

In the private sector, says Velji, even large, multi-division conglomerates have a single CEO who provides alignment and ensures that all divisions head in the same direction. The same alignment does not exist across the federal government. 'You work for your deputy or your minister,' says Velji. 'Those ministers will have competing interests and each department will have its own priorities. So the departments tend to remain microcosms of innovation.' Moreover, the rigid, hierarchical structures make many federal activities hard to reform: procurement and human resource processes operate in a system where different constituent elements do not fully align. And so, at the federal level, the government is frequently stuck, as it finds translating policy into practice hard to pull off. As a result, a lot of high-level innovation becomes more about transforming the organisation than about changing how services are provided.

Nigel Jacob of MONUM agrees. According to him, cities are better placed than states or federal governments to introduce new services and new ways of engaging with citizens. 'The challenge at the state or federal level is that those governments don't have customers. We in Boston have 650,000 residents who on any day can get in touch with us about what we should do and how.' Citizens don't access federal government services in same way. The main 'customers' of those who work for the central government are other departments. There is no direct connection with ordinary people and no 'tight feedback loops' with citizens. 'At the local government level,' says Jacob, 'we can understand the value of what we're doing better than the federal government can.'

Changing the DNA of government is hard

In Canada, the Policy and Innovation Branch where Velji works is trying out different approaches to transform the federal government from within. On a corporate level, the branch sends people on training courses, and brings external organisations in to show government employees what innovation looks like. 'The School of Public Service', says Velji, 'brings in social entrepreneurs and tech start-ups to help us learn. We make a concerted effort to go out to organisations that are fostering that creativity.'

In all this, the role of the leadership is key. Government hierarchy determines what employees can see and navigate, and so it is necessary for leaders to help their people find a balance between following the rules and being creative. Often, Velji feels, the top and bottom layers of the federal government 'get it', but there is a middle 'clayey' layer that's hard to shift. 'Your team', she says, 'is key: the people you have around you and who you can take along with you. And the support you get from your boss.' Thanks to such leaders and teams, there are a number of small spaces where innovation is happening. 'Micro actors are making change,' says Velji, 'but changing the DNA of the system is harder.'

This is where the real challenge for federal governments lies. How is it possible to change a large, rigid structure that has worked in a hierarchical, cautious way for so long? Moreover, how can these sprawling structures not only work out how to change the game in theory but also bring about this change in practice? 'We see plenty of modifications to the current system,' says Velji, 'but we really haven't changed the financial organisation or how we leverage money and resources in a different way. Civil servants should be asking those questions, because that's what they are meant to do. But because the world is moving so fast, they are not able to keep up.'

Sometimes, it might take a sudden external shock to the system to bring about such change. For instance, a threat like the Covid-19 pandemic, with the potential to upend the foundations of a society and economy, can have a galvanising effect on the government. As *The Economist* argues, the pandemic, like war, seems to have forced 'innovation on a scale and at a pace that no government would normally contemplate. Across the public sector, what was previously unthinkable is happening', resulting in an 'overhaul of decades or even centuries of procedures and habits'.[14] As one UK Treasury official put it, his department quickly switched from being one that 'looks for reasons to say no, to one that looks for ways to make things work'.

Meanwhile in Greece, despite a decade-long debt crisis that weakened the economy and health system, the government managed the pandemic with competence and efficiency. It emphasised science over politics and adopted a managerial approach that the prime minister, Kyriakos Mitsotakis, described as relying on 'state-sensitivity, coordination, resolve and swiftness'.[15] Importantly, the pandemic acted as a catalyst for innovation. As the country went into lockdown, the government pushed through digital reforms to both protect citizens' health and modernise the state. 'When the pandemic broke, the need to simplify government processes became paramount,' says Kyriakos Pierrakakis, the minister of digital governance. 'One of the first things we did to limit the incentives for people to exit their homes was to enable them to receive prescriptions on their phones. That, alone, has saved 250,000 citizens from making visits to the doctor in the space of 20 days.'[16] Further, official documents that used to require showing up at government offices and grappling with labyrinthine bureaucracy were made available online, saving Greeks thousands of daily trips and wasted hours. 'By changing the nature of the interaction of citizens with the state,' says Pierrakakis, 'our hope is that ultimately public trust in institutions will be further regained.'

In Greece, as in the UK, however, the question remains: is such change merely temporary or is it systemic, and can it last long after the crisis has passed? How can a government embed a culture of innovation deep into its institutions and ways of working and can this be done even when resources are scarce?

The case of Bangladesh

Some countries have attempted to leapfrog the West in driving a culture of innovation at all levels of government. An example is Bangladesh which in 2007 launched the Access to Information (a2i) Programme with the support of the United Nations Development Programme (UNDP). Implemented within the Prime Minister's Office, the objective was to build a digital nation that delivered services to the citizen's doorstep. The delivery of public services would be decentralised, leading to wider access and improved quality, responsiveness and transparency. The programme aimed to achieve these objectives in four ways. First, it would use mobile and internet delivery of public services to reduce the cost to citizens and the distance they had to travel, while reducing the corruption they encountered along the way. Second, it would develop the skills and capacity of the service providers through training courses for government officials. Third, it would promote innovation in public service delivery via Service Innovation Centres that identified, supported and designed innovative solutions closer to citizens. Finally, it would create a supportive culture and environment for service delivery in government.

Anir Chowdhury, who heads the programme, has been involved with it since almost the beginning. A native of Bangladesh, Chowdhury had spent nearly two decades in the US before moving back in the early 2000s. 'In the US,' he says, 'I had focused on the ICT industry and built two tech companies from scratch in the Boston area. Then, through a set of happy coincidences I made the transition back to Bangladesh.'[17]

Between 1998 and 2002, Chowdhury had volunteered in the US with Tech Bangla, an NGO designed to involve expatriate Bangladeshis in creating a technological ecosystem in their homeland. The idea was inspired by the way in which 'non-resident' Indians had made Bangalore a tech hub in the 1990s. It soon became clear to Chowdhury that if he was serious about this objective he would have to quit his cushy life in Boston and spend more time in Bangladesh. This led him to cast around for opportunities that would allow this. In 2002, driven by family considerations, he decided to focus on education, and move away from tech per se. With his mother, a university lecturer, he started an NGO to develop educational content for secondary schools in Bangladesh. While working on the NGO, he had a further revelation: at the rate he was making progress on his own, it would be several years before he would be able to achieve the scale needed to make a real impact in the education sector in Bangladesh. Even a partnership with BRAC, the country's largest NGO (see pages 129–30), might at best accelerate his growth, but would ultimately be insufficient to achieve significant change. It was increasingly clear that it would be necessary to work with the government. 'Without the backing of the state,' says Chowdhury, 'especially in a country like Bangladesh, impact isn't really possible.' Soon afterwards, Chowdhury signed up with the UNDP programme to run workshops designed to change the mindset and approach of senior civil servants in Bangladesh.

Access to information

In 2006, when the a2i programme began, there was a belief in government that digitisation held many potential benefits for citizens. Accordingly, the programme started out as a classic e-governance project. The UNDP support and funding acted as an initial catalyst for the digitisation drive, and the decision was taken to locate the team in the Prime Minister's Office.

'By 2007,' says Chowdhury, 'there had been a number of roundtable discussions. Members of the team had made many presentations. But it was all very much a top-down view.'

The team had developed vision documents for various sectors: health, education, agriculture, civil administration and local government. The belief was that these were the key sectors that could be transformed with technology. Much of the preliminary work involved scanning and reporting on what was already being done in Bangladesh at that time, and using this understanding to make projections for the future. 'We soon realised', says Chowdhury, 'that what we had was no more than a clutch of documents. We had no action plans and little or no buy-in from government at large.'

A glaring omission in all the initial plans was the citizen. This changed in April 2008 when the prime minister in the caretaker government of the time asked the a2i team the critical question: what are you doing for the citizen? None of the plans until then had a description of how change would take place from the citizen's point of view. The plans for agriculture, for instance, failed to account for the farmer. In education, the plans lacked a view on the process by which pupils came to school or entered tertiary education: what were the skills they needed to get a job or navigate life? Similarly, in health, there was no clear understanding of how patients viewed the way the health system was serving them. 'All our plans', says Chowdhury, 'had been supply-centric, from the point of view of government.'

To correct this, the team began a series of workshops with the most senior bureaucrats in the government. In the first round, a small team from a2i met for an hour or so with four to five senior leaders and guided them towards identifying one idea for change ('a quick win') that digitisation could bring about within their departments from the perspective of citizens. These conversations led in turn to larger workshops involving all fifty-three secretaries who headed the various ministries. These secretaries had, over their careers, moved across departments and so had wide experience of how government worked. But it had been some time since they had worked in the field in direct contact with citizens. So the workshops also brought in junior officers who still worked in the field at lower levels of government. The input of these junior officers helped remind the senior ones what government felt like from the perspective of citizens. In the workshops, the senior and junior civil servants worked in a collegial atmosphere to critique the ideas they had come up with in the previous round. 'The emphasis at these workshops', says Chowdhury, 'was on honest, constructive criticism. There was a high level of camaraderie. Attendees had the confidence to be sincere in their views and feedback.' The main focus throughout was on solving the problems of citizens rather than the problems of government. At the end of the process, each secretary had a single refined idea to take forward within their ministry, leading to fifty-three quick wins across government. The next step was to take these ideas forward and launch them. Working with the ministries involved, a2i eventually oversaw the launch of twenty ideas. Some of the other ideas had failed to make the grade, but in the process, important lessons had been learned, the most significant of which was the importance of collaboration across different levels of government.

Digital Bangladesh

At the end of 2008, soon after it won the general elections, the Awami League, one of the nation's two leading national parties, launched Digital Bangladesh: a flagship programme that it had outlined in its manifesto. This provided the political backing for change at the highest levels. Soon after the new government was formed, Chowdhury made a presentation to Sheikh Hasina, the prime minister, on how the a2i team would deliver Digital Bangladesh. In it, he fleshed out both the vision for the programme as well as its actual implementation. He explained how it would build on the fifty-three quick wins already identified across government as well as another 200 that had been identified in a subsequent phase.

This plan prepared the ground for the next few years for a2i. In 2009–10, the team worked on two things. First, even though the focus was on delivering digital services, the harsh reality was that the internet was still not widely available in Bangladesh. Penetration in the country at that time was a mere 1 per cent. But even if access could be provided, there was the issue of who would provide the services to citizens on a digital platform. To address this issue, the team took the radical decision to involve local, private entrepreneurs in selling public services from digital service centres to citizens for a fee. At first the idea was resisted by the bureaucracy. But it had the prime minister's support, and her son, who had a background in the private sector, believed that marrying private sector incentive with a public service ethos had the potential to work. Eventually the civil service came on board.

In 2010, a2i went country-wide with this new approach. The World Bank earmarked $50 million for the project, with support from the Prime Minister's Office and the cabinet. The money was spent on setting up over 400 digital service centres in towns and villages across the country. These would act as one-stop shops for services that brought the entire government together. Public–private partnerships (PPP) had previously been carried out at the macro, national level, typically on big infrastructure projects. Now a2i was seeking to extend the approach to the micro, village level.

The entrepreneurs in most cases were ordinary folk from the countryside. These 'jobs' did not come with salaries. Instead, the entrepreneurs would earn an income from the fees they charged and run their centres like micro-businesses: they would engage in their own promotion, marketing and accounting. They would receive permission to provide certain government services such as birth and death certificates, land records and exam results, and could rent a room in local government offices. But that was all the support they could expect from the state.

'This was PPP to achieve the last mile integration of government services through digitisation,' says Chowdhury. Creating these centres brought private citizens in as agents of change as well as beneficiaries, providing them with employment and a social safety net in the process. It also reduced the distance between officialdom and the citizen. Importantly, while programmes of this sort can sometimes be a recipe for corruption, this programme actually increased transparency and cut down on corruption. It did so through the use of market prices regulated by competition and through the presence of an electronic paper trail. Crucially, if citizens complained of irregularities, the third-party providers could lose their license to operate.

Overall, the programme improved service delivery to citizens and increased the credibility of government on the whole. As a sign of its success, by 2020, there were over 5,000 such centres throughout the country, offering over 150 services – 70 public and 80 private – to between 5 and 6 million citizens per month, and employing over 25,000 local entrepreneurs.

Building an innovation framework for government

To support these front-end digital services in 2010, a2i needed to build the back-end systems. At that time, digitisation was still a foreign, scary thing for most civil servants. It had the potential to challenge the very foundations of the control and power they had enjoyed for decades. In one fell swoop, it might cause much of the power they had always enjoyed to drain away.

The task before a2i therefore became the creation of a framework that would assuage the fears of the bureaucracy and motivate the relevant government agencies and their leaders. In building this framework, the vocabulary they used would prove crucial. Chowdhury had already learned how important it was for him and his team to adapt business terminology to suit the government. For instance, they had noticed that civil servants did not like the term 'business process re-engineering'; so this became 'service process simplification'. 'E-governance' was renamed 'service at the doorstep'. And 'corruption' and 'transparency' were reincarnated as 'time, cost, and visits' (TCV), from the citizen's perspective.

A further source of inspiration for the framework came in 2013 when Chowdhury read *Drive* by Dan Pink. In the book, Pink argued that human motivation, particularly in organisations, was driven by three things: purpose, autonomy and mastery.[18] Impressed by this argument, Chowdhury began to think about how to adapt these ideas to government. First, he thought about what might constitute *purpose* in government. Through conversations with his team and various civil servants, Chowdhury came to the conclusion that purpose in government had to be a shared credo: something that was so simple and compelling that civil servants could quickly and easily explain it to one another and citizens alike. In time, a2i settled on the government's overarching purpose as being the reduction in TCV for citizens as they accessed government services. The term soon became a byword for civil servants across the bureaucracy. The cabinet secretary began to review progress across the entire government based on how individual departments had reduced TCV for the services they offered, a practice that continues to this day. Citizens were at the heart of all this. When someone applied for a birth certificate or a pension, the question for the relevant department became: how much time does that citizen have to wait, how much money do they have to spend, and how many visits do they have to make to get the service they need? This clear, shared, citizen-centric purpose not only generated huge political support but it also motivated the bureaucracy to do their work better. Moreover, it was suited to measuring, tracing and recognising progress, and helped with the granting of awards to particularly successful departments and personnel.

Second came autonomy. Chowdhury and his team had realised that civil servants could achieve a lot if they were given some space to experiment. 'We knew that if we allowed our people to try things they had not tried before – things they might even have considered outside the rules – then they would come up with solutions that were interesting and made a difference. Provided, of course, they kept the overarching purpose in mind.'

In time, Chowdhury and the a2i team would encounter people across government who were particularly responsive to such autonomy. 'A number of people rose to the challenge and proved really entrepreneurial. We called them "govpreneurs". They were willing to take risks, not in the pursuit of profit, of course, but because they were focused on minimising TCV.'

a2i provided civil servants with a licence to experiment and fail that came directly from the prime minister and the Cabinet Office. If they failed, there were no negative consequences to their actions. If they succeeded, a2i would put their interventions through a quality control process and scale them up. 'Left to their own devices, these entrepreneurs were unlikely to be able to go beyond their sphere of influence. Most might only be able to operate within their *upazila* or district.' But Bangladesh has sixty-four districts or *zilas* and nearly 500 sub-districts or *upazilas*. Typically, administrators only have influence over their *upazillas*. Even the sixty-four district administrators can only bring about change within their districts. 'Letting them experiment within their sphere,' says Chowdhury, 'and then taking their tested ideas and scaling them up nationally with the help of the appropriate central ministry – agriculture or education – resulted in a lot of interesting stuff happening across the government as a whole.'

The final element of the a2i framework was what Dan Pink termed 'mastery'. Seeing that the word did not mean much to civil servants, a2i redubbed it 'capacity'. Over time, the team would work to develop many capacities across the government. To do so, it adopted two approaches: training and platforms.

Training

The most successful a2i training programme to date has been one that improves civil servants' capacity to redesign public services by building their empathy for citizens. To create the programme, a2i drew on materials developed by NESTA, a UK public policy think tank, and Stanford University's Design School. The a2i team simplified and customised these materials to suit their context and translated everything into Bengali.

Empathy training has proved popular and powerful. Over five days, a variety of public servants – doctors, teachers, public officials – are put through various experiential learning and reflection exercises that help them place themselves in the shoes of citizens in order to rethink the design of the services they offer. On the first day, participants are taught the basic principles of design thinking and given time to practise using the relevant tools and approaches. On the second day, they are given a chance to apply these tools in a live setting. The objective is to get them to understand what might be wrong with the delivery of a particular public service from the citizen's perspective.

In the first iteration of the programme, the team sent participants back to their own place of work to observe and reflect on how services were delivered there. Thus, doctors went sent back to their hospitals, teachers to their schools, and land officers to the land office in their sub-district. But this approach didn't prove too successful. 'We realised that our people needed to learn how to observe and develop a critical eye. Habit had made them immune to seeing things differently in their own place of work. We wondered if it might be better instead for them to go, not to their own offices, but to someone else's place of work.' So, in the second iteration of the programme, on day two, doctors were sent to the land office, teachers to the hospital, and so on. Now everyone was truly on par with the ordinary citizen. When a doctor went to obtain a land record, he had no clue how the process worked. He had to stand in line just like everybody else and work things out for himself. The a2i team made sure he didn't call and ask a friend for help.

After being placed on a par with the ordinary citizen, trainees return to the training venue at the end of the second day for a period of reflection. Many come back with scathing views about what is wrong with the service they were involved with obtaining. Armed with the tools from day one, and their direct evidence from day two, the doctors, for instance, see plenty that is wrong with the land office (even while in an earlier iteration they had been unable to find fault with their own hospital).

On the third day, delegates are sent to their own place of work: doctors to their hospitals, land officers to the land office, and so on. Having seen someone else's place of work, and heard from someone else about their own office, the scales tend to fall from their eyes and they are able to observe things afresh. The period of reflection that follows at the end of the third day is typically emotionally charged. 'During the reflection period,' says Chowdhury, 'some people cry, while others say: "I don't know how I have not been able to see all this even though I've been in my outfit for ten years." This is hugely moving.'

On the fourth and fifth days, based on their experiences and insights from the previous days, the participants develop a prototype for a new design or solution. They are then taught how to pitch their ideas to a panel, how to garner support for it, and how to bid for and raise funds for their scheme.

'It is a rapidly moving five days,' says Chowdhury. 'We cover a lot of stuff.' Twenty-five per cent of those who attend these training sessions start something new when they go back to work. Somewhat less than 25 per cent are able to actually see their new initiative through. A full 75 per cent completely drop out. When they go back, they do not take any action, or lead any sort of change whatsoever.

But a2i's work is far from done. The final step is to take the prototype interventions of those who do start something new and roll them out nationally. This involves bringing in the relevant ministries and getting them to introduce the interventions across the country. There follows a six- to nine-month period of execution. In the end, if all goes well, a2i hosts a celebratory event which brings together all the successful teams with the relevant ministers and secretaries. During the event, the senior officials walk round the room while the 'govpreneurs' explain their vision, how they came up with their ideas, and how they are being taken forward across the country.

Some of these interventions, says Chowdhury, are very person dependent. When the officials behind the idea move on through promotion, transfer or retirement, institutionalising their innovations is hard. 'We have not been able to solve this. We need to know how the change happened and why the particular institution where the idea was first tried out didn't take it forward,' he says. A further challenge is taking the new idea countrywide. Doing so often requires a totally different mindset, a different set of people, and an entirely new process of funding the project and improving it. In the process of adaptation, a lot of the zeal that made the innovation happen in the first place melts away. The project becomes run of the mill. Now, more often than not, it needs collaboration of a new kind. Sometimes this might involve public–private partnership, but it almost always needs to be taken through a standard government process. All this often only serves to kill it.

Out of the nearly 1,800 pilots the a2i process has identified and run, only about 40 to 50 have been scaled up. The team has a large amount of data on these projects. It is now analysing these data to understand better the profile of people who can make change happen, who can drive scaling, and how the people who come up with the innovation differ from those who can scale it up.

Platforms and digital Lego for government

A second aspect of building capacity for change across the government involves the creation of enabling platforms. These platforms, often digital in nature, act as a breeding ground for new ideas. Govpreneurs can use them to try out a redesigned service, get feedback on it, improve it and encourage its adoption by others. These digital platforms can also involve others, such as the local entrepreneurs in the digital service centres. Indeed, in many cases, it is easier for the local entrepreneurs to make change happen than it is for officials within the government. Government officials can often be unsupportive of change. For instance, district administrators who are asked to change the process of accessing land records are very likely to say: 'We're not authorised to do that.'

But entrepreneurs are unlikely to feel so constrained. They are likely to be more eager to support change and say: 'We'll take it!' Indeed, such platforms give them a place to express their innate eagerness for change.

The a2i team's use of digital platforms has matured over time. In 2010, when it launched a district portal, it didn't have much of the technical infrastructure required. Nevertheless, as Chowdhury explains, the portal served as the 'first peg on which to hang a digital space'. Since 2010, however, portal frameworks have matured worldwide, helping the team realise its Digital Bangladesh ambitions. But to do so, a2i has had to look at what others have done, and then develop its own model, often through experimentation. For instance, the idea of public digital service first came out of the UK's Government Digital Service, a unit that was formed in 2011 to transform the provision of online public services there. 'We found a lot of synergy with the UK,' says Chowdhury, 'and also with the US government's United States Digital Service, an elite technology unit within the Executive Office of the President.'

Over time, the a2i team has built several different modules for the digital platform to perform different tasks. For instance, the team built a specific module for the verification of national identity. 'You could think of this', says Chowdhury, 'as being the way that Lego works: little units that you bring together to create your new service, and prototype stuff. These modules act as the building blocks for the different ministries. Every ministry comes up with its own building blocks and modules that together add to the overall digital platform.'

A different approach to the use of digital platforms has involved bringing public servants together to learn from each other. The Teachers' Portal, for instance, is a Facebook-based platform created in 2011 for teachers in government schools across Bangladesh. Starting with just twenty-three teachers from seven schools, the portal had over 400,000 teachers by 2020. No one curates the platform or the content on it. It is entirely run by teachers for teachers: they share digital content with each other with a focus on what their students need. The platform also uses 'gamification' to bring about change: teachers play games and are rewarded based on their scores. These scores might then be used to choose the best teacher of the week or even of the year.

Another variant was a Facebook page specifically for civil servants. At its peak, the page had over 10,000 bureaucrats posting their stories, leading to shared learning and providing the basis for rewards and recognition. For Ishtiaque Hussain, the head of exploration and innovation strategy at a2i, the webpage was an important part of the drive to create a culture of innovation in government. 'We wanted to create ownership and champions for change within government, from the rank and file all the way up to cabinet secretary and the prime minister herself. We wanted to say publicly to all our people: "Go out and learn, failure is OK, make change possible." But how do you spread that message throughout government, down to the grassroots?'[19]

The team decided to use Facebook rather than other platforms like Twitter because, according to Hussain: 'Facebook equals the internet in Bangladesh.' To run the webpage, a2i hired Manik Mahmud who came from the development sector and had a background in participatory activism. Mahmud was trained in social methodology and knew how to create excitement and a sense of ownership among the members online. 'Manik', says Hussain, 'used Facebook like a surgeon uses his instruments. He was clinical in spreading the culture of innovation. He knew how to provoke those who were inactive and encourage those who were active.'[20]

In its first three years, the portal was a success. There was constant activity on it, with people posting stories and others 'liking' them and suggesting further ideas. But then there was a boomerang effect, as the portal's early success worked against it later. Hussain refers to the experience as the 'Facebook debacle'. 'The initiative championed by Manik', he says, 'showed great potential.

It enabled mentorship. It showed that people were doing interesting stuff and had passion at the grassroots. But then everything got out of hand.'[21] The members became so prolific that the webpage became impossible to manage in the systematic way in which the team had managed other initiatives. It began to generate jealousy and ill feeling. 'For every ten members who shared a story of what they had done,' says Hussain, 'there were ninety others who were liable to get resentful.'

The question then became: how do you assess what people are saying in an unbiased and objective way? How do you objectively compare stories and use them to decide who should be civil servant of the month? Unable to find satisfactory answers to these questions, the a2i team eventually closed down the webpage four years after it had been launched.

Log frames and log jams

The Facebook story highlights just one of a whole set of challenges faced by the a2i team in driving a culture of innovation within the Bangladeshi government. Perhaps the most persistent and deep-seated challenge is that all new development interventions in Bangladesh inevitably come up against the 'log frame' approach to decision-making in the state. The log frame, Hussain explains, is a tool used for improving the planning, implementation, management, monitoring and evaluation of projects. It provides a way of structuring the main elements of a project and highlighting the logical linkages between them.

The use of the log frame approach is typically driven by the need to meet the requirements of donors or the legal obligations that all governments are under to make the best use of public money. The approach helps address the need for accountability and provides an audit trail. But it also results in governments being suffused with rigid structures and linear processes that all officials have to follow: five-year plans that require a clear sense in advance of the likely inputs in terms of investment and outputs in terms of impact and return on investment.

Chowdhury and Hussain both believe that the approach is fundamentally at odds with the drive to innovate. Often, it acts as a straitjacket that, while it holds public officials to account, also constrains them to a rigid and time-consuming process. Whether in health, education, or law and order, such an approach forces officials to have a well-laid-out plan with a logical framing in advance of anything they actually do. 'It pushes you', says Hussain, 'to find a clear path to your destination, and lay out in advance all the steps you have to take with no uncertainty involved.' But what plan comes without uncertainty or shocks? 'Such a logical framework only works for an assembly line operation,' says Hussain. 'It doesn't help when you need to innovate, when circumstances are rapidly changing and you need to respond quickly and efficiently.'[22]

Chowdhury concurs. 'We are still stuck in the log frame. And this is a major reason why we are so often unable to come up with meaningful alternatives to how things are currently done.'

The key challenges that government therefore faces remain: how does one create a culture of innovation within a bureaucracy? How does one introduce continuous innovation in government? How can one measure innovation and develop metrics that objectively separate the good from the bad? 'Without such metrics,' says Chowdhury, 'any attempts to build an innovation culture will remain incomplete.'

Building a culture of innovation in government

The a2i experience in Bangladesh, alongside the initiatives in Boston and Canada, suggests that three ingredients are crucial to any attempt to build a culture of public service innovation. A first vital ingredient is the focus on citizens. For instance, the a2i team's emphasis shifted over the years from an initial focus on technology and e-governance to the creation of a government that was responsive to citizens and a civil service that knew what was needed to make that happen. Doing so meant creating a culture of innovation: one that helps the bureaucracy think differently, enables risk-taking and spreads a shared purpose that puts the citizens first.

A second ingredient is the need to form partnerships and be flexible and pragmatic. The a2i team, for instance, did not have a clear plan that was slavishly followed from the start. Rather, like successful start-ups, the team was flexible and learned over time how to respond to citizens' demands by partnering with the civil service and citizens themselves. Even the team itself reflects this diversity; it has hired people from three sectors: NGOs (who help bring in the citizen's perspective), bureaucrats (who know how to navigate the maze of government bureaucracy) and the private sector (which brings in a focus on metrics and results).

The final ingredient is the need for political support to drive change. Any attempt to bring about systemic change is likely to be stillborn without political will and support. This was true of MONUM in Boston and with the federal government's Innovation and Policy Services Branch in Canada. And it was also crucial to a2i's existence and success in Bangladesh. As Chowdhury puts it: 'In 2008–09, the Digital Bangladesh platform of the Awami League's manifesto provided that political agenda and momentum. Without it, we would not have been able to accomplish much. We might have created some innovation but taking it to scale and spreading it across government would have been hard.'

If political leadership is so important, then it is equally vital to be able to find and vote for the right political leaders. But how does one identify leaders who will pay attention to the need for change and support it? How does one then hold them to account and ensure that, once they are in government, they will be ever more responsive to the changing needs of citizens? Most importantly, what is the citizen's role in all this? We turn to these questions in the final chapter of this book.

10

How should citizens be?

'We get the leaders we vote for. We get the policies we
vote for. And when we don't vote, that's when we wind
up with government of, by and for other people.'

Michelle Obama

'Never doubt that a small group of thoughtful,
committed citizens can change the world; indeed, it's the
only thing that ever has.'

Margaret Mead

In July 2018, based on joint research, *The Atlantic* magazine and
the Public Religion Research Institute concluded that Americans
were 'living in two separate worlds'. In one world, the US was
headed in the wrong direction, with billionaires controlling politics, foreign governments interfering in elections, and not enough
people voting for change. In the other, things were looking up,
with a good president in office, but a broken media that was politically biased against their own candidates. Most Democrats lived
in the first world, while Republicans mostly populated the latter.
Thus, 82 per cent of Democrats versus 42 per cent of Republicans felt that the influence of money in politics was a big issue;
78 per cent of Democrats versus 58 per cent of Republicans said
low voter turnout was a problem; and 81 per cent of Republicans versus 41 per cent of Democrats said that media bias toward
certain political candidates was a major problem.[1] Further, many

respondents didn't care about the issues that journalists, scholars and officials considered important, suggesting a gap between the elites and everyone else.   I DON'T like that

As the American journalist George Packer puts it, American politics today requires a word as primal as 'tribe' to get at the 'blind allegiances and huge passions of partisan affiliation'.[2] 'Tribes demand loyalty,' writes Packer, 'and in return they confer the security of belonging. In a way, they make thinking unnecessary, because they do it for you, and may punish you if you try to do it for yourself.' Dan Kahan, a professor at Yale, concurs. Both liberal and conservative Americans today, he says, are driven more by 'loyalty to important affinity groups' than by individual self-interest.[3] What voters appear to care about most is having their political tribe win.

Such tribalism isn't of course unique to the US. We see it across the world today, in North and South America, Europe and Asia. Moreover, such tribalism should not be a surprise to us. In evolutionary terms, the roots of group behaviour go far deeper than those of individual rationality. Indeed, our very brains may be partisan, as recent research suggests. In a 2016 study, Jonas Kaplan of the University of Southern California placed forty liberal voters in functional magnetic resonance imaging (fMRI) scanners and asked them to read liberal statements such as 'abortion should be legal' and conservative statements such as 'ten times more people are murdered with kitchen knives each year than are killed by guns'. Reading statements that challenged their liberal views resulted in a greater flow of blood to parts of the brain linked to basic beliefs and personal identity, suggesting that political tribalism may be hard-wired into our brains.[4]

Other research backs this up. After the 2012 US presidential elections, Jeremy Frimer of the University of Winnipeg found that voters were not only uninterested in hearing why anyone would back the other side, they were positively averse to it. Over a third of those who voted for Barack Obama and more than half who voted

bad way of describing blind allegiance

for Mitt Romney 'compared the experience of listening to the other side's voters to having a tooth pulled'.[5] Frimer replicated the study in Canada before the 2015 election and found similar results.

People seem to either refuse to accept inconvenient facts or dismiss them entirely. Brendan Nyhan of the University of Michigan and Ethan Porter of George Washington University ran an online study during America's presidential debates in 2016 in which they asked 1,500 people to rate the candidates' statements for accuracy.[6] When Trump made a misleading claim, the team sent corrections to only half the group. Those who received the corrections adjusted their opinion of Trump's accuracy relative to those who did not. But this made no difference to their overall opinion: Trump's favourability ratings remained the same among those who got the corrections relative to those who did not.[7]

This type of tribalism isn't limited to ethno-nationalists and libertarians on the right or campus radicals and the so-called 'antifa' on the left. David Adler, a political researcher, believes that it is just as rife among people in the centre. His research shows that, across Europe and North America, centrists are among the least supportive of democracy and the most supportive of authoritarianism. Adler argues that this isn't just a Western phenomenon. Strongmen in the developing world have historically found support in the centre. 'From Brazil and Argentina to Singapore and Indonesia,' Adler says, 'middle-class moderates have encouraged authoritarian transitions to bring stability and deliver growth. Could the same happen in mature democracies like Britain, France and the United States?'[8]

A central premise of this book is that governments are improvable. But the relationship between the state and its citizens is symbiotic: the rulers serve the people, at the pleasure of those they serve. This is true of all states: even autocrats need the approval and support of their people. But it is especially true in democracies where citizens have a special role in improving their governments.

What, then, is the role of citizens in making their governments better? Clearly, good citizens must be politically engaged and informed. Even more importantly, when they can, they must choose their political leaders wisely and hold those leaders to account. Accordingly, this chapter will look at how voters can choose good leaders. Setting aside, as far as possible, questions of substantive politics, it will ask the question: what do leaders who know how to run a twenty-first-century government look like? It will also look at how citizens can create a virtuous circle whereby governments become more responsive to pressures to change in real time. Of course, when all else fails, citizens must be prepared to make change themselves. If informed, engaged citizens can't 'beat 'em', how can they 'join 'em' to make change happen? This chapter will end with an analysis of the role of citizens in driving protest movements and political activism around the world.

Citizens: the basics

Even in an autocratic society, citizens must be vigilant. They must constantly assess and re-assess the terms of the social contract. As John Locke advised, they must push for getting as much from the state as they can without giving up more of their freedom than is necessary. In the worst circumstances, they must even be prepared to overthrow their governments to achieve their ends.

As well as being engaged, citizens must also be informed. Civic education has always been essential to systems of government: Plato, Cicero, Machiavelli and Rousseau all emphasised the importance of instilling political virtue in the young. As James Madison put it: 'A people who mean to be their own Governors must arm themselves with the power which knowledge gives ... A popular Government, without popular information, or the means of acquiring it, is but a Prologue to a Farce or a Tragedy; or, perhaps both.'

Thus, the proper functioning of states depends on citizens faithfully performing their civic duties. Above all, they must regularly participate in elections. 'Boil it down,' says Barack Obama. 'If we don't vote, then this democracy doesn't work.'

It is easy enough to exhort citizens to be informed and engaged and to vote. Indeed, it almost goes without saying that citizens should be and do all these things. Providing such advice is akin to saying to a student: 'Study hard, get good grades, be intelligent.' But how can citizens go beyond such pieties and learn how to choose their leaders better? How can they learn to spot good politicians from bad ones?

Citizens: choose your leaders well

Contemporary theories of leadership are clear on the broad outlines. Good leaders have a vision. They can communicate this vision to their followers. And they can build trust and maintain a special relationship with their followers through thick and thin. But in politics, this alone may be insufficient. Political leaders must be able to talk the talk and then walk the walk. It is not enough for them to know *what* to do; they must also know *how* to do it and have the required motivation to put their plans into action. Being able to walk the walk requires many things: knowledge, experience, commitment, perseverance, pragmatism, the ability to work with others (including opponents), and the willingness to experiment and admit failures. It requires clarity about the ends, but pragmatism about the means to achieving them.

Good leaders on their own cannot make a government good. Even the smartest, most experienced leaders can't know or do everything themselves. This recognition brings into focus the team that leaders put in place to help them achieve their goals. Does the leader's team have people whose strengths and weaknesses complement their own? Citizens, in choosing leaders, must take a leaf out of the book of venture capitalists who invest in start-up *teams* over their *ideas*. 'Pick the riders, not the horse' is the advice given when investing in new companies. This is because even mediocre ideas can be polished by a good team. And even great ideas are likely to be botched by a poor team. Quality leaders attract quality people to them, and citizens must learn how to look out for and recognise this ability. Citizens should also be able to look beyond the leader's immediate team, to the wider organisation: the leader's party itself.

What should citizens look for in an individual leader and their immediate and wider team? Consistent with the principles of good government explored in this book, I argue that citizens should ask the following questions of their potential leaders. How good are they at balancing pragmatism and ideology? How well do they organise and lead teams? How good are they at taking many tribes along? Included within these themes are related questions such as how good they are at understanding the role of technology – not only in winning elections but in governing and driving inclusive growth – and how able they are to create a culture of innovation, both within the government and in the economy at large.

How good are leaders at balancing pragmatism and ideology?

In the political sphere, it goes without saying that citizens should look for leaders with clear principles and well thought-out plans. In many cases, these principles and plans are laid out in the manifestos of leaders' parties and made clear during election campaigns.

But what happens *after* a successful campaign, when the elected leader actually has to implement these plans? What happens when these principles and plans collide with reality, as is invariably the case?

Here it becomes crucial that the leader is able to balance principles and ideology against the constraints of the real world. Flexibility and the ability to rethink and modify plans are of paramount importance. Does the leader have it in them to do this? In politics, people often set great store by leaders who don't change tack. Margaret Thatcher once said with pride, as if it were a good thing: 'You turn if you want to ... The lady is not for turning.' Tony Blair famously claimed that he did not have a reverse gear. But such rigidity can be an impediment in the rough and tumble of government.

'Plans are worthless,' said Dwight D. Eisenhower, 'but planning is everything.' At best, planning can help with an intelligent start to work. But in an emergency, Eisenhower advised that 'the first thing to do is to take all the plans off the top shelf and throw them out the window'. Good leaders are able to balance principles and plans, even ideology, with the need for pragmatism. As Peter Cannellos of *Politico* puts it: 'The virtue and weakness of ideology is that it's fixed: The same program applies in good times and bad, regardless of changing conditions.'[9]

Increasingly, the ability to be pragmatic is also about the willingness to experiment and conduct evidence-based policy. Citizens should ask whether their potential leaders will make decisions by the seat of their pants or based on the facts and following rational principles. Are they flexible about testing new ideas and reworking them if needed? Do they have the self-awareness and judgement to learn from failure and not just from their successes?

Crucially, how can citizens know in advance what their leaders will be like *before* they take office? Some of the characteristics of leaders are visible when they are on the campaign trail. Citizens can observe candidates in live hustings and televised debates, and ask these questions of their prospective leaders: Who are their supporters? Where do they get their money from? Who are they beholden to? But even more important than the campaign trail is their prior experience and track record. When faced with potential leaders, citizens must know what they have done before. Have they run an organisation of note? And how good are their organisational and team-building skills?

How well do they organise and lead teams?

(handwritten margin note: are we running for career politicians than ???)

Good leaders must have a grasp of new possibilities and a track record that demonstrates this throughout their careers. Have they run large organisations in the public or the private sector? Do they have a track record of having done this before as politicians? Have they managed teams of people? Have they used technology to do this better?

Candidates who have governed before, at lower levels of government for instance, are more likely to be able to govern well when elected to higher office. Candidates who have run states as governors or chief ministers in federal nations, or have been mayors of cities, can use this record as evidence of their ability to be good leaders once in power. If prospective leaders have served in Congress or Parliament, citizens can look to evaluate their voting record and their ability to work across party lines to draft and pass new legislation.

Increasingly, citizens have the option of voting for 'outsiders': candidates who do not come from politics but have had careers in civil society or the private sector. The benefit of choosing those with a third sector background is that they have been close to citizens' lives and may well have a commitment to solving social problems. *(handwritten margin note: should gov run for the people by the people)* Those from the private sector, however, may have a deeper appreciation of performance under pressure and working to targets within financial and time constraints. Undoubtedly, there are pros and cons of choosing such outsiders. On the plus side, they are likely to have fresh ideas and be willing to shake things up in a way that dyed-in-the-wool politicians might not. On the other hand, outsiders might underestimate the challenges of working in politics. They may lack the credibility to get other politicians to work with them. And they may lack an understanding or appreciation of the processes and protocols.

Citizens should therefore be careful not to vote for outsiders merely as a form of protest against the status quo or against elites and the establishment. While the consequences of such protest votes might not be too damaging when all is going well, they might prove disastrous if things should take a turn for the worse. During times of crisis – such as economic downturns or pandemics – the competence of even the most staid insider might prove more valuable than the exciting incompetence of the flashy outsider. During the Covid-19 crisis, for instance, no less an oracle than Jared Kushner, Donald Trump's son-in-law and right-hand man, pointed out that '[w]hat a lot of the voters are seeing now is that when you elect somebody to be a mayor or governor or president, you're trying to think about who will be a competent manager during the time of crisis. This is a time of crisis and you're seeing certain people are better managers than others.'[10] In many ways, the best candidates might be those who have experience of two or more sectors: those who have worked in the business world or civil society as well as in government. Such hybrid careers might help such candidates bring the best of their prior experience to their new job while avoiding the pitfalls.

A key issue that citizens should pay attention to is the ability of leaders to work with their immediate team and others more generally. Even the smartest, most experienced leaders can't know or do everything themselves. The question then becomes: are they sufficiently self-aware to know what they don't know, and humble enough to accept their limitations? Also: what sort of team have they put in place to overcome them? Does the team have people whose strengths and weaknesses complement the leader's own? Good leaders must be good at delegation and bringing talent on. Citizens must assess whether their candidates are willing and able to devolve power within their organisations, to other levels of government, and eventually to citizens themselves. Specifically: do they have autocratic versus democratic instincts and how well can they handle power?

Citizens should ask themselves which candidates are likely to delegate authority and mentor others to do their work better. Research on contemporary forms of leadership suggests that it is no longer possible, necessary or desirable for one person to do everything or to centralise power. Doing so only paves the way for authoritarianism and reactionism. And while such an approach might have worked in a prior epoch, in today's flat, non-hierarchical world, in which problems are complex and expertise is distributed, it is important that leaders are able to distribute power and responsibility. And so citizens must look to their potential leader's track record for evidence that they can do all this. Are they able to give credit to others in their team but take the blame when things go wrong?

As I argued in the previous chapter, leaders must also be able to lead in a way that fosters innovation and systemic change, not only in the economy but within the government itself. Citizens must choose leaders who can empower others to make change happen. They should ask: can the candidate deal with organisational reform by flattening hierarchies, breaking down silos, allowing risk-taking and experimentation, enabling the scaling of new ideas and getting the government to deliver?

Increasingly, along with organisational capability, potential leaders must also have a grasp of technology and its uses. The failure of contemporary politicians to understand, for instance, how large digital platforms work was embarrassingly clear when Mark Zuckerberg testified before the joint Senate judiciary and commerce committee over the US elections of 2016. During the five-hour hearing, the senators seemed clueless and beaten into submission. Not surprising, Zuckerberg capitalised on committee members' lack of knowledge and their superficial questions.

Political candidates are increasingly good at using technology to win elections. Barack Obama used crowdfunding and digital technologies to win the presidential election twice. Donald Trump made extensive use of social media during his campaign and continued to do so while in power. Likewise Narendra Modi in India and Emmanuel Macron in France. Indeed, Macron's La République En Marche! movement employed an army of young people who built and used sophisticated digital tools to organise campaign efforts across the country leading up to the 2017 elections. Called the NationBuilder Network, this 'out-of-the-box' set of organising and campaigning tools was built to include everything a campaign needed to succeed.[11] Using it, the new party rapidly created a digital infrastructure across campaigns that allowed hundreds of candidates from various backgrounds and positions on the political spectrum to run their campaigns their own way while remaining united under the En Marche! banner. In effect, the NationBuilder system was a network of individual sites for each candidate that integrated fully with a database of supporters to manage key events, volunteers and communications. The system was also deeply integrated with social networks such as Facebook and Twitter.

While candidates might be good at using technology to win elections, the bigger question is whether they know how to use it to govern once in office. Citizens should ask themselves whether candidates and members of their team have the ability to use technology to make things happen once they assume power.

Further, it's not just the ability to use technology *in* government that matters, but also the ability to understand the role of technology in society more generally. Does the candidate understand about regulation and how to engage with industry to get the best from new breakthroughs while minimising the risks? Are they able to balance letting go (steering) with holding on to power (rowing)? Do they have a sense of industrial strategy and the ability to engage with all levels of industry – from large firms to small start-ups and grassroots innovators – without being beholden to them? Most importantly, do they know how to use technology not to divide the public but to be inclusive and take everyone along?

How good are they at taking many tribes along?

Tribalism can have a pernicious effect on the body politic. People are likely to remain in their bubbles and only care about the opinions of others in their tribe. Thus those on the right clash with those on the left (and vice versa), and the elites in the centre scorn everyone else. Moreover, divisive leaders can exacerbate such tribal tendencies. While this might help galvanise their core supporters and even help them win elections, the long-term effects can be hugely damaging. The ultimate casualty is likely to be democracy, which requires everyone to know and care about everyone else. As John Stuart Mill wrote in *Considerations on Representative Government*, democracy is undermined when people cast a 'base and mischievous vote ... from the voter's personal interest or class interest, or some mean feeling in his own mind'. Political scientists claim that some people even vote simply to cancel out their spouse's contribution.

There is much that citizens can do to overcome such tribalism. They need to be aware of their tribal tendencies and the various accompanying biases. They must seek to overcome the attitudes and behaviours that reinforce such biases. They must look across groups and transcend old categories of left–right, young–old, black–white, and think in holistic terms. They need to actively engage with those with opposing views, see things from their perspective, and seek common ground. Doing all this is undoubtedly hard but it is crucial to the long-term success of societies and economies. More importantly, perhaps, citizens must choose leaders who are able to transcend ideologies and tribal sentiments themselves. How can we assess candidates for this ability?

Observing candidates on the campaign trail can help. Physical presence can both build support and dissolve the political polarities on which tribalism feeds. As Alexandria Ocasio-Cortez, the youngest member of the US Congress, puts it: 'When someone actually knocks on your door or goes to your civic association meeting and you actually touch their hand, it really does change everything.'[12]

Good leaders know how to communicate well and take different groups along with them. Citizens should therefore ask: which of the candidates can balance multiple viewpoints and is willing to take on vested interests if they are a barrier to progress?

Citizens: hold your leaders to account

Even the best leaders can waver in the commitments they make to their people. Once in office, they may forget the promises they made on the campaign trail. Or, despite their best intentions, they may fail in the messy process of implementation and struggle to make the hard decisions that change entails. They may succumb to opposition or prove incapable of taking dissenters along.

Of course, citizens, if they are unhappy with what their leaders do in office, can dispense with them at the next elections. But four to five years can be a long time to wait: what can citizens do in the interim?

It isn't enough for people to choose the right leaders and then sit back and do nothing until they get to vote again. Citizens must also pay attention to what is happening *between* elections. They must hold leaders to account after they have elected them into office. They must keep the pressure on through the press, through town hall meetings, and through protests, if necessary.

Citizens can use the power of crowds and mobilise the support of others to force change. They can do this by joining parties and using the party machinery to exert pressure on their elected officials. Or they can join new movements which create the conditions that force politicians to adopt new policies. In the late nineteenth century, for instance, the Progressive movement in the US gave rise to the antitrust policies of Theodore Roosevelt and Woodrow Wilson in the early twentieth century. In Britain, the Fabian movement paved the way for the welfare state in the early to mid-twentieth century. Again, in the 1960s, the Civil Rights movement in the US led on to Lyndon Johnson's Great Society. As the political scientists Roberto Stefan Foa and Yascha Mounk argue, ever since Gabriel Almond and Sidney Verba wrote *The Civic Culture* in 1963, studies have shown that 'civic engagement affects democracy's ability to deliver public goods, to hold officials accountable, and to provide effective government'.[13]

Distraction and withdrawal from public action can have adverse effects on the body politic over time. In the US, for instance, increasing budget deficits have been part of the price that citizens have paid for apathy and distraction. Voters may find it expedient to delegate to the state the chores that they do not have the time or the willingness to take care of by themselves. But if they do so, the state can misuse their money, deprive them of the services they should expect for their taxes, and drive many into poverty.

In recent years, the young have shown themselves to be particularly adept at holding leaders to account. For decades, the response to American mass shootings, for instance, was predictable: intense media coverage for a few days, the inevitable 'thoughts and prayers' from politicians, and the eventual inability of Congress to pass any gun control laws of substance. But at least since the February 2018 shooting in Parkland, Florida, a new wave of student activism has shaken things up. There have been school walkouts involving millions of students and die-ins outside the White House and elsewhere. Less than six months after the shooting, The March for Our Lives, a demonstration in Washington called by a Parkland student, ended up being the third biggest in US history. Now, any new attack results in an immediate response from school shooting survivors and other teenage activists. Calls for new protests are quickly shared and amplified on social media.[14]

Teenage gun control activists are also registering young people to vote. Survivors of the shooting in Parkland spent the summer of 2018 on a national Road to Change bus tour, during which they registered young voters at stops all over the country. Their eventual goal is to ensure that lawmakers who block gun control legislation are voted out of office. In Arizona, high school gun control advocates too young to vote helped organise a campaign across the state to register their eighteen- and nineteen-year-old classmates and friends.

As with gun control, so too with public activism against inequality, climate change and racial injustice. Hence the Occupy movement after the financial crisis and, more recently, the Extinction Rebellion and the Black Lives Matter movements that have spread throughout the world.

Protesting is important. But civil uprising alone is not enough. Sometimes it can even be counterproductive. If protest movements are to effect long-term change, they must learn how to build and nurture the machinery of government. Transforming grassroots movements into political parties and governments can, however, be hard.

Take the case of France's En Marche! Despite its spectacular success in taking power in 2017, the movement has dissipated since. The party's campaign headquarters used to be a lively hub with takeaway boxes everywhere and young people huddled over laptops. The moment Mr Macron was elected, however, members of his team melted away into government jobs or, passed over by the party, went back to business or academia. Meanwhile, Macron's approval ratings have been less than impressive.

As in France, so too in Italy. The Five Star Movement produced mayors for two of Italy's biggest cities: Turin and Rome. But in both cities, they have run into trouble. In Turin, residents are unhappy with Chiara Appendino who became mayor in June 2016. 'There is a very strong feeling, even among those who voted for Appendino, that Turin is a city which is no longer being managed,' says Pietro Occhetto, a shop owner in the city centre.[15] And in Rome, Virginia Raggi has presided over a city of potholes, uncollected rubbish, inefficient transport and rat infestations. While some of these problems preceded her election, Raggi has been plagued by scandal and criticisms over her failure to solve them. To top it all, in June 2018 she faced trial for cronyism.

Meanwhile, in the Arab world, the anger that drove the Arab spring is flaring up again. In Tunisia, the lone country where democracy has taken root, the economy has faltered even as democracy has blossomed. Many middle-class citizens feel economically worse off than they were under former dictator Ben Ali. Corruption and red tape get in the way of setting up businesses, and the education system continues to produce graduates for jobs in the public sector rather than in companies looking for those with science skills and vocational training.

So: citizens must protest but be careful not to see civil resistance as superior to the mundane business of government. When they use it against a regime, citizens must be alert to a credible plan for governing the country if they do bring about regime change. In the absence of such a plan, civil resistance can end up becoming part of the problem rather than the solution. Unfortunately, many grassroots movements around the world have been unsuited to the tedious task of running political parties and governments. And the citizens who supported them have ended up paying the price.

Citizens: Be the solution yourselves

In the end, citizens may not simply be able to rely on others to do the job of governing for them. When all else fails, they may have to take matters into their own hands and solve social problems themselves. They can do this in two ways: <u>outside government, in civil society, or from within government itself.</u>

In the UK, the last few years have seen many occasions when citizens have stepped in to solve local problems where governments have failed. As Aditya Chakrabortty, a *Guardian* journalist, puts it, austerity, centralisation and the lowest local government budgets in the OECD have meant that ordinary citizens across the UK have had to 'take back control'.[16] There have been huge budget cuts across the board. This has been made worse by the fact that, while local government delivers a quarter of all public services, it controls a mere 1.6 per cent of GDP (compared with 6, 11 and 16 per cent in France, Germany and Sweden respectively). Councils have slashed spending on nurseries, libraries, care homes, visits to the elderly, public parks and road repairs.

To study the consequences, Chakrabortty spent several months in 2018 examining how local communities have responded to these pressures. With rare exceptions, what is most noticeable is 'how minor is the role played by formal local government' and how important citizens have been in keeping their communities afloat.

In Liverpool, Chakrabortty met residents of abandoned streets who had brought them back to life by developing social housing. In Oldham, he saw how school caterers were feeding schoolchildren award-winning organic meals. In Witney, he spoke to Andrew Lyons, who quit his job with Stagecoach, a transport company, to help run community buses because he did not like the idea of pensioners being trapped in their homes. In Brighton, local residents set up Brighton's Bevy to be a pub as well as a community centre where neighbours can meet and address local issues or rally against school cuts and housing problems. In Plymouth, he found an entire ecosystem of social enterprises and cooperatives. In all these places, ordinary citizens who care about their homes and neighbours have found ways to make things better. Participation has been key: many of the solutions depend on others getting involved. These organisations, says Chakrabortty, are noisy and energetic.[17]

But citizens aren't only driven by desperation. In many cases, they are also positively empowered by access to new tools that help them get involved and make a difference. In Boston, Massachusetts, a group of millennials called TransitMatters are working with the local government to improve the city's transit system.[18] Drawing on a network of government insiders and freely available data on train schedules, the group has used data-driven approaches to increase citizen engagement while improving traffic outcomes and saving the city money. TransitMatters has, for instance, persuaded the city to launch an overnight bus service for the first time in decades, and add a bus lane to a renovated bridge over the Charles river to speed up some of the most overcrowded bus lines.

In São Paulo, Sergio Andrade founded Agenda Pública (Public Agenda) in 2009 to improve public management. The NGO drives social participation through partnerships between local government, society and private companies to address problems such as housing and basic sanitation. In Cape Town, Francois Petousis set up Lumkani to make and sell a heat detector to reduce shack fires in slums. A network of Lumkani devices in the slum uses radio frequency to send text messages and notify people in case of emergency. A central device locates the GPS coordinates of the blaze and liaises with the fire department for immediate action. In Delhi, architect Bhavya Singh launched #LightUpDelhi to improve women's safety through better street lighting in the city. She then led She Creates Change, a year-long online programme of support, training and community-building for women campaigners for social change across India.

If citizens feel that social enterprise is too precarious or unsystematic to bring about change, they can solve social problems from *within* government instead. Unfortunately, there is a common perception that there are more opportunities to innovate in the private rather than the public sector. This belief persists despite the fact that the public sector offers greater potential for systemic change and thus has the greater need for innovative employees.

[handwritten margin note: why! that service has a lot of privilege to it...]

288

Dismissing the public sector's ability to be innovative from within can result in a self-fulfilling prophesy. As Mariana Mazzucato puts it in *The Entrepreneurial State*: 'the smartest young graduates think that it will be more exciting and fun to work at Goldman Sachs or Google than a state investment bank or a ministry for innovation'.[19] As a result, the best young talent gives the state a wide berth. The only way to rebalance this problem, Mazzucato says, is to upgrade the status of government.

Alternatively, citizens can work for political parties. Political scientist Olof Petersson argues that one of the distinctive features of Swedish political culture for most of the twentieth century was mass membership of political parties. In 1983, nearly a quarter of the population was enrolled in a political party: the parties functioned like social media do today, with young people joining to meet others, especially in the countryside. Because they were so embedded in everyday life, party officials had a good idea of what ordinary people were talking about. Since then, though, membership has collapsed. About half the membership of the Social Democrats vanished with the abolition of collective membership through the unions. By 2010 the party, which once boasted 1 million members, was down to barely over 100,000. As a result, there was no longer a mechanism by which the leadership in Stockholm could be told things they did not want to hear.[20]

When all else fails, citizens can run for office. They can run locally, regionally or at the national level. This is exactly what Alexandria Ocasio-Cortez did in Queens, New York, in the 2018 mid-term elections. A working-class Latina activist, Ocasio-Cortez was as an organiser for Bernie Sanders' presidential campaign in 2016. After the election, she travelled across America, to places like Flint, Michigan, and Standing Rock, North Dakota, and spoke to people affected by the Flint water crisis and the Dakota Access Pipeline. Standing Rock, says Ocasio-Cortez, was a tipping point for her. Before the visit, she felt that the only way to run for office was to have access to wealth, influence and power.

AOC

But when she saw others 'putting their whole lives and everything that they had on the line for the protection of their community', she felt inspired to give it a go herself.[21]

On 26 June 2018, Ocasio-Cortez won the Democratic primary in New York's 14th congressional district, defeating the incumbent, Democratic caucus chair Joe Crowley, in the biggest upset of the 2018 mid-term election primaries. When she took office on 3 January 2019, at the age of twenty-nine, Ocasio-Cortez was the youngest woman to serve in Congress in the history of the United States.

Running for office is also what Leila Ali Elmi, aged thirty, did in another part of the world. Elmi – who arrived in Sweden as a child after her family fled Somalia's civil war – won a surprise victory in the autumn 2018 elections, on a platform of providing a voice for immigrants facing growing hostility. Prior to the elections, Elmi had worked as an interpreter, helping immigrants and refugees to navigate the administrative processes of their adopted homeland. Subsequent to that, she had been a city councillor for the Greens. Her political inspiration, she says, was Shirley Chisholm, the first black woman elected to the US Congress.

A nation: a 'fragile vase' held together by its people

The relationship between governments and their people is a special one. This is particularly true in democracies where 'we the people' are, in a very real sense, sovereign. Citizens in democracies vote for and hold governments to account. Governments in turn serve the people, at the pleasure of the people.

This social contract, which has worked for so long in the West, and which has more recently emerged in the developing world, seems today to be on the point of breaking down everywhere. Governments appear powerless, leaden and disconnected in the face of powerful demands from people. Opportunistic leaders and parties appear to be pursuing their own interests and those of the elites over their countries and citizens at large. The people themselves, apparently empowered by social media, are at once more aware of the foibles and failings of their governments and less able to change the status quo. This has bred dissatisfaction on a grand scale. More often than not it has led to apathy. From time to time it has bred the opposite: protest and a knee-jerk rejection of a sensible middle ground in favour of the extremes. In their bid to shake things up or register their frustration, people have taken to supporting disruptive populists who, in the long run, will only make matters worse.

For the social contract to work properly, the people need to do their part. They need to be engaged and informed. They need to choose their leaders well and hold them to account during and after elections. When all else fails, they must choose to work within the government or solve social problems with the government from the vantage of civil society. Above all, they must resist the seductions of tribalism and an 'us versus them' mindset.

In December 2018, the Dutch prime minister, Mark Rutte, wrote an open letter to the people of the Netherlands warning them about what happens when a nation fails to work together for the common good. In the letter, Rutte admitted that the Netherlands wasn't perfect but that progress did nevertheless take place. The country was a 'precious possession', he said, that belonged to everyone. But it 'was brittle ... and can easily break', like 'a fragile vase' held by its millions of 'ordinary and exceptional' citizens who 'do not only want a good life for themselves and those around them, but also want to contribute to the happiness of others'.[22] It was especially important to ensure that the vase remained in one piece, but this required 'compromises ... in which difficult problems are solved in a sensible way'. Those who refused to work together could end up 'gripping the vase so tightly that it breaks'. Pointing to Brexit Britain, he added: 'There, the country's politicians and people have forgotten what they have achieved together. And now they are caught up in chaos.'

Barack Obama, speaking before the 2018 mid-term elections, sounded a different warning. For him, the biggest threat to democracy was indifference. '[T]he story of America …,' he said, '… wasn't achieved by just a handful of famous leaders making speeches' but by 'countless quiet acts of heroism and dedication by citizens, by ordinary people'.[23] Rather than act as bystanders to history, ordinary people had time and again fought, marched, mobilised and voted to make America what it was.

The same of course could be said about practically any other country in the world today. Now is the moment of the people, and the people must address the many challenges they face together. They must choose and act wisely. The future of their societies depends on that.

Acknowledgements

I would like to thank the many people who have made this book possible: Paul Lewis, who introduced me to Patrick Walsh, my agent; Clare Grist Taylor, who worked with me on an initial proposal and handed over the project to Ed Lake; Ed for believing in the idea, commissioning the book, and then providing me with incisive input throughout the writing process; Fiona Screen for copy-editing, Philippa Logan for proofreading, and Paul Forty for managing the editorial work; James Jones, the jacket designer; Steve Panton, the art director; Jane Pickett, my publicist; and the rest of the marketing team at Profile Books.

I would also like to thank the many people I interviewed for the book: Beatrice Andrews, Jos de Blok, Kris Carter, Anir Chowdhury, Kevan Collins, Marco Daglio, Tomas Diez, David Halpern, Ishtiaque Hussain, Nigel Jacob, Sanjay Jain, Per Kongshøj Madsen, Liz McKeown, Nandan Nilekani, Anna Malaika Nti-Asare-Tubbs, Gerald Nyaoma, Vivek Raghavan, Robyn Scott, Ram Sewak Sharma, Rohan Silva, Andrea Siodmok, Michael Talbot, Mark Thompson, Lisa Witter and Aleeya Velji. Their stories and insights make the book what it is.

I thank my colleagues and students with whom I have discussed aspects of the book over the years. I am especially grateful to the civil servants from various countries whose inputs have enlivened and deepened the ideas here.

Most of all, I thank my family for their care and support throughout the process. I could not have done any of this without them.

Notes

The author and publisher assume no responsibility for the content of websites that are not the publisher's own. While care has been taken to ensure that the web links in the Notes section of this book are accurate at the time of publication, the publisher cannot guarantee that these links remain viable.

Introduction
1. Chopra, A., *Innovative State: How New Technologies can Transform Government*. Open Road+ Grove/Atlantic, 2014.

Chapter 1: Foundations
1. 'From Narayana Murthy to Salil Parekh: how chief executives have steered Infosys over the years', *Economic Times*, 4 December 2017.
2. Friedman, T., 'Builders & titans: Nandan Nilekani,' *Time*, 8 May 2006.
3. All quotations from Nandan Nilekani, former founder and CEO of UIDAI, are taken from an interview with the author on 31 March 2017.
4. Raghavan, V., biometric architect, UIDAI, interview with the author, 1 April 2017.
5. Jain, S., chief product officer, UIDAI, interview with the author, 31 March 2017.
6. Sharma, R. S., director general, UIDAI, interview with the author, 6 April 2017.
7. Rebello, K., 'Narendra Modi, from Aadhaar critic to champion: a FactCheck', *BOOM Live*, 11 April 2017.
8. 'Future of UIDAI was uncertain', *Economic Times*, 24 July 2014.
9. Mishra, A. R., 'NDA govt kicks off PDS reforms with direct cash transfers', *LiveMint*, 3 July 2015.
10. Ibid.
11. 'Prime Minister to launch Pradhan Mantri Jan Dhan Yojana tomorrow', Press Information Bureau, Government of India, 24 August 2014.

12. 'Need reforms backed by growth to end poverty', *Deccan Herald*, 6 July 2015.

Chapter 2: How should a government be?

1. Hayek, F. A., 'Reflections on the Pure Theory of Money of Mr. J. M Keynes', *Economica*, 11(33), pp. 270–95, 1931.
2. Ibid.
3. Hayek, F. A., *Prices and Production and Other Works*, Ludwig von Mises Institute, 2008.
4. Keynes, J. M., 'The Pure Theory of Money. A reply to Dr. Hayek', *Economica*, 11(34), pp. 387–97, 1931.
5. Ibid.
6. Von Mises, L., *Economic Calculation in the Socialist Commonwealth*. Lulu Press, 2016.
7. Hayek, F. A., 'Economics and knowledge,' *Economica*, 4(13), pp. 33–54, 1937.
8. Hayek, F. A., *The Road to Serfdom: Text and Documents: The Definitive Edition*. Routledge, 2014.
9. Ebenstein, A., *Friedrich Hayek: A Biography*. St. Martin's Press, 2014.
10. Tebble, A. J., *F. A Hayek*. A&C Black, 2013.
11. Orwell, G., Davison, P. H., Angus, I., and Davison, S., *I Have Tried to Tell the Truth: 1943–1944* (Vol. 16). Secker & Warburg, 1998.
12. Micklethwait, J., and Wooldridge, A., *The Fourth Revolution: The Global Race to Reinvent the State*. Penguin UK, 2014.
13. Matthijs, M. M., *Ideas and Economic Crises in Britain from Attlee to Blair (1945–2005)*. Routledge, 2012.
14. Kotler, P., *Advancing the Common Good: Strategies for Businesses, Governments, and Nonprofits*. ABC-CLIO, 2019.
15. Madrick, J., *Age of Greed: The Triumph of Finance and the Decline of America, 1970 to the Present*. Vintage, 2012.
16. Reis, R., 'How do countries differ in their response to the coronavirus economic crisis?' *Guardian*, 3 April 2020.

Chapter 3: Lean Leviathan

1. Gelb, A., Mukherjee, A., Navis, K., Thapliyal, M., and Giri, A., 'What a new survey of Aadhaar users can tell us about digital reforms: initial insights from Rajasthan', Center for Global Development, December 2017. Available at: www.cgdev.org/publication/

what-a-new-survey-aadhaar-users-can-tell-us-about-digital-reforms-initial-insights

2. 'Of 42 "hunger-related" deaths since 2017, 25 "linked to Aadhaar issues"', *Wire*, 21 September 2018.

3. 'Uniquely vulnerable: a watertight store of Indians' personal data proves leaky', *The Economist*, 11 January 2018.

4. Ibid.

5. Ibid.

6. Choudhary, M., 'Viewpoint: the pitfalls of India's biometric ID scheme', *BBC News*, 23 April 2018.

7. Ibid.

8. Ibid.

9. Tharoor, S., 'Why link mobiles, bank accounts to Aadhaar?' *Week*, 8 April 2018.

10. Abraham, R. and Bennett, E., 'Viewpoint: world's biggest ID scheme Aadhaar still poses risks', BBC News, 26 September 2018.

11. 'Centre saved Rs 90,000 crore through digital transfer: Amitabh Kant', *Economic Times*, 19 June 2018.

12. Mitter, S. 'India world's second biggest fintech hub, with Mumbai and Bengaluru leading the charge: study', *YourStory*, 4 March 2019.

13. KPMG, 'Fintech in India: a global growth story', June 2016. Available at: assets.kpmg/content/dam/kpmg/pdf/2016/06/FinTech-new.pdf

14. 'Aadhaar helped government save $9 billion: Nandan Nilekani', *Hindustan Times*, 13 October 2017.

15. Nilekani, N., 'Aadhaar: universal access is for the greater good', *LiveMint*, 13 February 2018.

16. Ibid.

17. Ibid.

18. Ibid.

19. Ibid.

20. 'When Nobel winner Paul Romer praised India's Aadhaar scheme', *India Today*, 8 October 2018.

21. Wetzel, D., 'Bolsa Família: Brazil's Quiet Revolution', The World Bank, 4 November 2013. Available at: www.worldbank.org/en/news/opinion/2013/11/04/bolsa-familia-Brazil-quiet-revolution

22. Ibid.

23. Ibid.

24. Lowe, J., 'Three ways Latin America can make dealing with government less painful', *Apolitical*, 3 September 2018.

25. Roseth, B., Reyes, A., Farias, P., Porrúa, M., Villalba, H., Acevedo, S., Peña, N., Estevez, E., Lejarraga, S. L. and Fillotrani, P., *Wait No More: Citizens, Red Tape, and Digital Government*. Inter-American Development Bank, 2018.

26. Lowe, J., 'Three ways Latin America can make dealing with government less painful', *Apolitical*, 3 September 2018.

27. Burke, J., 'e-ID saves Estonia 2% of GDP a year. It's time America caught up', *Apolitical*, 7 December 2018.

28. Mistreanu, S., 'Life inside China's social credit laboratory', *Foreign Policy*, 3 April 2018.

29. Ibid.

30. Kuo, L. 'China bans 23m from buying travel tickets as part of "Social Credit" system', *Guardian*, 1 March 2019.

31. Kobie, N., 'The complicated truth about China's Social Credit System', *Wired*, 7 June 2019.

32. Wang, M., 'China's chilling "Social Credit" blacklist', *Human Rights Watch*, 12 December 2017. Available at: www.hrw.org/news/2017/12/12/chinas-chilling-social-credit-blacklist

33. Kobie, N., 'The complicated truth about China's Social Credit System', *Wired*, 7 June 2019.

34. Ibid.

35. Ibid.

36. Kostka, G., 'China's social credit systems are highly popular – for now', Mercator Institute for China Studies blog, 17 September 2018. Available at: www.merics.org/en/blog/chinas-social-credit-systems-are-highly-popular-now

37. Kobie, N., 'The complicated truth about China's Social Credit System', *Wired*, 7 June 2019.

38. Ibid.

39. Ibid.

40. Tan, C. K., 'China spending puts domestic security ahead of defense: budget rise highest in western regions of Xinjiang and Tibet', *Nikkei Asia Review*, 14 March 2018.

41. 'China due to introduce face scans for mobile users', *BBC News*, 1 December 2019.

42. Wang, M., 'China's algorithms of repression: reverse engineering a Xinjiang police mass surveillance app', *Human Rights Watch*, 1 May 2019. Available at: www.hrw.org/report/2019/05/02/chinas-algorithms-repression/reverse-engineering-xinjiang-police-mass

43. Ibid.
44. Mistreanu, S. '"Seldom uses front door": report reveals how China spies on Muslim minority', *Guardian*, 1 May 2019.
45. Davidson, H., 'Asian countries face possible second wave of coronavirus infections', *Guardian*, 2 April 2020.
46. Kobie, N., 'The complicated truth about China's social credit system', *Wired*, 7 June 2019.
47. Rolley, C., 'Is Chinese-style surveillance coming to the west?' *Guardian*, 7 May 2019.
48. Mozur, P., Kessel, J. M., and Chan, M., 'Made in China, exported to the world: the surveillance state', *New York Times*, 24 April 2019.
49. Ibid.
50. Kobie, N., 'The complicated truth about China's social credit system,' *Wired*, 7 June 2019.

Chapter 4: The responsive state

1. All quotations from Jos de Blok, founder and CEO of Buurtzorg, are taken from an interview with the author on 20 March 2018.
2. Laloux, F., *Reinventing Organizations: A Guide to Creating Organizations Inspired by the Next Stage in Human Consciousness.* Nelson Parker, 2014.
3. Ibid.
4. Buurtzorg. Available at: www.buurtzorg.com/about-us/our-organisation
5. Laloux, F., *Reinventing Organizations: A Guide to Creating Organizations Inspired by the Next Stage in Human Consciousness.* Nelson Parker, 2014.
6. Gray, B., Sarnak, D. O., and Burgers, J. 'Home care by self-governing nursing teams: the Netherlands' Buurtzorg model', The Commonwealth Fund, 29 May 2015. Available at: www. commonwealthfund.org/publications/case-study/2015/may/ home-care-self-governing-nursing-teams-netherlands-buurtzorg-model
7. Laloux, F., *Reinventing Organizations: A Guide to Creating Organizations Inspired by the Next Stage in Human Consciousness.* Nelson Parker, 2014.
8. Gray, B., Sarnak, D. O., and Burgers, J. 'Home care by self-governing nursing teams: the Netherlands' Buurtzorg model', The Commonwealth Fund, 29 May 2015. Available at: www.

commonwealthfund.org/publications/case-study/2015/may/
home-care-self-governing-nursing-teams-netherlands-buurtzorg-model

9. KPMG, *The Added Value of Buurtzorg Relative to Other Providers of Home Care: A Quantitative Analysis of Home Care in the Netherlands in 2013* [in Dutch], Jan. 2015.

10. All quotations from Mark Thompson, professor in digital economy, University of Exeter, are taken from an interview with the author on 9 April 2018, unless otherwise stated.

11. Amin-Smith, N., Phillips, D., and Simpson, P., 'Adult social care funding: a local or national responsibility?' The Institute for Fiscal Studies, March 2018.

12. 'Interface between health and adult social care', Sixty-Third Report of Session 2017–19, House of Commons Committee of Public Accounts, 19 October 2018. Available at: publications.parliament.uk/pa/cm201719/ cmselect/cmpubacc/1376/1376.pdf

13. Fishenden, J., Thompson, M., and Venters, W., 'Better Public Services: The Green Paper accompanying Better Public Services, A Manifesto', March 2018. Available at: digitizinggovernment.weebly.com/ uploads/1/3/0/7/13071055/green_paper_interactive_pdf_compressed.pdf

14. 'Government and IT – "a recipe for rip-offs": time for a new approach', Twelfth Report of Session 2010–12, House of Commons Public Administration Select Committee, 18 July 2011. Available at: publications.parliament.uk/pa/cm201012/cmselect/cmpubadm/715/715i. pdf

15. Micklethwait, J., and Wooldridge, A., *The Fourth Revolution: The Global Race to Reinvent the State*. Penguin UK, 2014.

16. Thompson, M., 'UK voters are being sold a lie. There is no need to cut public services', *Guardian*, 12 February 2015.

17. Ibid.

18. Fishenden, J., Thompson, M., and Venters, W., 'Better Public Services: The Green Paper Accompanying Better Public Services: A Manifesto', March 2018. Available at: digitizinggovernment.weebly.com/ uploads/1/3/0/7/13071055/green_paper_interactive_pdf_compressed.pdf

19. Oltermann, P., 'Germany's devolved logic is helping it win the coronavirus race', *Guardian*, 5 April 2020.

20. 'France's Napoleonic approach to covid-19', *The Economist*, 4 April 2020.

21. 'Bring on the mayors', *The Economist*, 27 April 2017.

22. Rotheram, S., 'My global lesson in how mayors can change the world for cities', *Evening Standard,* 10 August 2017.

23. O'Reilly, T., 'Government as a platform', *Innovations: Technology, Governance, Globalization,* 6(1), pp. 13–40, 2011.

24. Berdou, E., Lopes, C. A., Sjoberg, F. M., and Mellon, J., 'The case of UNICEF's U-Report Uganda', *Civic Tech in the Global South*, p. 97, 2015.

25. D-CENT, NESTA. Available at: www.nesta.org.uk/project/d-cent

26. 'Trust in OECD governments back at pre-crisis levels as governments seek to be more open and engaged', OECD, 14 November 2019. Available at: www.oecd.org/newsroom/trust-in-oecd-governments-back-at-pre-crisis-levels-as-governments-seek-to-be-more-open-and-engaged.htm

27. Friedman, U., 'Trust in government is collapsing around the world?' *Atlantic*, 1 July 2016.

28. Ibid.

29. Ibid.

Chapter 5: The inclusive state

1. Dovere, E.-I., 'Can this millennial mayor make Universal Basic Income a reality?' *Politico*, 24 April 2018. Available at: www.politico.com/magazine/story/2018/04/24/michael-tubbs-stockton-california-mayor-218070

2. Hubert, C., 'Michael Tubbs, one of America's youngest mayors, aims to lift his hometown of Stockton', *Sacramento Bee,* 12 April 2017. Available at: www.sacbee.com/news/local/article144077954.html

3. Dovere, E.-I., 'Can this millennial mayor make Universal Basic Income a reality?' *Politico*, 24 April 2018. Available at: www.politico.com/magazine/story/2018/04/24/michael-tubbs-stockton-california-mayor-218070

4. Ibid.

5. Ibid.

6. Ibid.

7. Ibid.

8. Ibid.

9. Ibid.

10. Christie, J., 'How Stockton went broke: a 15-year spending binge', *Reuters*, 3 July 2012.

11. Dovere, E.-I., 'Can this millennial mayor make Universal Basic Income a

reality?' *Politico*, 24 April 2018. Available at: www.politico.com/ magazine/story/2018/04/24/michael-tubbs-stockton-california-mayor- 218070

12. Ibid.
13. Nti-Asare-Tubbs, A. M., writer and PhD student, University of Cambridge, interview with the author, 14 June 2018.
14. Advance Peace. Available at: www.drkfoundation.org/organization/ advance-peace
15. Shapiro, T. M., and Loya, R., 'Michael Tubbs on universal basic income: "The issue with poverty is a lack of cash"', *Guardian*, 21 March 2019.
16. Yoon-Hendricks, A., and Anderson, B., 'Stockton is giving people $500 a month, no strings attached. Here's how they're spending it', *Sacramento Bee*, 3 October 2019.
17. Dovere, E-I., 'Can this millennial mayor make Universal Basic Income a reality?' *Politico*, 24 April 2018. Available at: www.politico.com/ magazine/story/2018/04/24/michael-tubbs-stockton-california-mayor- 218070
18. 'Stockton mayor touts experimental program that pays families $500 a month', CBS, 1 February 2018. Available at: sanfrancisco.cbslocal. com/2018/02/01/stockton-mayor-tubbs-touts-universal-income- experiment/
19. Madsen, P. K., emeritus professor of political science at Aalborg University, interview with the author, 15 June 2018.
20. 'Flexicurity: a model that works', *The Economist*, 7 September 2006.
21. Bredgaard, T., and Madsen, P. K., 'Farewell flexicurity? Danish flexicurity and the crisis', *Transfer: European Review of Labour and Research*, 24(4), pp. 375–86, 2018.
22. Madsen, P. K., emeritus professor of political science at Aalborg University, interview with the author, 15 June 2018.
23. Ibid.
24. Katzenstein, P. J., *Small States in World Markets: Industrial Policy in Europe*. Cornell University Press, 1985.
25. Madsen, P. K., emeritus professor of political science at Aalborg University, interview with the author, 15 June 2018.
26. *Christensen, E.,* 'Basic income ("Borgerløn") in Denmark – status and challenges in 2017', BIEN Denmark, 13 October 2017. Available at: basisindkomst.dk/ basic-income-borgerloen-in-denmark-status-and-challenges-in-2017

27. Henley, J., 'Money for nothing: is Finland's universal basic income trial too good to be true?' *Guardian*, 12 Jan 2018.
28. Ibid.
29. Colson, T., 'The economist behind Universal Basic Income: Give all citizens UBI to help combat a "neofascist wave of populism"', *Business Insider*, 5 January 2017.
30. Goldin, I., 'Five reasons why universal basic income is a bad idea', *Financial Times*, 11 February 2018.
31. ibid.
32. Ibid.
33. Ibid.
34. Ibid.
35. Ibid.
36. Madsen, P. K., emeritus professor of political science at Aalborg University, interview with the author, 15 June 2018.
37. Henley, J., 'Finland to end basic income trial after two years', *Guardian*, 23 April 2018.
38. Loew, J., 'What a big tech executive learned transforming Italy's government', *Apolitical*, 12 November 2018.
39. Cottam, H., 'More money will not fix our broken welfare state. We need to reinvent it', *Guardian*, 21 June 2018.
40. Smillie, I., *Freedom from Want: The Remarkable Success Story of BRAC, the Global Grassroots Organization that's Winning the Fight against Poverty*, Kumarian Press, 2009.
41. Cottam, H., 'More money will not fix our broken welfare state. We need to reinvent it', *Guardian*, 21 June 2018.
42. Dudman, J., '"The NHS would collapse without them": the growing role of volunteers', *Guardian*, 4 July 2018.
43. Ibid.
44. Murphy, S., 'More than 500,000 people sign up to be NHS volunteers', *Guardian*, 25 March 2020.
45. Gayle, C., 'The truth about black unemployment in America', *Guardian*, 7 July 2018.
46. Ibid.
47. Ibid.
48. Cochrane, E., and Fandos, N., 'Senate approves $2 trillion stimulus after bipartisan deal', *New York Times*, 25 March 2020.
49. Beckett, L., 'One California mayor has tried universal basic income. His advice for Trump: "Think big"', *Guardian*, 20 March 2020.

50. Ibid.

Chapter 6: The experimental state

1. Wintour, P., 'Clegg and Gove in spending review battle over free nursery education', *Guardian*, 24 June 2013.
2. Burton, M., 'The politics of public sector reform: from Thatcher to the Coalition', in M. Burton, *The Politics of Public Sector Reform* (pp. 1–13). Palgrave MacMillan, London, 2013.
3. Silva, R., senior policy adviser to the prime minister 2010–13, interview with the author, 5 March 2018.
4. Ibid.
5. Ibid.
6. Osborne, G., 'Nudge, nudge, win, win', *Guardian*, 14 July 2008.
7. Silva, R., senior policy adviser to the prime minister 2010–13, interview with the author, 5 March 2018.
8. Ibid.
9. Ibid.
10. Halpern, D., CEO of the Behavioural Insights Team, interview with the author, 14 February 2018.
11. Ibid.
12. Ibid.
13. Ibid.
14. Ibid.
15. Halpern, D., *Inside the Nudge Unit: How Small Changes Can Make a Big Difference*. Random House, 2015.
16. Ibid.
17. Ibid.
18. Ibid.
19. Ibid.
20. Ibid.
21. Halpern, D., CEO of the Behavioural Insights Team, interview with the author, 14 February 2018.
22. Halpern, D., *Inside the Nudge Unit: How Small Changes Can Make a Big Difference*. Random House, 2015.
23. Ibid.
24. Halpern, D., CEO of the Behavioural Insights Team, interview with the author, 14 February 2018.
25. Ibid.

26. Silva, R., senior policy adviser to the prime minister 2010–13, interview with the author, 5 March 2018.
27. Ibid.
28. Ibid.
29. Halpern, D., CEO of the Behavioural Insights Team, interview with the author, 14 February 2018.
30. Cochrane A. L., *Effectiveness and Efficiency. Random Reflections on Health Services*. London: Nuffield Hospitals Trust, 1972.
31. Dollery, C. T., '*Constructive Attack. Effectiveness and Efficiency. Random Reflections on Health Services (A. L. Cochrane)*' Book Reviews. *British Medical Journal*, 2(5804), p. 56, 1972.
32. 'About What Works', UK Cabinet Office blogs. Available at: whatworks. blog.gov.uk/about-the-what-works-network
33. Halpern, D., CEO of the Behavioural Insights Team, interview with the author, 14 February 2018.
34. All quotations from Kevan Collins, chief executive of the Education Endowment Foundation, are taken from an interview with the author on 9 March 2018.
35. Guay, J., 'Evidence-based policymaking: is there room for science in politics?' *Apolitical*, 7 October 2018.
36. Cairney, P., *The Politics of Evidence-Based Policy Making*. Springer, 2016.
37. Yates, T., 'Why is the government relying on nudge theory to fight coronavirus?' *Guardian*, 13 March 2020.

Chapter 7: The entrepreneurial state: regulating the economy

1. Nayak, B. B., *The Synergy of Microfinance: Fighting Poverty by Moving Beyond Credit*. SAGE Publishing India, 2014.
2. Ndung'u, N., 'Digital technology and state capacity in Kenya', *Center for Global Development Policy Paper*, 154, 2019.
3. Burns, S., 'Mobile money and financial development: the case of M-PESA in Kenya', November 2015. Available at: papers.ssrn.com/so13/ papers.cfm?abstract_id=2688585
4. All quotations from Gerald Nyaoma, Bank Supervision Department, Central Bank of Kenya, are taken from an interview with the author on 20 April 2018.
5. 'Financial access in Kenya: results of the 2006 national survey', FSD Kenya, October 2007. Available at: www.centralbank.go.ke/uploads/

financial_inclusion/410963334_FinAccess%20%20Household%20
2006%20Key%20Results%20Report.pdf

6. Burns, S., 'Mobile money and financial development: the case of
   M-PESA in Kenya', November 2015. Available at: papers.ssrn.com/so13/
   papers.cfm?abstract_id=2688585

7. 'Enabling mobile money transfer: The Central Bank of Kenya's
   treatment of M-Pesa', Alliance for Financial Inclusion. Available at:
   www.afi-global.org/publications/1577/Case-Study-1-The-Central-Bank-
   of-Kenya%E2%80%99s-treatment-of-M-Pesa

8. Ibid.

9. Ibid.

10. Ibid.

11. 'FinAccess National Survey 2009: dynamics of Kenya's changing financial
    landscape', FSD Kenya, June 2009. Available at: www.centralbank.
    go.ke/uploads/financial_inclusion/2025116444_FinAccess%20%20
    Household%202009%20Key%20Results%20Report.pdf

12. 'Enabling mobile money transfer: The Central Bank of Kenya's
    treatment of M-Pesa', Alliance for Financial Inclusion. Available at:
    www.afi-global.org/publications/1577/Case-Study-1-The-Central-Bank-
    of-Kenya%E2%80%99s-treatment-of-M-Pesa

13. Rolfe, A., 'Mobile money transactions equivalent of half of Kenya's
    GDP', *Payments Cards and Mobiles*, 25 January 2019.

14. Cook, T., and McKay, C., 'How M-Shwari works: the story so far',
    Consultative Group to Assist the Poor (CGAP) and Financial Sector
    Deepening (FSD) Kenya, 2015. Available at: www.cgap.org/sites/default/
    files/Forum-How-M-Shwari-Works-Apr-2015.pdf

15. Mader, P., 'Rise and fall of microfinance in India: the Andhra Pradesh
    crisis in perspective', *Strategic Change*, 22(1–2), pp. 47–66, 2013.

16. Oransky, I., 'Albert Hofmann', *Lancet*, 371(9631), p. 2168, 2008.

17. Tweney, D., 'LSD inventor Albert Hofmann dead at age 102', *Wired*, 29
    April 2008.

18. Delaney, T., *Social Deviance*. Rowman & Littlefield, 2017.

19. Gasser, P., Kirchner, K., and Passie, T., 'LSD-assisted psychotherapy for
    anxiety associated with a life-threatening disease: a qualitative study of
    acute and sustained subjective effects', *Journal of Psychopharmacology*,
    29(1), pp. 57–68, 2015.

20. Jacobs, J., '"They broke my mental shackles": could magic mushrooms
    be the answer to depression?', *Guardian*, 10 June 2019.

21. Griffiths, R. R., Johnson, M. W., Carducci, M. A., Umbricht, A.,

Richards, W. A., Richards, B. D., Cosimano, M. P., and Klinedinst, M. A., 'Psilocybin produces substantial and sustained decreases in depression and anxiety in patients with life-threatening cancer: a randomized double-blind trial', *Journal of Psychopharmacology*, 30(12), pp. 1181–97, 2016.

22. Jacobs, J., '"They broke my mental shackles": could magic mushrooms be the answer to depression?' *Guardian*, 10 June 2019.

23. Paarlberg, R., 'A dubious success: the NGO campaign against GMOs', *GM Crops & Food*, 5(3), pp. 223–28, 2014.

24. Ibid.

25. Ibid.

26. Ibid.

27. Ibid.

28. European Commission, 'A decade of EU-funded GMO research 2001–2010', *Directorate-General for Research and Innovation, Biotechnologies, Agriculture, Food*, 2010. Available at: ec.europa.eu/research/biosociety/pdf/a_decade_of_eu-funded_gmo_research.pdf

29. 'Facebook: a timeline of the social network', *Daily Telegraph*, 1 February 2012.

30. MacManus, R., 'Facebook mobile usage set to explode', *ReadWriteWeb*, 27 October 2011.

31. Clement, J., 'Number of Facebook users worldwide 2008–2019', Statista, 30 January 2020. Available at: www.statista.com/statistics/264810/number-of-monthly-active-facebook-users-worldwide

32. Olsen, P., 'Exclusive: the rags-to-riches tale of how Jan Koum built WhatsApp into Facebook's new $19 billion baby', *Forbes*, 2 February 2014.

33. Patil, S., 'India has a public health crisis. It's called fake news', *New York Times*, 29 April 2019.

34. Ibid.

35. Ibid.

36. Ibid.

37. Isaac, M., and Wakabayashi, D., 'Russian influence reached 126 million through Facebook alone', *New York Times*, 30 October 2017.

38. Ibid.

39. Lewis, P., '"Fiction is outperforming reality": how YouTube's algorithm distorts truth', *Guardian*, 2 February 2018.

40. Ibid.

41. Stewart, E., 'Lawmakers seem confused about what Facebook does – and how to fix it', *Vox*, 10 April 2018.
42. Ibid.
43. Helmore, E., 'Google made $4.7bn from news sites in 2018, study claims', *Guardian*, 10 June 2019.
44. Ibid.
45. Solon, O., 'George Soros: Facebook and Google a menace to society', *Guardian*, 26 January 2018.
46. Gabbatt, A., and Paul, K. 'Facebook cofounder calls for company to break up over "unprecedented' power"', *Guardian*, 9 May 2019.
47. Scott, M., Cerulus, L., and Kayali, L., 'Six months in, Europe's privacy revolution favors Google, Facebook', *Politico*, 19 April 2019.
48. Scott, M., Cerulus, L., Overly, S., 'How Silicon Valley gamed the world's toughest privacy rules', *Politico*, 25 May 2019.
49. Shieber, J., 'Alphabet, Apple, Amazon and Facebook are in the crosshairs of the FTC and DOJ', *Tech Crunch*, 3 June 2019.
50. Aleem, Z., 'Why London is banning Uber from its streets', *Vox*, 24 September 2017.
51. Burns, E., 'London is open ... except for Uber – Mayor Sadiq Khan says firm should "play by the rules"', *Computer Business Review*, 22 September 2017.
52. 'Connected and Autonomous Vehicle industry worth £28bn to the UK by 2035', *Catapult Transport Systems*, 8 September 2017. Available at: ts.catapult.org.uk/news-events-gallery/news/connected-autonomous-vehicle-industry-worth-28bn-uk-2035
53. Garston, E., 'Sharp growth in autonomous car market value predicted but may be stalled by rise in consumer fear', *Forbes*, 13 April 2018.
54. Simons, R. A., *Driverless Cars, Urban Parking and Land Use*. Routledge, 2020. This cites an *Economist* article that refers to the UBS study. See www.economist.com/the-economist-explains/2018/03/05/why-driverless-cars-will-mostly-be-shared-not-owned
55. All quotations from Michael Talbot, former head of industrial strategy, Centre for Connected and Autonomous Vehicles, are taken from an interview with the author on 15 May 2018.
56. 'Code of Practice: Automated vehicle trialling', Centre for Connected & Autonomous Vehicles,' February 2019. Available at: assets.publishing.service.gov.uk/government/uploads/system/uploads/attachment_data/file/776512/invitation-to-comment-code-of-practice-automated-vehicle-trialling.pdf

57. Karsten, J., and West, D., 'The state of self-driving car laws across the U.S.', *Brookings*, 1 May 2018.
58. Ibid.
59. Ibid.
60. Ohnsman, A., 'Arizona governor bans self-driving Ubers after pedestrian fatality', *Forbes*, 26 March 2018.

Chapter 8: The entrepreneurial state: cultivating the economy

1. All quotations from Michael Talbot, former head of industrial strategy, Centre for Connected and Autonomous Vehicles, are taken from an interview with the author on 15 May 2018.
2. Bender, B., 'A new moon race is on. Is China already ahead?' *Politico*, 13 June 2019.
3. 'A new age of space exploration is beginning', *The Economist*, 18 July 2019.
4. Bender, B., 'A new moon race is on. Is China already ahead?' *Politico*, 13 June 2019.
5. Losier, T., 'The race to the red planet: how NASA, SpaceX are working to get to Mars', AccuWeather. Available at: https://www.accuweather.com/en/weather-news/the-race-to-the-red-planet-how-nasa-spacex-are-working-to-get-to-mars/358844
6. Feldscher, J., '"We want access to every part of the moon, at any time"', *Politico*, 13 June 2019.
7. Fishman, C., *One Giant Leap: The Impossible Mission that Flew Us to the Moon*. Simon & Schuster, 2019.
8. Fishman, C., 'Five lessons from Apollo for the new space age', *Politico*, 13 June 2019.
9. Ibid.
10. Ibid.
11. Mazzucato, M., *The Entrepreneurial State: Debunking Public vs. Private Sector Myths*. Penguin, 2018.
12. Ibid.
13. Losier, T., 'The race to the red planet: how NASA, SpaceX are working to get to Mars', AccuWeather. Available at: www.accuweather.com/en/weather-news/the-race-to-the-red-planet-how-nasa-spacex-are-working-to-get-to-mars/358844
14. Mazzucato, M., *The Entrepreneurial State: Debunking Public vs. Private Sector Myths*. Penguin, 2018.

15. 'Challenge prizes', NESTA. Available at: www.nesta.org.uk/feature/ innovation-methods/challenge-prizes

16. All quotations from Tomas Diez, director, Fab Lab Barcelona, are taken from an interview with the author on 25 July 2019.

17. Gershenfeld, N., *Fab: The Coming Revolution on your Desktop – From Personal Computers to Personal Fabrication*. Basic Books, 2008.

18. Rosen, Z., 'From Fab Labs to Fab Cities', *Shareable*, 16 December 2014. Available at: www.shareable.net/from-fab-labs-to-fab-cities

19. Riley, T., 'The FABulous Sherry Lassiter', *SKF*, 14 May 2018. Available at: evolution.skf.com/the-fabulous-sherry-lassiter

20. Ibid.

21. Rosen, Z., 'From Fab Labs to Fab Cities', *Shareable*, 16 December 2014. Available at: www.shareable.net/from-fab-labs-to-fab-cities

22. Riley, T., 'The FABulous Sherry Lassiter', *SKF*, 14 May 2018. Available at: evolution.skf.com/the-fabulous-sherry-lassiter

23. Ibid.

24. 'How to make (almost) anything', *The Economist*, 11 June 2005.

25. Corsini, L., 'The Maker Movement responds to Covid-19', *Medium*, 30 March 2020.

26. Fried, B., and Wetstone, K., 'The White House Maker Faire: "Today's D.I.Y. is tomorrow's "Made in America",' White House Blog, 18 June 2014. Available at: obamawhitehouse.archives.gov/blog/2014/06/18/ president-obama-white-house-maker-faire-today-s-diy-tomorrow-s-made-america

27. Ibid.

28. Ibid.

29. Ibid.

Chapter 9: The innovative state

1. Seelye, K., 'Thomas M. Menino, mayor who led Boston's renaissance, is dead at 71', *New York Times*, 30 October 2014.

2. Ibid.

3. All quotations from Nigel Jacob, co-chair, Mayor's Office of New Urban Mechanics, Boston, are taken from an interview with the author on 5 September 2019.

4. Schreckinger, B., 'Boston: there's an app for that: "civic hacking" and the transformation of local government', *Politico*, 10 June 2014.

5. All quotations from Kris Carter, co-chair, Mayor's Office of New Urban

Mechanics, Boston, are taken from an interview with the author on 5 September 2019.

6. Schreckinger, B., 'Boston: there's an app for that: "civic hacking" and the transformation of local government', *Politico*, 10 June 2014.

7. Glaeser, E., 'New Urban Mechanics, keep tinkering', *Boston Globe*, 9 January 2014.

8. Schreckinger, B., 'Boston: there's an app for that: "civic hacking" and the transformation of local government', *Politico*, 10 June 2014.

9. Crabtree, J., 'Civic hacking: a new agenda for e-democracy', *OpenDemocracy*, 12 June 2007.

10. 'Boston's innovation lab teaches government to take risks. Here's how', *Apolitical*, 21 August 2018.

11. 'Distributed ledger technology: beyond block chain', A report by the UK government chief scientific adviser, 19 January 2016. Available at: assets.publishing.service.gov.uk/government/uploads/system/uploads/ attachment_data/file/492972/gs-16-1-distributed-ledger-technology.pdf

12. 'Boston's innovation lab teaches government to take risks. Here's how', *Apolitical*, 21 August 2018.

13. All quotations from Aleeya Velji, analyst, Strategic Design and Innovation, Treasury Board of Canada Secretariat, are taken from an interview with the author on 24 June 2019.

14. 'How Covid-19 is driving public-sector innovation', *The Economist*, 4 April 2020.

15. Smith, H., 'How Greece is beating coronavirus despite a decade of debt', *Guardian*, 14 April 2020.

16. Ibid.

17. All quotations from Anir Chowdhury, policy adviser, UNDP Bangladesh, government of Bangladesh, are taken from an interview with the author on 11 October 2019.

18. Pink, D. H., *Drive: The Surprising Truth about What Motivates Us*. Penguin, 2011.

19. Hussain, I., policy analyst, UNDP Bangladesh, interview with the author, 11 October 2019.

20. Ibid.

21. Ibid.

22. Ibid.

Notes

Chapter 10: How should citizens be?

1. Green, E., 'One country, two radically different narratives', *Atlantic*, 17 July 2018.
2. Packer, G., 'A new report offers insights into tribalism in the Age of Trump', *New Yorker*, 13 October 2018.
3. Kahan, D. M., 'Ideology, motivated reasoning, and cognitive reflection: an experimental study', *Judgment and Decision Making*, 8, pp. 407–24, 2012.
4. Kaplan, J. T., Gimbel, S. I., and Harris, S., 'Neural correlates of maintaining one's political beliefs in the face of counterevidence', *Scientific Reports*, 6, p. 39589, 2016. Available at: www.ncbi.nlm.nih.gov/pmc/articles/PMC5180221
5. 'The partisan brain: what psychology experiments tell you about why people deny facts', *The Economist*, 8 December 2018.
6. Nyhan, B., Porter, E., Reifler, J., and Wood, T. J., 'Taking fact-checks literally but not seriously? The effects of journalistic fact-checking on factual beliefs and candidate favorability', *Political Behavior*, 11, pp. 1–22, 2019.
7. 'The partisan brain: what psychology experiments tell you about why people deny facts', *The Economist*, 8 December 2018.
8. Adler, D., 'Centrists are the most hostile to democracy, not extremists', *New York Times*, 23 May 2018.
9. Canellos, P., 'What FDR understood about socialism that today's Democrats don't', *Politico*, 16 August 2019.
10. McCarthy, T., 'Jared Kushner and his shadow corona unit: what is Trump's son-in-law up to?' *Guardian*, 5 April 2020.
11. 'Emmanuel Macron's La République En Marche!' Tectonica blog. Available at: www.tectonica.co/la_republique_en_marche
12. Smarsh, S., 'They thought this was Trump country. Hell no', *Guardian*, 26 July 2018.
13. Foa, R. S., and Mounk, Y., 'The danger of deconsolidation: the democratic disconnect', *Journal of Democracy*, 27(3), pp. 5–17, 2016.
14. Younge, G., 'What happened next? How teenage shooting survivor David Hogg became a political leader', *Guardian*, 12 December 2018.
15. Giuffrida, A., 'How Turin turned against its Five Star Movement mayor', *Guardian*, 4 February 2018.
16. Chakrabortty, A., 'Yes, there is an alternative. These people have shown how to "take back control"', *Guardian*, 26 September 2018.
17. Ibid.

18. Trickey, E., '"They're bold and fresh": the millennials disrupting Boston's transit system', *Politico*, 25 October 2018.
19. Mazzucato, M., *The Entrepreneurial State: Debunking Public vs. Private Sector Myths*, Penguin, 2018.
20. Brown, A., 'Sweden's far right has flourished because the elite lost touch with the people', *Guardian*, 26 August 2018.
21. Aspinall, G., '12 reasons why we love Alexandria Ocasio-Cortez', *Grazia*, 7 November 2018.
22. Henley, J., 'Netherlands PM uses Britain's Brexit "chaos" as cautionary tale', *Guardian*, 17 December 2018.
23. Obama, B., 'Barack Obama: you need to vote because our democracy depends on it', *Guardian*, 18 September 2018.

Index

Index

Index

Index

Index

Index